Milestone Documents in the National Archives

National Archives and Records Administration
Washington, DC

Published for the
National Archives and Records Administration
By the National Archives Trust Fund Board
1995

Library of Congress Cataloging-in-Publication Data

United States. National Archives and Records Administration.
Milestone documents in the National Archives.
p. cm.
Rev. ed. of The written word endures. 1978.
Includes bibliographical references.
ISBN 0-911333-98-3
1. United States—History—Sources. I. United States. National Archives and Records Service. Office of Educational Programs.
Written word endures. II. Title.
E173.U62 1995 93-23047
973—dc20 CIP

Designed by Serene Feldman Werblood, National Archives

Cover: Deed of gift of the Statue of Liberty, 1876. The statue was a Centennial gift from France to the American people. It symbolized this nation's openness to the "huddled masses" of the world and served as a welcoming beacon to generations of immigrants entering New York Harbor. *21 1/8 by 26 5/8 inches.*

Table of Contents

Acknowledgments

Many persons have contributed their talents to this publication, which was prepared under the direction of Linda N. Brown, Charles W. Bender, Sandra Glasser, and Henry J. Gwiazda II in the Office of Public Programs, National Archives and Records Administration. Principally responsible for the text of the original edition were Virginia C. Purdy and Lee Scott Theisen and, under their direction, Lillian E. Grandy, Mark Samuelson, and Cece A. Byers. Sandra M. Tilley compiled new text for this edition, with assistance from Joan A. Platten of the Environmental Protection Agency; Evan Duncan, Phil Ellis, Paul Claussen, and Phil Peters of the Department of State; William Nary of the Arms Control and Disarmament Agency; Tom McCray of the U.S. Senate Library; and Pat Reilly of the National Women's Political Caucus. The revision was copyedited by Sandra M. Tilley, with the assistance of Julie Feltz, and designed by Serene Feldman Werblood. Special appreciation is also due to Archives staff members Lisa Auel, Rick Blondo, Barbara Burger, Bruce I. Bustard, Stuart Butler, Mike Carter, Wayne Cook, Robert Coren, Robert Ellis, Mary Finch, Tom Fortunato, Richard Fusick, Robert Gruber, Milton O. Gustafson, Beth Haverkamp, Elizabeth Hill, Maida Loescher, Darlene McClurkin, Nancy Malan, Michael Meier, Paula Nassen Poulos, Jimmy Rush, Mary C. Ryan, Richard B. Smith, Richard H. Smith, Richard Snyder, David Stanhope, Douglas L. Thurman, Angie Vandereedt, John Vandereedt, John Vernon, and James D. Zeender.

Foreword

The National Archives of the United States preserves and makes available those records of the federal government that have continuing value for the necessary processes of government, that provide protection of public and private rights, and that contain useful information for researchers and the general public. These records take many forms: textual documents, maps, still photographs, sound recordings, motion pictures, architectural drawings, information stored on electronic media, and others. The National Archives Building in Washington, DC, the National Archives at College Park, MD, 13 regional archives, and 9 Presidential libraries throughout the United States hold the records of the federal government, which document our history from the First Continental Congress to the present.

Some of the most important of these records are reproduced in this book, originally published in 1976 in conjunction with a National Archives exhibit entitled "The Written Word Endures." This revised edition includes additional text, which covers events that occurred after the original publication date. Even a quick perusal of this book will kindle a spark of recognition in most Americans: Many of the documents in it have been familiar since grade school, and others mark events that we have experienced directly. A thoughtful reading of *Milestone Documents in the National Archives* may lead to a new appreciation of our nation's rich documentary heritage as it is preserved and made available by the National Archives. I hope you enjoy it.

JOHN W. CARLIN
Archivist of the United States

Introduction

Littera scripta manet, the motto on the National Archives seal, may be loosely translated as "the written word endures." Millions of documents in the Archives of the United States of America testify to the continuing importance of written words in the life of the nation.

From the Revolutionary period of American history emerged three great documents whose concepts are as valid today as they were when they were written: the Declaration of Independence, the Constitution, and the Bill of Rights. In a sense, the rest of American history is an outgrowth of these documents—relating the development and application of the precepts laid down by the Revolutionary War generation. Further, those who came later carried on that generation's tradition of expressing ideas and ideals on paper.

The struggles to adapt unchanging principles to ever-changing events and conditions gave rise to other great written documents. These former colonists, who had rebelled against what they deemed an arbitrary and distant central government, devised means to prevent any part of their own national government from becoming too powerful—and wrote the necessary checks into the law. The government of a people stretching across a continent entered into treaties to establish boundaries and developed ways of distributing land and attracting settlers—and put those actions into words. Expanding from its beginnings as an agrarian nation, the United States built factories based on inventions duly patented and recorded; a growing urban population met its social and economic problems by writing new laws and giving new legal interpretations to old laws. The United States as a world power prepared statements to explain its policies toward other nations and entered into written agreements to make alliances and end wars.

Yet all the documents of American history preserved in the National Archives are not in written form. Important words have been recorded to be heard, not read; others have entered the record in forms that only a computer can interpret. Many documents have very few written words, or none at all; film, maps, drawings, and photographs provide vivid records of events or ideas. Thus the recorded history of the American people as it is preserved in the National Archives takes many forms.

From this vast accumulation of documents, a few stand out as milestones on the road connecting the past with the present. Most of these milestones represent steps toward the ideals established in the three founding documents; most have benefited the majority of the American people; most have helped to establish this nation as a leader among the nations of the world.

The pages that follow present some of these great documents, which in one way or another have shaped American history. Many have heralded new departures or marked closed chapters. Most represent turning points; the nature of American life was altered after their appearance. To underscore the significance of each milestone document, other records from the National Archives have been grouped with the central document to show its background and origins or to demonstrate its far-reaching consequences. All illustrations are from the holdings of the National Archives.

IN CONGRESS, JULY 4, 1776.

A DECLARATION

BY THE REPRESENTATIVES OF THE

UNITED STATES OF AMERICA,

IN GENERAL CONGRESS ASSEMBLED.

WHEN in the Course of human Events, it becomes necessary for one People to dissolve the Political Bands which have connected them with another, and to assume among the Powers of the Earth, the separate and equal Station to which the Laws of Nature and of Nature's God entitle them, a decent Respect to the Opinions of Mankind requires that they should declare the causes which impel them to the Separation.

WE hold these Truths to be self-evident, that all Men are created equal, that they are endowed by their Creator with certain unalienable Rights, that among these are Life, Liberty, and the Pursuit of Happiness—That to secure these Rights, Governments are instituted among Men, deriving their just Powers from the Consent of the Governed, that whenever any Form of Government becomes destructive of these Ends, it is the Right of the People to alter or to abolish it, and to institute new Government, laying its Foundation on such Principles, and organizing its Powers in such Form, as to them shall seem most likely to effect their Safety and Happiness. Prudence, indeed, will dictate that Governments long established should not be changed for light and transient Causes; and accordingly all Experience hath shewn, that Mankind are more disposed to suffer, while Evils are sufferable, than to right themselves by abolishing the Forms to which they are accustomed. But when a long Train of Abuses and Usurpations, pursuing invariably the same Object, evinces a Design to reduce them under absolute Despotism, it is their Right, it is their Duty, to throw off such Government, and to provide new Guards for their future Security. Such has been the patient Sufferance of these Colonies; and such is now the Necessity which constrains them to alter their former Systems of Government. The History of the present King of Great-Britain is a History of repeated Injuries and Usurpations, all having in direct Object the Establishment of an absolute Tyranny over these States. To prove this, let Facts be submitted to a candid World.

HE has refused his Assent to Laws, the most wholesome and necessary for the public Good.

HE has forbidden his Governors to pass Laws of immediate and pressing Importance, unless suspended in their Operation till his Assent should be obtained; and when so suspended, he has utterly neglected to attend to them.

HE has refused to pass other Laws for the Accommodation of large Districts of People, unless those People would relinquish the Right of Representation in the Legislature, a Right inestimable to them, and formidable to Tyrants only.

HE has called together Legislative Bodies at Places unusual, uncomfortable, and distant from the Depository of their public Records, for the sole Purpose of fatiguing them into Compliance with his Measures.

HE has dissolved Representative Houses repeatedly, for opposing with manly Firmness his Invasions on the Rights of the People.

HE has refused for a long Time, after such Dissolutions, to cause others to be elected; whereby the Legislative Powers, incapable of Annihilation, have returned to the People at large for their exercise; the State remaining in the mean time exposed to all the Dangers of Invasion from without, and Convulsions within.

HE has endeavoured to prevent the Population of these States; for that Purpose obstructing the Laws for Naturalization of Foreigners; refusing to pass others to encourage their Migrations hither, and raising the Conditions of new Appropriations of Lands.

HE has obstructed the Administration of Justice, by refusing his Assent to Laws for establishing Judiciary Powers.

HE has made Judges dependent on his Will alone, for the Tenure of their Offices, and the Amount and Payment of their Salaries.

HE has erected a Multitude of new Offices, and sent hither Swarms of Officers to harrass our People, and eat out their Substance.

HE has kept among us, in Times of Peace, Standing Armies, without the consent of our Legislatures.

HE has affected to render the Military independent of and superior to the Civil Power.

HE has combined with others to subject us to a Jurisdiction foreign to our Constitution, and unacknowledged by our Laws; giving his Assent to their Acts of pretended Legislation:

FOR quartering large Bodies of Armed Troops among us:

FOR protecting them, by a mock Trial, from Punishment for any Murders which they should commit on the Inhabitants of these States:

FOR cutting off our Trade with all Parts of the World:

FOR imposing Taxes on us without our Consent:

FOR depriving us, in many Cases, of the Benefits of Trial by Jury:

FOR transporting us beyond Seas to be tried for pretended Offences:

FOR abolishing the free System of English Laws in a neighbouring Province, establishing therein an arbitrary Government, and enlarging its Boundaries, so as to render it at once an Example and fit Instrument for introducing the same absolute Rule into these Colonies:

FOR taking away our Charters, abolishing our most valuable Laws, and altering fundamentally the Forms of our Governments:

FOR suspending our own Legislatures, and declaring themselves invested with Power to legislate for us in all Cases whatsoever.

HE has abdicated Government here, by declaring us out of his Protection and waging War against us.

HE has plundered our Seas, ravaged our Coasts, burnt our Towns, and destroyed the Lives of our People.

HE is, at this Time, transporting large Armies of foreign Mercenaries to compleat the Works of Death, Desolation, and Tyranny, already begun with circumstances of Cruelty and Perfidy, scarcely paralleled in the most barbarous Ages, and totally unworthy the Head of a civilized Nation.

HE has constrained our fellow Citizens taken Captive on the high Seas to bear Arms against their Country, to become the Executioners of their Friends and Brethren, or to fall themselves by their Hands.

HE has excited domestic Insurrections amongst us, and has endeavoured to bring on the Inhabitants of our Frontiers, the merciless Indian Savages, whose known Rule of Warfare, is an undistinguished Destruction, of all Ages, Sexes and Conditions.

IN every stage of these Oppressions we have Petitioned for Redress in the most humble Terms: Our repeated Petitions have been answered only by repeated Injury. A Prince, whose Character is thus marked by every act which may define a Tyrant, is unfit to be the Ruler of a free People.

NOR have we been wanting in Attentions to our British Brethren. We have warned them from Time to Time of Attempts by their Legislature to extend an unwarrantable Jurisdiction over us. We have reminded them of the Circumstances of our Emigration and Settlement here. We have appealed to their native Justice and Magnanimity, and we have conjured them by the Ties of our common Kindred to disavow these Usurpations, which, would inevitably interrupt our Connections and Correspondence. They too have been deaf to the Voice of Justice and of Consanguinity. We must, therefore, acquiesce in the Necessity, which denounces our Separation, and hold them, as we hold the rest of Mankind, Enemies in War, in Peace, Friends.

WE, therefore, the Representatives of the UNITED STATES OF AMERICA, in GENERAL CONGRESS, Assembled, appealing to the Supreme Judge of the World for the Rectitude of our Intentions, do, in the Name, and by Authority of the good People of these Colonies, solemnly Publish and Declare, That these United Colonies are, and of Right ought to be, FREE AND INDEPENDENT STATES; that they are absolved from all Allegiance to the British Crown, and that all political Connection between them and the State of Great-Britain, is and ought to be totally dissolved; and that as FREE AND INDEPENDENT STATES, they have full Power to levy War, conclude Peace, contract Alliances, establish Commerce, and to do all other Acts and Things which INDEPENDENT STATES may of right do. And for the support of this Declaration, with a firm Reliance on the Protection of divine Providence, we mutually pledge to each other our Lives, our Fortunes, and our sacred Honor.

Signed by ORDER *and in* BEHALF *of the* CONGRESS,

JOHN HANCOCK, PRESIDENT.

ATTEST.
CHARLES THOMSON, SECRETARY.

PHILADELPHIA: PRINTED BY JOHN DUNLAP.

July 4, 1776, is the best known date in American history. It is the day when the Second Continental Congress adopted "A Declaration By the Representatives of the United States of America, in General Congress, Assembled." Drafted for the most part by Thomas Jefferson, the Declaration of Independence justified breaking the colonial tie to Great Britain by providing a basic philosophy of government and a list of grievances against the Crown.

Copies of the document were printed that same day to be distributed to legislative bodies in the 13 states and to commanding officers of the Continental Army. About a month later, an engrosser, probably Timothy Matlack, copied the text on parchment to be signed by the Members of Congress. By that time, the document could be designated "The unanimous Declaration of the thirteen united States of America."

On the same day the Declaration was adopted, the Continental Congress turned its attention to the symbols of an independent nation and resolved "That Dr. Franklin, Mr. J. Adams, and Mr. Jefferson be a committee to prepare a device for a Seal of the United States of America." Six years and two committees later, the design for the Great Seal was adopted. Meanwhile on June 14, 1777, Congress had provided another sign of nationhood in the resolution:

> *That the Flag of the thirteen united states be 13 stripes, alternate red and white, that the Union be 13 stars white in a blue field representing a new constellation.*

Yet these actions did not actually create a new nation in the eyes of the world. Even after France became the first nation to acknowledge the independence of the United States by joining with it in formal alliance in 1778, most other European governments refused to recognize America as a sovereign state. They not only wanted to avoid alienating powerful Britain, they disapproved of the rebellious colonies on principle. Although the victory of U.S. and French forces at Yorktown in 1781 struck a decisive blow for American independence, only with the Treaty of Paris of 1783 did "His Britannic Majesty acknowledge . . . said United States . . . to be free, sovereign, and independent States."

The first printing of the Declaration of Independence, made on July 4–5, 1776, by John Dunlap of Philadelphia, printer to the Continental Congress. One copy was attached with wafers of wax to the Journal of the Continental Congress to complete the record for July 4, 1776.
14 ¾ by 18 inches.

"Plan of the Attack of york in Virginia by the Allied Armies of America and France . . . ," 1781, signed by Lt. Col. Jean-Baptiste Gouvion, a French officer who joined the American Corps of Engineers in 1777. *29 by 38 inches, detail.*

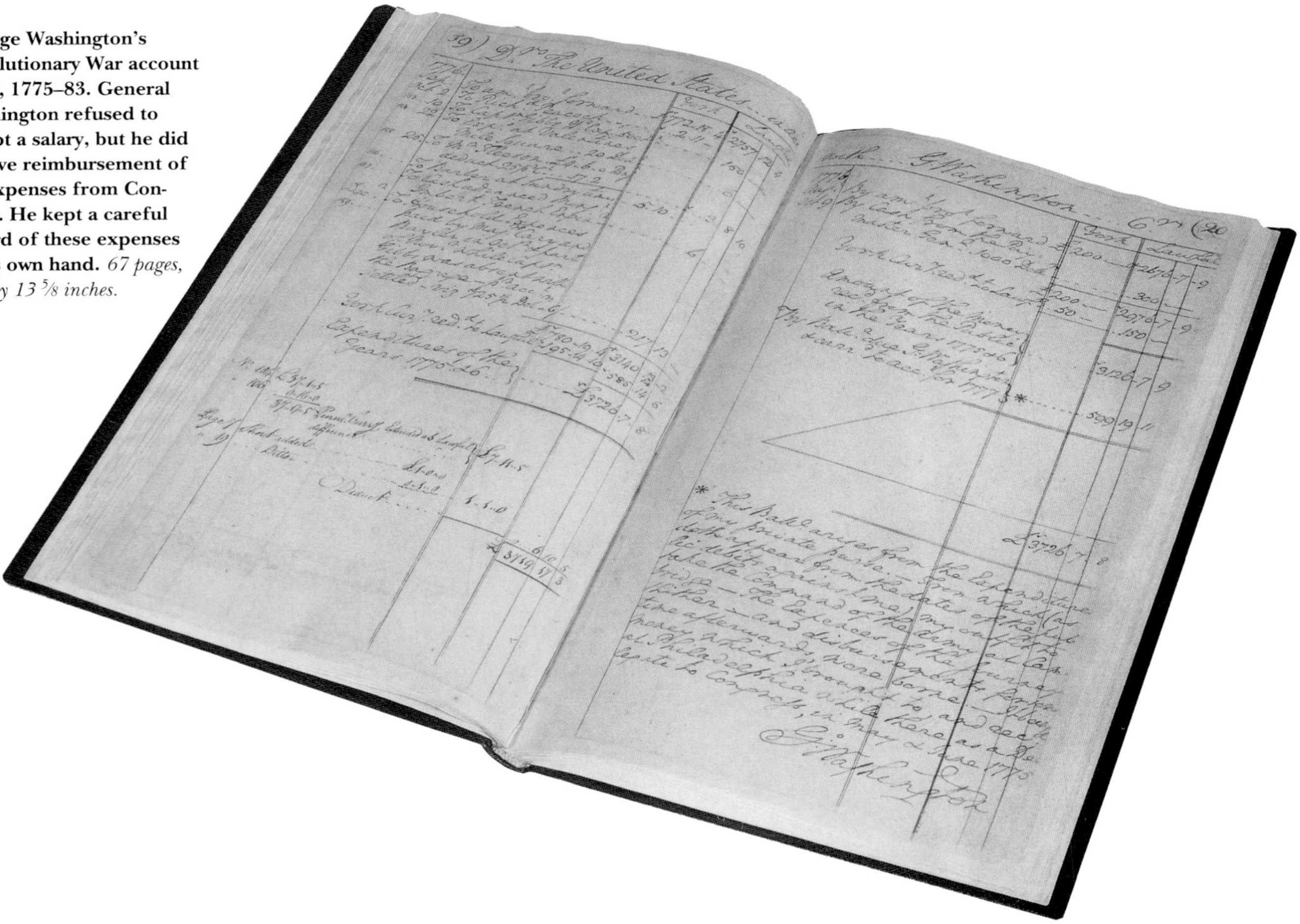

George Washington's Revolutionary War account book, 1775–83. General Washington refused to accept a salary, but he did receive reimbursement of his expenses from Congress. He kept a careful record of these expenses in his own hand. *67 pages, 8 5/8 by 13 5/8 inches.*

British skippet attached to the U.S. copy of the Treaty of Paris. Skippets—silver or gold boxes containing a wax impression of the signatory nation's official seal—formerly accompanied exchange copies of international treaties. *Silver gilt, 6 ¾ inches in diameter.*

The Treaty of Paris, 1783, sent to Congress by the American negotiators, formally ended the Revolutionary War when it was ratified on January 14, 1784. Congress was then sitting in Annapolis. *American original of treaty, pages 1 and 9 of 9 pages, 9 ¾ by 14 ¾ inches.*

Duplicate

Definitive Treaty of Peace with G. Britain 3. Sept. 1783.

In the Name of the most Holy and undivided Trinity.

It having pleased the Divine Providence to dispose the Hearts of the most Serene and most potent Prince George the Third, by the Grace of God, King of Great Britain, France and Ireland, Defender of the Faith, Duke of Brunswick and Lunebourg, Arch Treasurer and Prince Elector of the Holy Roman Empire &c.a And of the United States of America, to forget all past Misunderstandings and Differences that have unhappily interrupted the good Correspondence and Friendship which they mutually wish to restore, and to establish such a beneficial and satisfactory Intercourse between the two Countries upon the Ground of reciprocal Advantages and mutual Convenience as may promote and secure to both perpetual Peace & Harmony; and having for this desirable End already laid the Foundation of Peace and Reconciliation, by the Provisional Articles signed at Paris on the 30.th of November 1782, by the Commissioners empowered on each Part, which Articles were agreed to be inserted in and to constitute the Treaty of Peace proposed to be concluded between the Crown of Great Britain &

Article 10.

...Ratification of the present Treaty expedited in ... Form shall be exchanged between the contracting ... Space of six Months or sooner if possible, to be ... the Day of the Signature of the present Treaty ... whereof We the undersigned their Ministers ... tiary have in their Name and in Virtue of our ... signed with our Hands the present Definitive ... and caused the Seals of our Arms to be affixed thereto.

Done at Paris, this third Day of September In the Year of our Lord one thousand seven hundred and Eighty three.

D Hartley

John Adams.

B Franklin

John Jay

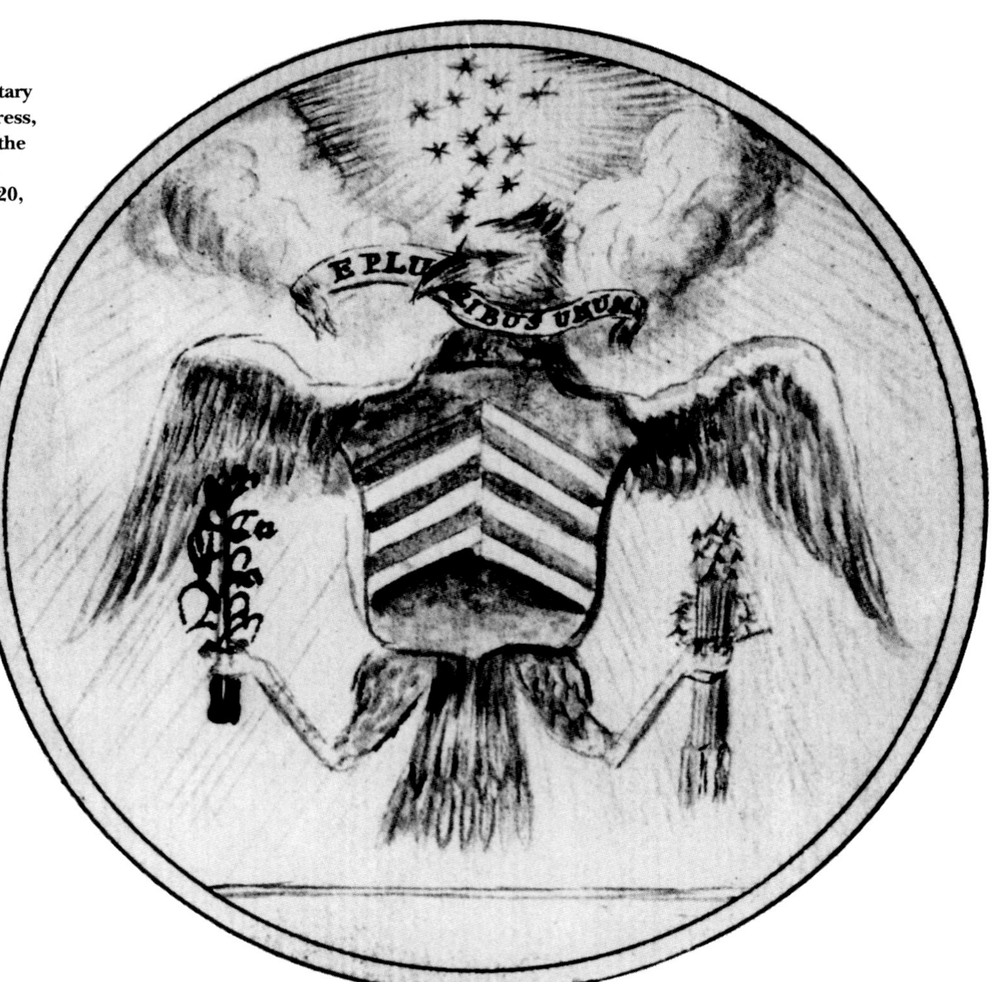

Charles Thomson, Secretary of the Continental Congress, designed the obverse of the Great Seal of the United States, adopted on June 20, 1782. *Ink and crayon, 3 7/8 inches in diameter.*

First die of the Great Seal of the United States, used on all official documents from 1782 through 1841. *Brass, 2 3/8 inches in diameter.*

William Barton proposed this design for the Great Seal of the United States in 1782. The small design in the upper right corner was adopted as the reverse of the seal; it also appears on the back of the current dollar bill. The rest of the design was rejected. *Watercolor, 14 1/2 by 11 7/8 inches.*

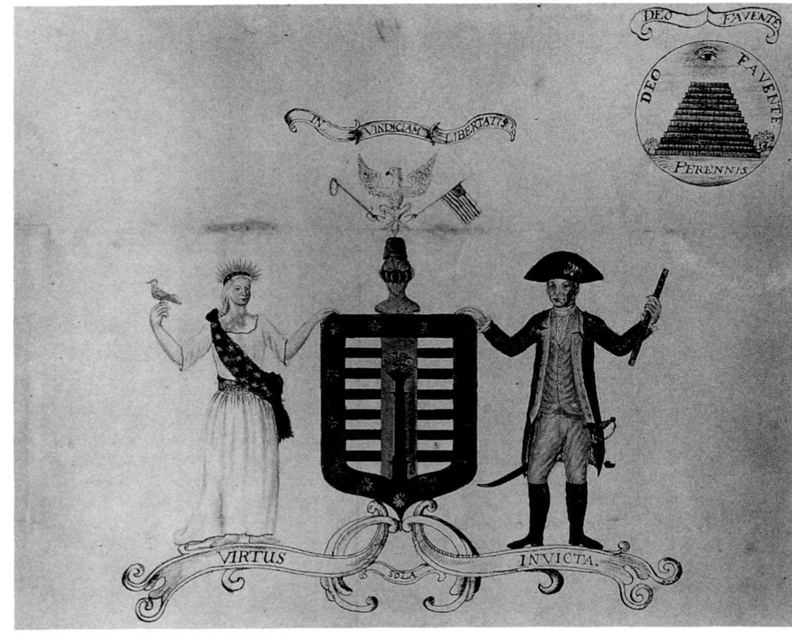

IN CONGRESS, JULY 4, 1776.

The unanimous Declaration of the thirteen united States of America,

When in the Course of human events, it becomes necessary for one people to dissolve the political bands which have connected them with another, and to assume among the powers of the earth, the separate and equal station to which the Laws of Nature and of Nature's God entitle them, a decent respect to the opinions of mankind requires that they should declare the causes which impel them to the separation. —— We hold these truths to be self-evident, that all men are created equal, that they are endowed by their Creator with certain unalienable Rights, that among these are Life, Liberty and the pursuit of Happiness. — That to secure these rights, Governments are instituted among Men, deriving their just powers from the consent of the governed, — That whenever any Form of Government becomes destructive of these ends, it is the Right of the People to alter or to abolish it, and to institute new Government, laying its foundation on such principles and organizing its powers in such form, as to them shall seem most likely to effect their Safety and Happiness. Prudence, indeed, will dictate that Governments long established should not be changed for light and transient causes; and accordingly all experience hath shewn, that mankind are more disposed to suffer, while evils are sufferable, than to right themselves by abolishing the forms to which they are accustomed. But when a long train of abuses and usurpations, pursuing invariably the same Object evinces a design to reduce them under absolute Despotism, it is their right, it is their duty, to throw off such Government, and to provide new Guards for their future security. — Such has been the patient sufferance of these Colonies; and such is now the necessity which constrains them to alter their former Systems of Government. The history of the present King of Great Britain is a history of repeated injuries and usurpations, all having in direct object the establishment of an absolute Tyranny over these States. To prove this, let Facts be submitted to a candid world. —— He has refused his Assent to Laws, the most wholesome and necessary for the public good. —— He has forbidden his Governors to pass Laws of immediate and pressing importance, unless suspended in their operation till his Assent should be obtained; and when so suspended, he has utterly neglected to attend to them. —— He has refused to pass other Laws for the accommodation of large districts of people, unless those people would relinquish the right of Representation in the Legislature, a right inestimable to them and formidable to tyrants only. —— He has called together legislative bodies at places unusual, uncomfortable, and distant from the depository of their public Records, for the sole purpose of fatiguing them into compliance with his measures. —— He has dissolved Representative Houses repeatedly, for opposing with manly firmness his invasions on the rights of the people. —— He has refused for a long time, after such dissolutions, to cause others to be elected; whereby the Legislative powers, incapable of Annihilation, have returned to the People at large for their exercise; the State remaining in the mean time exposed to all the dangers of invasion from without, and convulsions within. —— He has endeavoured to prevent the population of these States; for that purpose obstructing the Laws for Naturalization of Foreigners; refusing to pass others to encourage their migrations hither, and raising the conditions of new Appropriations of Lands. —— He has obstructed the Administration of Justice, by refusing his Assent to Laws for establishing Judiciary powers. —— He has made Judges dependent on his Will alone, for the tenure of their offices, and the amount and payment of their salaries. —— He has erected a multitude of New Offices, and sent hither swarms of Officers to harrass our people, and eat out their substance. —— He has kept among us, in times of peace, Standing Armies without the Consent of our legislatures. —— He has affected to render the Military independent of and superior to the Civil power. —— He has combined with others to subject us to a jurisdiction foreign to our constitution, and unacknowledged by our laws; giving his Assent to their Acts of pretended Legislation: — For Quartering large bodies of armed troops among us: — For protecting them, by a mock Trial, from punishment for any Murders which they should commit on the Inhabitants of these States: — For cutting off our Trade with all parts of the world: — For imposing Taxes on us without our Consent: — For depriving us in many cases, of the benefits of Trial by Jury: — For transporting us beyond Seas to be tried for pretended offences — For abolishing the free System of English Laws in a neighbouring Province, establishing therein an Arbitrary government, and enlarging its Boundaries so as to render it at once an example and fit instrument for introducing the same absolute rule into these Colonies: — For taking away our Charters, abolishing our most valuable Laws, and altering fundamentally the Forms of our Governments: — For suspending our own Legislatures, and declaring themselves invested with power to legislate for us in all cases whatsoever. — He has abdicated Government here, by declaring us out of his Protection and waging War against us. —— He has plundered our seas, ravaged our Coasts, burnt our towns, and destroyed the lives of our people. —— He is at this time transporting large Armies of foreign Mercenaries to compleat the works of death, desolation and tyranny, already begun with circumstances of Cruelty & perfidy scarcely paralleled in the most barbarous ages, and totally unworthy the Head of a civilized nation. —— He has constrained our fellow Citizens taken Captive on the high Seas to bear Arms against their Country, to become the executioners of their friends and Brethren, or to fall themselves by their Hands. —— He has excited domestic insurrections amongst us, and has endeavoured to bring on the inhabitants of our frontiers, the merciless Indian Savages, whose known rule of warfare, is an undistinguished destruction of all ages, sexes and conditions. In every stage of these Oppressions We have Petitioned for Redress in the most humble terms: Our repeated Petitions have been answered only by repeated injury. A Prince, whose character is thus marked by every act which may define a Tyrant, is unfit to be the ruler of a free people. Nor have We been wanting in attentions to our Brittish brethren. We have warned them from time to time of attempts by their legislature to extend an unwarrantable jurisdiction over us. We have reminded them of the circumstances of our emigration and settlement here. We have appealed to their native justice and magnanimity, and we have conjured them by the ties of our common kindred to disavow these usurpations, which, would inevitably interrupt our connections and correspondence. They too have been deaf to the voice of justice and of consanguinity. We must, therefore, acquiesce in the necessity, which denounces our Separation, and hold them, as we hold the rest of mankind, Enemies in War, in Peace Friends. ——

We, therefore, the Representatives of the united States of America, in General Congress, Assembled, appealing to the Supreme Judge of the world for the rectitude of our intentions, do, in the Name, and by Authority of the good People of these Colonies, solemnly publish and declare, That these United Colonies are, and of Right ought to be Free and Independent States; that they are Absolved from all Allegiance to the British Crown, and that all political connection between them and the State of Great Britain, is and ought to be totally dissolved; and that as Free and Independent States, they have full Power to levy War, conclude Peace, contract Alliances, establish Commerce, and to do all other Acts and Things which Independent States may of right do. —— And for the support of this Declaration, with a firm reliance on the protection of divine Providence, we mutually pledge to each other our Lives, our Fortunes and our sacred Honor.

Button Gwinnett
Lyman Hall
Geo Walton.

Wm Hooper
Joseph Hewes,
John Penn
Edward Rutledge 1.
Thos Heyward Junr.
Thomas Lynch Junr.
Arthur Middleton

John Hancock
Samuel Chase
Wm. Paca
Thos. Stone
Charles Carroll of Carrollton
George Wythe
Richard Henry Lee
Th Jefferson
Benja Harrison
Thos Nelson jr.
Francis Lightfoot Lee
Carter Braxton

Robt Morris
Benjamin Rush
Benja. Franklin
John Morton
Geo Clymer
Jas. Smith
Geo. Taylor
James Wilson
Geo. Ross
Caesar Rodney
Geo Read
Thos M:Kean

Wm Floyd
Phil. Livingston
Frans. Lewis
Lewis Morris
Richd. Stockton
Jno Witherspoon
Fras. Hopkinson
John Hart
Abra Clark

Josiah Bartlett
Wm. Whipple
Saml Adams
John Adams
Robt Treat Paine
Elbridge Gerry
Step. Hopkins
William Ellery
Roger Sherman
Saml Huntington
Wm. Williams
Oliver Wolcott
Matthew Thornton

W. J. STONE SC. WASHN.

The Declaration of Independence presented to Congress on August 2, 1776, for signing by the members. Some members signed at later dates. This impression is taken from an engraving made in 1823 by William J. Stone; the Stone engraved plate is in the National Archives. The original document, engrossed on parchment, is on permanent exhibition in the National Archives.
Stone's impression, 24 1/4 by 29 3/4 inches.

The Ordinance of 1787, known as the Northwest Ordinance, established the pattern by which territories were admitted into the Union as states. The signature is that of Charles Thomson of Pennsylvania, Secretary of the Continental and Confederation Congresses from 1784 to 1789.
2 pages, 8 by 12 ¾ inches.

An ORDINANCE for the GOVERNMENT of the TERRITORY of the UNITED STATES, North-West of the RIVER OHIO.

Cha Thomson Secy

Insignificant in appearance in the only form in which it has survived, the "Ordinance for the Government of the Territory of the United States North-West of the River Ohio" provided a policy for acquired territory that stands as a great American political innovation. After their experiences as colonists, the representatives of the 13 "United States in Congress assembled" decided that the new republic should not have a colonial empire. On October 10, 1780, a resolution to that effect was passed and properly recorded in the Journal of the Continental Congress:

> *That the unappropriated lands that may be ceded or relinquished to the United States . . . [shall be] formed into different republican states which shall become members of the federal Union and have the same rights of sovereignty, freedom, and independence as the other states.*

In 1787 the Confederation Congress confronted the problem of providing a government for territory that had been "ceded or relinquished" in what was then the Northwest Territory. In formulating the Northwest Ordinance during that year, Congress carried out the principle laid down in 1780.

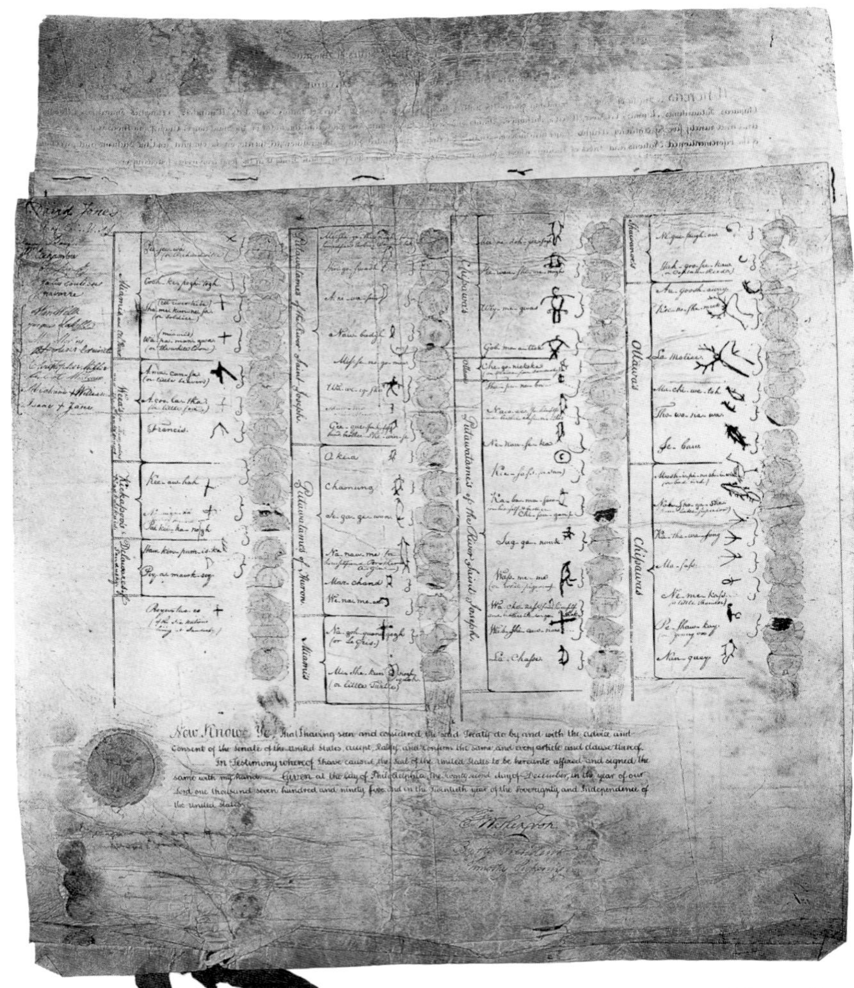

The Treaty of Greenville, 1795, negotiated by Gen. Anthony Wayne with several Indian tribes after the Battle of Fallen Timbers in 1794. The treaty opened the way for the first major influx of settlers into the Northwest Territory. *Page 3 of 3 pages, 26 by 32 inches.*

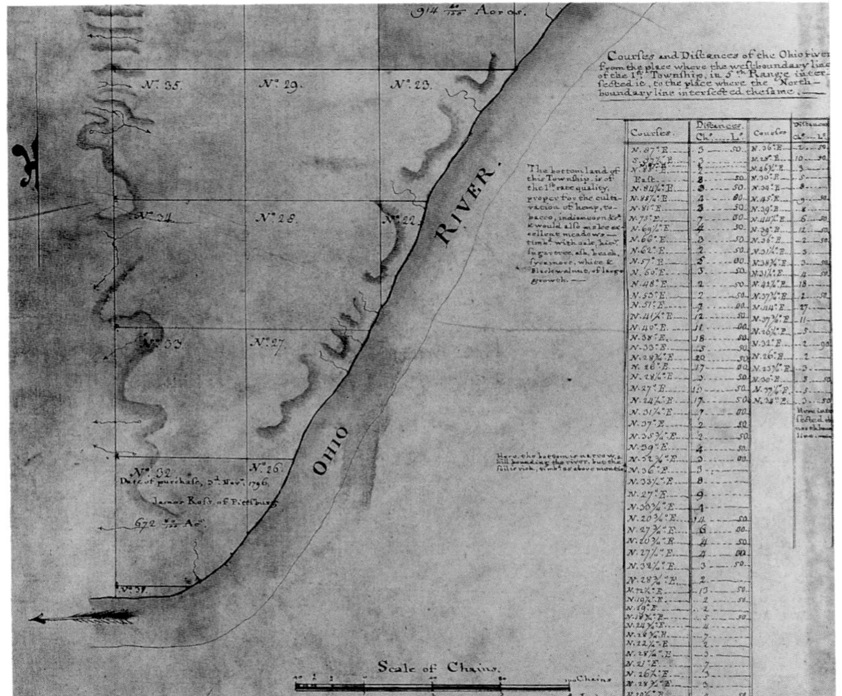

Map of Township 1, Range 5, Ohio's "Seven Ranges," the first land surveyed under the Land Ordinance of 1785, which provided that land would be marked out by a new grid system of sections, townships, and ranges. Government-owned land was to be surveyed before settlement. *25 1/8 by 16 1/4 inches, detail.*

БОЖІЕЮ
ПОСПѢШЕСТВУЮЩЕЮ МИЛОСТІЮ
МЫ
АЛЕКСАНДРЪ ВТОРЫЙ,
ИМПЕРАТОРЪ И САМОДЕРЖЕЦЪ
ВСЕРОССІЙСКІЙ,
МОСКОВСКІЙ, КІЕВСКІЙ, ВЛАДИМІРСКІЙ, НОВОГОРОДСКІЙ, ЦАРЬ КАЗАНСКІЙ,
ЦАРЬ АСТРАХАНСКІЙ, ЦАРЬ ПОЛЬСКІЙ, ЦАРЬ СИБИРСКІЙ, ЦАРЬ
ХЕРСОНИСА ТАВРИЧЕСКАГО, ЦАРЬ ГРУЗИНСКІЙ; ГОСУДАРЬ ПСКОВСКІЙ
И ВЕЛИКІЙ КНЯЗЬ СМОЛЕНСКІЙ, ЛИТОВСКІЙ, ВОЛЫНСКІЙ, ПОДОЛЬСКІЙ
И ФИНЛЯНДСКІЙ; КНЯЗЬ ЭСТЛЯНДСКІЙ, ЛИФЛЯНДСКІЙ, КУРЛЯНДСКІЙ И
СЕМИГАЛЬСКІЙ, САМОГИТСКІЙ, БѢЛОСТОКСКІЙ, КОРЕЛЬСКІЙ, ТВЕРСКІЙ, ЮГОРСКІЙ,
ПЕРМСКІЙ, ВЯТСКІЙ, БОЛГАРСКІЙ И ИНЫХЪ; ГОСУДАРЬ И ВЕЛИКІЙ КНЯЗЬ
НОВАГОРОДА НИЗОВСКІЯ ЗЕМЛИ, ЧЕРНИГОВСКІЙ, РЯЗАНСКІЙ, ПОЛОТСКІЙ, РОСТОВСКІЙ,
ЯРОСЛАВСКІЙ, БѢЛОЗЕРСКІЙ, УДОРСКІЙ, ОБДОРСКІЙ, КОНДІЙСКІЙ, ВИТЕБСКІЙ, МСТИСЛАВСКІЙ,
И ВСЕЯ СѢВЕРНЫЯ СТРАНЫ ПОВЕЛИТЕЛЬ; И ГОСУДАРЬ ИВЕРСКІЯ,
КАРТАЛИНСКІЯ И КАБАРДИНСКІЯ ЗЕМЛИ И ОБЛАСТИ АРМЕНСКІЯ; ЧЕРКАССКИХЪ И
ГОРСКИХЪ КНЯЗЕЙ И ИНЫХЪ НАСЛѢДНЫЙ ГОСУДАРЬ И ОБЛАДАТЕЛЬ; НАСЛѢДНИКЪ
НОРВЕЖСКІЙ, ГЕРЦОГЪ ШЛЕЗВИГЪ-ГОЛСТИНСКІЙ, СТОРМАРНСКІЙ, ДИТМАРСЕНСКІЙ
И ОЛЬДЕНБУРГСКІЙ, И ПРОЧАЯ, И ПРОЧАЯ, И ПРОЧАЯ. Объявляемъ чрезъ

The Alaska Purchase Treaty, 1867. Alaska, which became a state in 1959, was the first noncontiguous territory admitted subject to the principles of the Northwest Ordinance. *Russian exchange copy of the Treaty of Cession, signed by Tsar Alexander II, text in Russian, page 1 of 15 pages, 12 7/8 by 16 5/8 inches.*

The Northwest Ordinance outlined procedures by which land could be settled, organized as a territory, and prepared for eventual statehood. The system set up in 1787 was followed for every territory in the contiguous United States. Many states, such as Iowa, were part of more than one territory before they gained a population large enough to qualify for statehood. Texas was never a territory; it entered the Union directly by annexation. The territorial system, with modifications, reached as far as Alaska and Hawaii in 1959, when those two noncontiguous territories became states.

In a part of the ordinance designated as the "articles of compact between the original States and the people and States of the said territory," religious freedom and civil liberties were guaranteed, education encouraged, and slavery forbidden. In view of the bitter fate of the Native American population, one provision of the ordinance should be noted:

> *The utmost good faith shall always be observed towards the Indians; their lands and property shall never be taken from them without their consent; and, in their property rights, and liberty, they shall never be invaded or disturbed, unless in just and lawful wars authorized by Congress.*

Eskimo woman. *Watercolor by Russell W. Porter, ca. 1905, 12 3/4 by 18 1/2 inches.*

There is ample evidence that the federal government pursued an ambivalent policy toward Indians from the beginning. The government made some attempts to protect Native American rights. In 1777, when the Pennsylvania State Assembly reported that the Indians were "very uneasy on account of intrusion" of squatters, the Continental Congress instructed the legislature to "take proper measures to quiet the minds of the said Indians, . . . either by removal of the intruders, or by allowing them an adequate consideration for their soil, at the option of the Indians." In 1783 the Congress "strictly enjoined" against and then "prohibited" settling on Indian lands. The new government sent a force under the command of Col. Josiah Harmar to drive off squatters settled illegally on Indian lands in the Northwest Territory. At the same time, it instructed the governor of the Northwest Territory to neglect no opportunity for "extinguishing the Indian rights to the westward." The latter policy prevailed in a series of violent confrontations culminating in the Battle of Fallen Timbers in 1794 in the Ohio country. The subsequent Treaty of Greenville defined the first of many western lines beyond which white settlement should not advance. Indian tribes were thereafter repeatedly removed beyond such lines.

Harvesting pineapples in Mahiawa, Oahu, HI, ca. 1950.

2

NOW, THEREFORE, I, DWIGHT D. EISENHOWER, President of the United States of America, do hereby declare and proclaim that the procedural requirements imposed by the Congress on the State of Hawaii to entitle that State to admission into the Union have ...en complied with in all respects and that admission of the State ...Hawaii into the Union on an equal footing with the other States ...e Union is now accomplished.

...N WITNESS WHEREOF, I have hereunto set my hand and caused ...l of the United States of America to be affixed.

... at the City of Washington at four p.m. E.D.T. on this twenty-first day of August in the year of our Lord nineteen hundred and fifty-nine, and of the Independence of the United States of America the one hundred and eighty-fourth.

Dwight D. Eisenhower
Washington, D.C.

Secre... ...f State

AUG 24 11 17 AM '59
IN THE FEDERAL REGISTER DIVISION

3309

President Dwight D. Eisenhower's Proclamation of Hawaiian Statehood. In 1959 Hawaii became the last state to enter the Union.
2 pages, 8 by 13 inches.

We the People

of the United States, in Order to form a more perfect Union, establish Justice, insure domestic Tranquility, provide for the common defence, promote the general Welfare, and secure the Blessings of Liberty to ourselves and our Posterity, do ordain and establish this Constitution for the United States of America.

Article. I.

Section. 1. All legislative Powers herein granted shall be vested in a Congress of the United States, which shall consist of a Senate and House of Representatives.

Section. 2. The House of Representatives shall be composed of Members chosen every second Year by the People of the several States, and the Electors in each State shall have the Qualifications requisite for Electors of the most numerous Branch of the State Legislature.

No Person shall be a Representative who shall not have attained to the Age of twenty five Years, and been seven Years a Citizen of the United States, and who shall not, when elected, be an Inhabitant of that State in which he shall be chosen.

Representatives and direct Taxes shall be apportioned among the several States which may be included within this Union, according to their respective Numbers, which shall be determined by adding to the whole Number of free Persons, including those bound to Service for a Term of Years, and excluding Indians not taxed, three fifths of all other Persons. The actual Enumeration shall be made within three Years after the first Meeting of the Congress of the United States, and within every subsequent Term of ten Years, in such Manner as they shall by Law direct. The Number of Representatives shall not exceed one for every thirty Thousand, but each State shall have at Least one Representative; and until such enumeration shall be made, the State of New Hampshire shall be entitled to chuse three, Massachusetts eight, Rhode Island and Providence Plantations one, Connecticut five, New York six, New Jersey four, Pennsylvania eight, Delaware one, Maryland six, Virginia ten, North Carolina five, South Carolina five, and Georgia three.

When vacancies happen in the Representation from any State, the Executive Authority thereof shall issue Writs of Election to fill such Vacancies.

The House of Representatives shall chuse their Speaker and other Officers; and shall have the sole Power of Impeachment.

Section. 3. The Senate of the United States shall be composed of two Senators from each State, chosen by the Legislature thereof for six Years; and each Senator shall have one Vote.

Immediately after they shall be assembled in Consequence of the first Election, they shall be divided as equally as may be into three Classes. The Seats of the Senators of the first Class shall be vacated at the Expiration of the second Year, of the second Class at the Expiration of the fourth Year, and of the third Class at the Expiration of the sixth Year, so that one third may be chosen every second Year; and if Vacancies happen by Resignation, or otherwise, during the Recess of the Legislature of any State, the Executive thereof may make temporary Appointments until the next Meeting of the Legislature, which shall then fill such Vacancies.

No Person shall be a Senator who shall not have attained to the Age of thirty Years, and been nine Years a Citizen of the United States, and who shall not, when elected, be an Inhabitant of that State for which he shall be chosen.

The Vice President of the United States shall be President of the Senate, but shall have no Vote, unless they be equally divided.

The Senate shall chuse their other Officers, and also a President pro tempore, in the Absence of the Vice President, or when he shall exercise the Office of President of the United States.

The Senate shall have the sole Power to try all Impeachments. When sitting for that Purpose, they shall be on Oath or Affirmation. When the President of the United States is tried, the Chief Justice shall preside: And no Person shall be convicted without the Concurrence of two thirds of the Members present.

Judgment in Cases of Impeachment shall not extend further than to removal from Office, and disqualification to hold and enjoy any Office of honor, Trust or Profit under the United States: but the Party convicted shall nevertheless be liable and subject to Indictment, Trial, Judgment and Punishment, according to Law.

Section. 4. The Times, Places and Manner of holding Elections for Senators and Representatives, shall be prescribed in each State by the Legislature thereof; but the Congress may at any time by Law make or alter such Regulations, except as to the Places of chusing Senators.

The Congress shall assemble at least once in every Year, and such Meeting shall be on the first Monday in December, unless they shall by Law appoint a different Day.

Section. 5. Each House shall be the Judge of the Elections, Returns and Qualifications of its own Members, and a Majority of each shall constitute a Quorum to do Business; but a smaller Number may adjourn from day to day, and may be authorized to compel the Attendance of absent Members, in such Manner, and under such Penalties as each House may provide.

Each House may determine the Rules of its Proceedings, punish its Members for disorderly Behaviour, and, with the Concurrence of two thirds, expel a Member.

Each House shall keep a Journal of its Proceedings, and from time to time publish the same, excepting such Parts as may in their Judgment require Secrecy; and the Yeas and Nays of the Members of either House on any question shall, at the Desire of one fifth of those Present, be entered on the Journal.

Neither House, during the Session of Congress, shall, without the Consent of the other, adjourn for more than three days, nor to any other Place than that in which the two Houses shall be sitting.

Section. 6. The Senators and Representatives shall receive a Compensation for their Services, to be ascertained by Law, and paid out of the Treasury of the United States. They shall in all Cases, except Treason, Felony and Breach of the Peace, be privileged from Arrest during their Attendance at the Session of their respective Houses, and in going to and returning from the same; and for any Speech or Debate in either House, they shall not be questioned in any other Place.

No Senator or Representative shall, during the Time for which he was elected, be appointed to any civil Office under the Authority of the United States, which shall have been created, or the Emoluments whereof shall have been encreased during such time; and no Person holding any Office under the United States, shall be a Member of either House during his Continuance in Office.

Section. 7. All Bills for raising Revenue shall originate in the House of Representatives; but the Senate may propose or concur with Amendments as on other Bills.

Every Bill which shall have passed the House of Representatives and the Senate, shall, before it become a Law, be presented to the President of the

Whether the Constitution of the United States is "the most wonderful work ever struck off at a given time by the brain and purpose of man," as the British statesman William Gladstone said, or is "what the Supreme Court says it is," as Charles Evans Hughes described it, it is the oldest written document of its kind in the world. George Washington, who presided over the Constitutional Convention, thought it "little short of a miracle, that Delegates from so many different States . . . should unite in forming a system of national Government so little liable to well founded objections." Thomas Jefferson called the men gathered at Philadelphia in 1787 an "assembly of demigods." But the Constitution did not spring full blown from the minds of the delegates. They were, after all, able to draw on 170 years as colonies with considerable autonomy plus 11 years as an independent nation founded on republican principles. In addition, most knew well the works of philosophers and political writers from ancient Greece to the Enlightenment.

From 1781 until the adoption of the Constitution, the country had been governed under a set of "articles of Confederation and perpetual Union" for the "United States in Congress assembled." Wary of a strong central government after

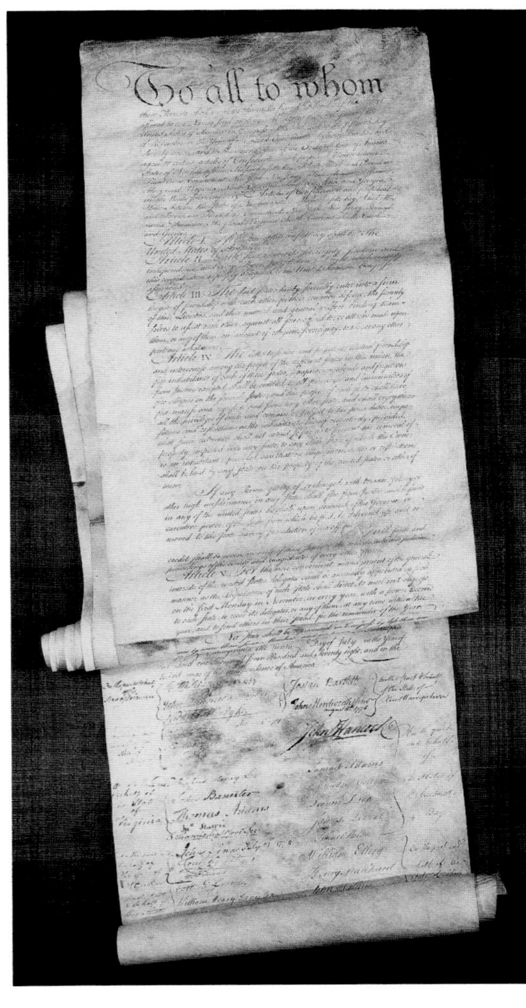
To all to whom

The Articles of Confederation, ratified March 1, 1781, when Maryland became the 13th state to approve them. The confederation form of government vested virtually all power in the states. Congress could make laws, but there was no independent executive to enforce them or courts to interpret them. *Engrossed on 6 parchment sheets stitched together and fastened to a wooden roller to form a scroll; each leaf, 15 3/8 by 23 1/2 inches.*

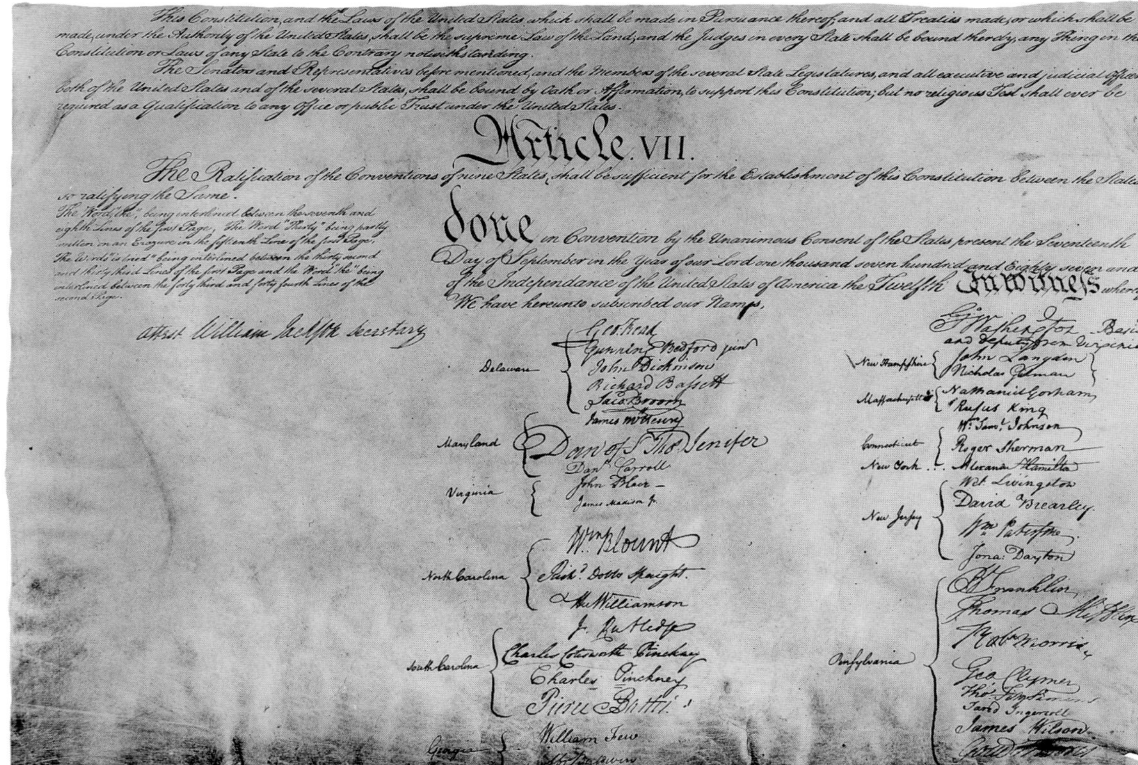
This Constitution, and the Laws of the United States which shall be made in Pursuance thereof; and all Treaties made, or which shall be made, under the Authority of the United States, shall be the supreme Law of the Land; and the Judges in every State shall be bound thereby, any Thing in the Constitution or Laws of any State to the Contrary notwithstanding.

The Senators and Representatives before mentioned, and the Members of the several State Legislatures, and all executive and judicial Officers, both of the United States and of the several States, shall be bound by Oath or Affirmation, to support this Constitution; but no religious Test shall ever be required as a Qualification to any Office or public Trust under the United States.

Article. VII.

The Ratification of the Conventions of nine States, shall be sufficient for the Establishment of this Constitution between the States so ratifying the Same.

The Word, "the," being interlined between the seventh and eighth Lines of the first Page, The Word "Thirty" being partly written on an Erazure in the fifteenth Line of the first Page, The Words "is tried" being interlined between the thirty second and thirty third Lines of the first Page and the Word "the" being interlined between the forty third and forty fourth Lines of the second Page.

Attest William Jackson Secretary

Done in Convention by the Unanimous Consent of the States present the Seventeenth Day of September in the Year of our Lord one thousand seven hundred and Eighty seven and of the Independance of the United States of America the Twelfth In witness whereof We have hereunto subscribed our Names,

Go: Washington—Presidt. and deputy from Virginia

Delaware: Geo: Read, Gunning Bedford jun, John Dickinson, Richard Bassett, Jaco: Broom

Maryland: James McHenry, Dan of St Thos. Jenifer, Danl Carroll

Virginia: John Blair—, James Madison Jr.

North Carolina: Wm Blount, Richd. Dobbs Spaight., Hu Williamson

South Carolina: J. Rutledge, Charles Cotesworth Pinckney, Charles Pinckney, Pierce Butler.

Georgia: William Few, Abr Baldwin

New Hampshire: John Langdon, Nicholas Gilman

Massachusetts: Nathaniel Gorham, Rufus King

Connecticut: Wm. Saml. Johnson, Roger Sherman

New York: Alexander Hamilton

New Jersey: Wil: Livingston, David Brearley, Wm. Paterson, Jona: Dayton

Pensylvania: B Franklin, Thomas Mifflin, Robt Morris, Geo. Clymer, Thos. FitzSimons, Jared Ingersoll, James Wilson, Gouv Morris

Signatures on the Constitution. George Washington was unanimously chosen president of the Constitutional Convention. Of the 62 delegates appointed to the Convention, 7 had been state Governors, almost 30 had served in Congress, and 8 had signed the Declaration of Independence. *Page 4, detail.*

Opposite: **The Constitution of the United States, signed September 17, 1787. It provided that "the ratification of the conventions of nine states shall be sufficient" to establish a government. The ninth ratification came when New Hampshire approved the Constitution on June 21, 1788, making it part of the "supreme law of the land." The other four states ratified the Constitution later.** *4 pages, 23 5/8 by 28 3/4 inches.*

experience with a distant king and parliament in England, the Continental Congress agreed only to a loose confederation of independent states, each yielding little of its claimed sovereignty. There was, to be sure, a national legislative body—the Congress—but it had no power to tax or to regulate commerce. It soon became apparent that a government that can make laws but has no machinery to enforce or interpret them is incomplete.

Under the Articles of Confederation, such national government as existed was created by the states. But under the Constitution, the source of power became "We the People." Augmented by federal laws and treaties, the Constitution was soon recognized as the "supreme law of the land," taking precedence over state and local ordinances. Yet it established a federal system, with many rights reserved to the states.

When the Constitution was ratified, Benjamin Rush of Philadelphia wrote, "'Tis done. We have become a nation." But many felt that the Constitution did not give sufficient protection for individual rights. George Mason, author of the Virginia Bill of Rights, refused to sign the Constitution because he feared an unfavorable impact on individual liberty. North Carolina would not ratify it until a bill of rights was added.

In *The Federalist,* a series of articles written by James Madison, Alexander Hamilton, and John Jay to persuade voters to support ratification, Madison pledged that a bill of rights protecting individual liberties would be added. As a member of the first Congress under the new Constitution, Madison kept his promise and introduced 12 amendments. The 10 that were initially ratified by the states were added to the Constitution as the Bill of Rights in 1791. The Bill of Rights guaranteed free speech and freedom of religion, press, and assembly and further restricted the power of the federal government over the individual and the states.

By 1804 two more amendments had been added, but there were no further changes for 60 years. Altogether, only 27 amendments have been passed in the first 200 years of the Constitution, and the 27th amendment was one of Madison's proposed 12. The Founding Fathers did their work well.

Seals of some of the states, 1800.

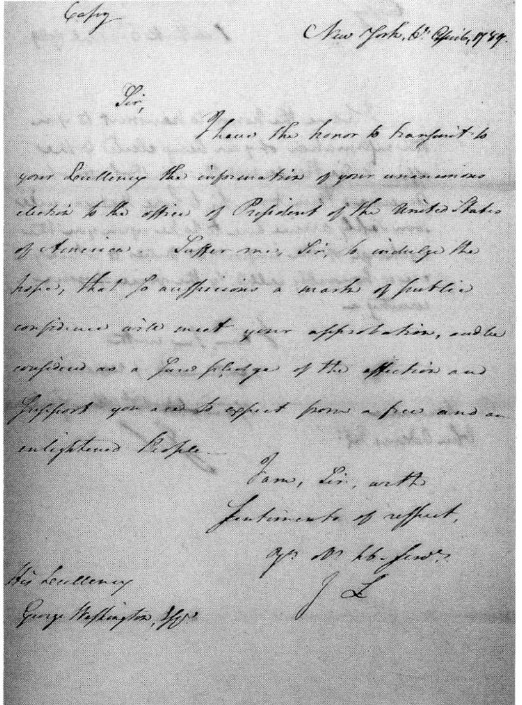

Copy

New York, 6th April, 1789.

Sir,

I have the honor to transmit to your Excellency the information of your unanimous election to the office of President of the United States of America. Suffer me, Sir, to indulge the hope, that so auspicious a mark of public confidence will meet your approbation, and be considered as a sure pledge of the affection and support you are to expect from a free and an enlightened People.

I am, Sir, with sentiments of respect, Yr. Ob. Servt.

J L

His Excellency George Washington, Esqr.

Letter notifying George Washington of his unanimous election as President of the United States, April 6, 1789. The initials are those of John Langdon, President pro tempore of the Senate. *Records of the U.S. Senate, National Archives; 7 7/8 by 12 3/4 inches.*

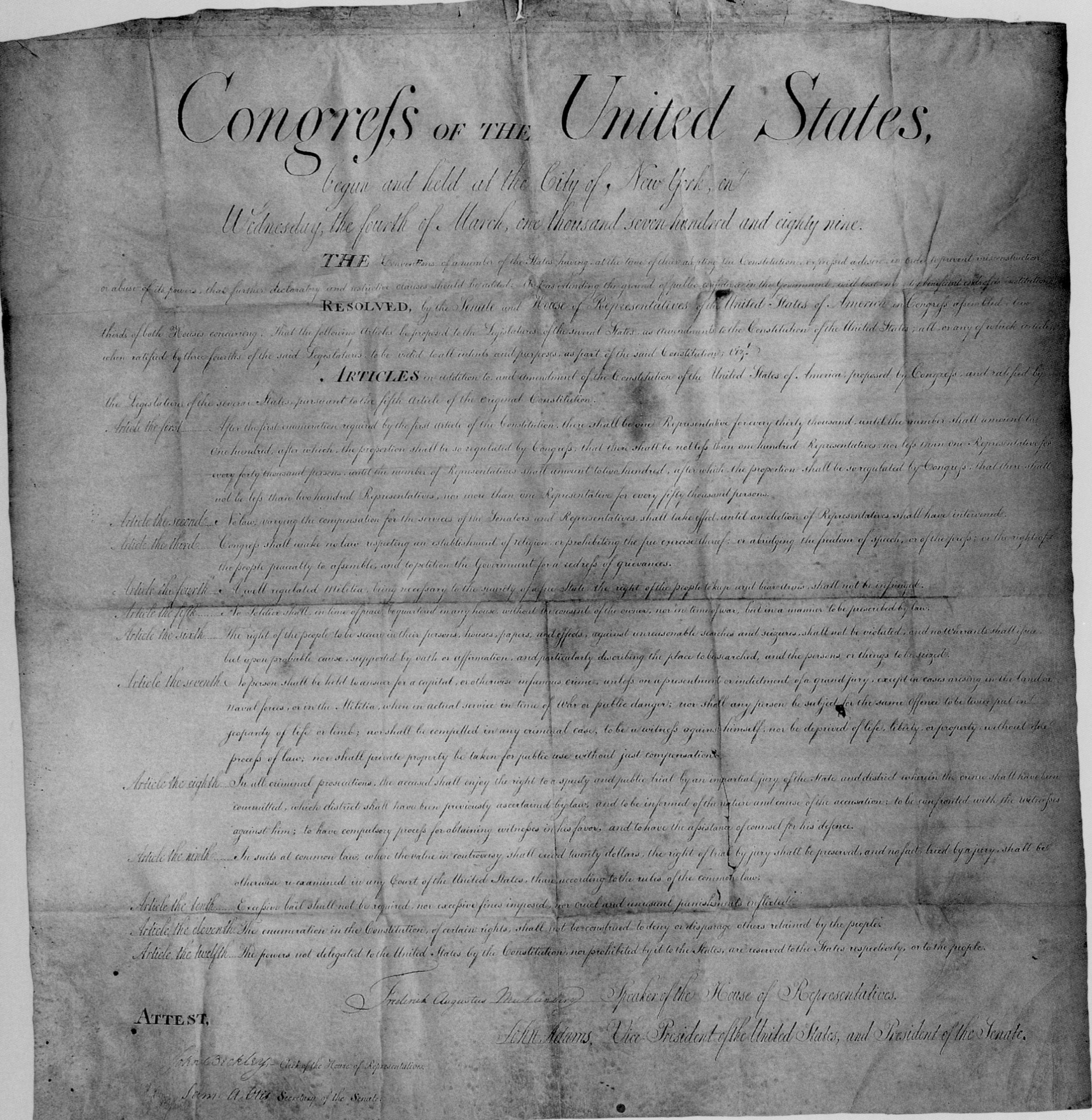

Congress of the United States,

begun and held at the City of New-York, on
Wednesday, the fourth of March, one thousand seven hundred and eighty nine.

THE Conventions of a number of the States, having at the time of their adopting the Constitution, expressed a desire, in order to prevent misconstruction or abuse of its powers, that further declaratory and restrictive clauses should be added: And as extending the ground of public confidence in the Government, will best ensure the beneficent ends of its institution.

RESOLVED, by the Senate and House of Representatives of the United States of America in Congress assembled, two thirds of both Houses concurring, that the following Articles be proposed to the Legislatures of the several States, as amendments to the Constitution of the United States, all, or any of which Articles, when ratified by three fourths of the said Legislatures, to be valid to all intents and purposes, as part of the said Constitution; viz.

ARTICLES in addition to, and Amendment of the Constitution of the United States of America, proposed by Congress, and ratified by the Legislatures of the several States, pursuant to the fifth Article of the original Constitution.

Article the first.... After the first enumeration required by the first article of the Constitution, there shall be one Representative for every thirty thousand, until the number shall amount to one hundred, after which, the proportion shall be so regulated by Congress, that there shall be not less than one hundred Representatives, nor less than one Representative for every forty thousand persons, until the number of Representatives shall amount to two hundred, after which the proportion shall be so regulated by Congress, that there shall not be less than two hundred Representatives, nor more than one Representative for every fifty thousand persons.

Article the second.... No law, varying the compensation for the services of the Senators and Representatives, shall take effect, until an election of Representatives shall have intervened.

Article the third.... Congress shall make no law respecting an establishment of religion, or prohibiting the free exercise thereof; or abridging the freedom of speech, or of the press; or the right of the people peaceably to assemble, and to petition the Government for a redress of grievances.

Article the fourth.... A well regulated Militia, being necessary to the security of a free State, the right of the people to keep and bear Arms, shall not be infringed.

Article the fifth.... No Soldier shall, in time of peace be quartered in any house, without the consent of the owner, nor in time of war, but in a manner to be prescribed by law.

Article the sixth.... The right of the people to be secure in their persons, houses, papers, and effects, against unreasonable searches and seizures, shall not be violated, and no Warrants shall issue, but upon probable cause, supported by oath or affirmation, and particularly describing the place to be searched, and the persons or things to be seized.

Article the seventh.... No person shall be held to answer for a capital, or otherwise infamous crime, unless on a presentment or indictment of a Grand Jury, except in cases arising in the land or naval forces, or in the Militia, when in actual service in time of War or public danger; nor shall any person be subject for the same offence to be twice put in jeopardy of life or limb; nor shall be compelled in any criminal case, to be a witness against himself, nor be deprived of life, liberty, or property, without due process of law; nor shall private property be taken for public use without just compensation.

Article the eighth.... In all criminal prosecutions, the accused shall enjoy the right to a speedy and public trial, by an impartial jury of the State and district wherein the crime shall have been committed, which district shall have been previously ascertained by law, and to be informed of the nature and cause of the accusation; to be confronted with the witnesses against him; to have compulsory process for obtaining witnesses in his favor, and to have the assistance of counsel for his defence.

Article the ninth.... In suits at common law, where the value in controversy shall exceed twenty dollars, the right of trial by jury shall be preserved, and no fact, tried by a jury, shall be otherwise re-examined in any Court of the United States, than according to the rules of the common law.

Article the tenth.... Excessive bail shall not be required, nor excessive fines imposed, nor cruel and unusual punishments inflicted.

Article the eleventh.... The enumeration in the Constitution, of certain rights, shall not be construed to deny or disparage others retained by the people.

Article the twelfth.... The powers not delegated to the United States by the Constitution, nor prohibited by it to the States, are reserved to the States respectively, or to the people.

Frederick Augustus Muhlenberg Speaker of the House of Representatives.

ATTEST,

John Adams, Vice-President of the United States, and President of the Senate.

John Beckley, Clerk of the House of Representatives.

Sam. A. Otis Secretary of the Senate.

The Bill of Rights. A joint resolution proposing 12 amendments (a bill of rights) to the Constitution was submitted to all the states on September 25, 1789. Without the promise to safeguard certain basic rights, the Constitution might not have been ratified by the necessary number of states. Articles III through XII were ratified by the requisite three-fourths of the state legislatures and became the first 10 amendments to the Constitution. *28 1/4 by 28 1/2 inches.*

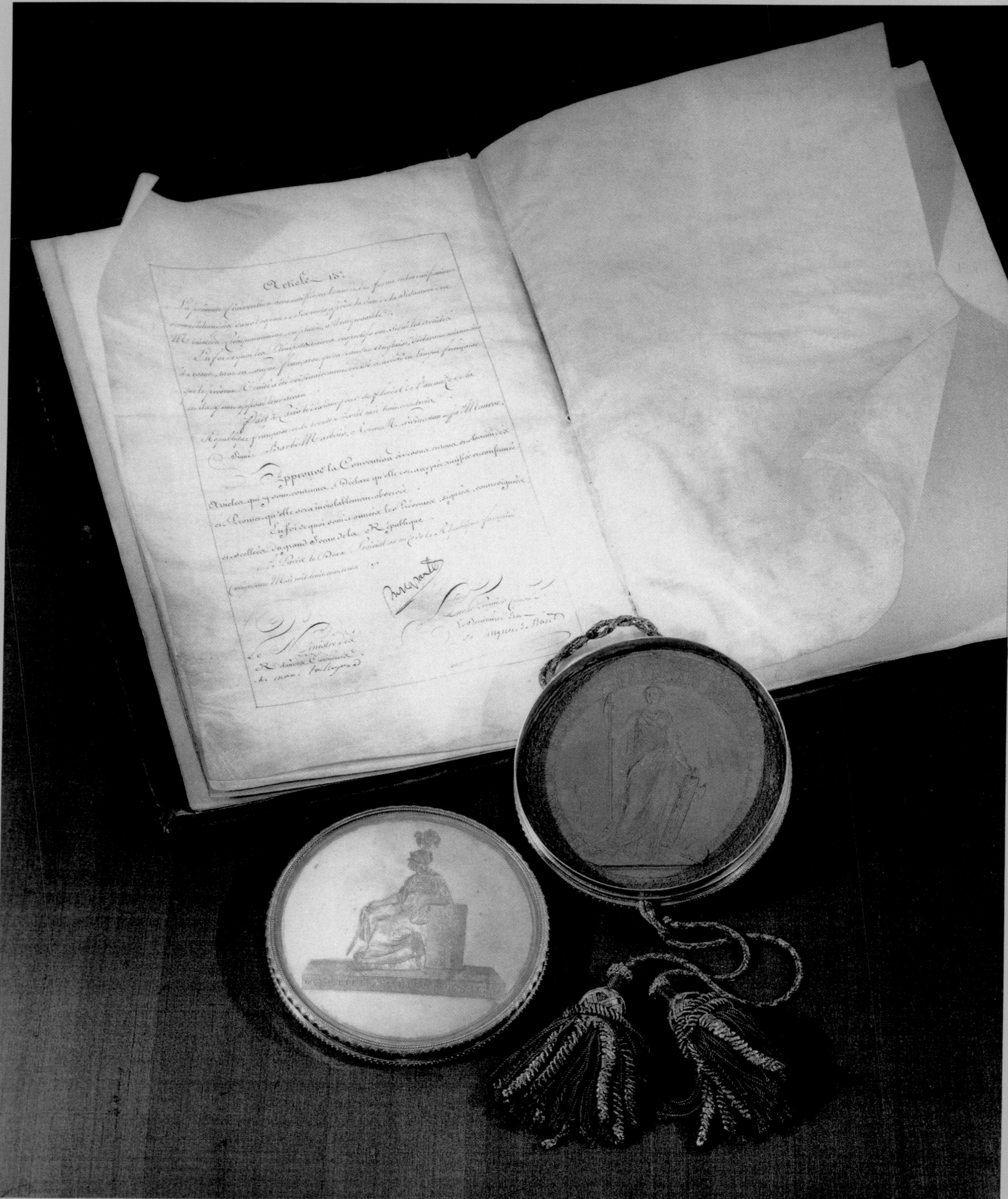

The Louisiana Purchase, obtained from Napoleon Bonaparte of France in 1803, was the first step toward building a nation as wide as the continent. The new territory doubled the size of the United States, advancing its boundary westward from the Mississippi River to an ill-defined line along the uncharted Rocky Mountains. President Thomas Jefferson sent Capt. Meriwether Lewis and Lt. William Clark to explore this vast territory in 1803. The expedition, 1804–6, mapped the new land, added to scientific knowledge, and ultimately helped open the area to settlement.

Eager settlers poured into the lower part of the territory on the wave of nationalist optimism and economic depression that followed the War of 1812. In 1812 Louisiana became the first state to be created from the Louisiana Purchase. Missouri applied for statehood in 1819 and thereby precipitated the first national crisis over the extension of slavery. The Missouri Compromise established a line across the Louisiana Purchase that was intended to settle this question forever: Except for Missouri, there would be no new slave states north of 36° 30´, which was the southern boundary of the new state.

"The Tetons—Snake River," Glacier National Park, WY, 1942. *Ansel Adams photograph.*

Louis de Kerlérec

Sur Les bons Temoignages

Nous L'avons Etabli

Okana-Stoté

Kerlérec

Commission appointing a Cherokee Indian, Okana-Stoté, as a captain in the French Army, 1761. Before the Louisiana Purchase, the French made allies of many Indian tribes. *19 ⅞ by 15 ⅜ inches.*

Opposite: **The Louisiana Purchase Treaty, signed for France by Napoleon Bonaparte, then First Consul, and by Talleyrand, his Foreign Minister, 1803. The treaty was the first and most important of a series that led to the expansion of the nation westward across the continent.** *French exchange copy, 8 pages, 10 ¼ by 15 ¼ inches; skippet, 5 ¼ inches in diameter.*

William Marbury
vs
James Madison
Secretary of State &c

Sup. Court of the
December Term

On the motion of Wi
Marbury for a rule upon
Madison Secretary of Sta
United States to shew cause why a Man
should not be Issued to the said James
Secretary of State of the Unit
Commanding him to cause to
said William Marbury a Commission
of the peace in the County of Washingt
the District of Columbia, it appearing to
Court that Notice of this motion has been g
to the said James Madison Secretary of St
the United States, and it further appearing
Affidavit of the said William Mar
has been credibly informed and
that John Adams President of the Unite
nominated the said William Marbury
Senate of the United States for their adv
and Consent to be a Justice of the pe
in the County of Washington in the Di
of Columbia and that the Senate

MESSAGE TO THE CONGRESS

I am returning without my approval Bill No. 3896 originating in the House of Representatives providing for the immediate payment to veterans of the face value of their adjusted service certificates, and for other purposes.

Eighteen years ago this Nation of one hundred twenty million people was united in the purpose of victory. The millions engaged in agriculture toiled to provide the raw materials and foodstuffs for our armies and for the Nations with whom we were associated. Other millions engaged in industry toiled to create the material for the active conduct of the War on land and sea.

Four and three-quarter million men volunteered or were drafted into the armed forces of the United States. Of these, about one-half remained within the continental limits of the United States. Of the others, one million four hundred thousand saw service in actual combat. In line with our national policy, the people and the government of the United States have shown a proper and generous regard for the sacrifices and patriotism of all of the four and three-quarter million men who were in uniform During the World War, the President and the Congress sought an entirely new principle, however, to guide the granting of financial aid to veterans. Recognizing the unfortunate results that came from a lack of a veterans' policy after the Civil War, they determined that the prudent principle of insurance should supplant the uncertainties and unfairness of bounties. At the same time, their policy recognized the most complete care for those who had

President Franklin D. Roosevelt's veto of the soldier's bonus bill, May 22, 1935, the first veto to be delivered in person before Congress. Of Roosevelt's 635 vetoes, only 9 were overridden. The possession of veto power gives the President considerable leverage over Congress. *From the Franklin D. Roosevelt Library; 13 pages, 8 by 10 ½ inches.*

"A law repugnant to the Constitution is void." With these words, written by Chief Justice John Marshall in the 1803 case of *Marbury* v. *Madison,* the Supreme Court for the first time declared unconstitutional a law passed by Congress and signed by the President. Nothing in the Constitution gave the Court this specific power. Marshall, however, believed that the Supreme Court should have a role equal to that of the other two branches of government in the system of "checks and balances" created to prevent any one branch from becoming too powerful.

When James Madison, Alexander Hamilton, and John Jay wrote a defense of the Constitution in *The Federalist,* they explained their judgment that a strong national government must have built-in restraints: "You must first enable government to control the governed; and in the next place oblige it to control itself." The writers of the Constitution had given the executive and legislative branches powers that would limit each other as well as the judiciary branch. The Constitution gave Congress the power to impeach and remove officials, including judges or the President himself. The President was given the veto power to restrain Congress and the authority to appoint members of the Supreme Court with the advice and consent of the Senate. In this intricate system, the role of the Supreme Court had not been defined. It therefore fell to a strong Chief Justice like Marshall to complete the triangular structure of checks and balances by establishing the principle of judicial review. Although no other law was declared unconstitutional until the Dred Scott decision of 1857, the role of the Supreme Court to invalidate federal and state laws that are contrary to the Constitution has never been seriously challenged.

As the Founding Fathers had foreseen, the principal struggle for dominance within the government was between the Congress and the President. In the aftermath of the Civil War, confronting the tensions of Reconstruction, for example, the House of Representatives impeached President Andrew Johnson when he tried to test the constitutionality of an act restricting Presidential powers.

Opposite: **Show-cause order served on James Madison, Secretary of State in the Cabinet of President Thomas Jefferson, 1802. Madison had refused to deliver William Marbury's commission as justice of the peace that had been issued by outgoing President John Adams, and Marbury sued to obtain it. With his decision in *Marbury* v. *Madison,* Chief Justice John Marshall for the first time declared unconstitutional a law passed by Congress and signed by a President, thus establishing the principle of judicial review, an important addition to the system of checks and balances in the federal government. The order bears the marks of the Capitol fire of 1898.** *Page 1 of 4 pages, 7 ⅜ by 9 ½ inches.*

Andrew Jackson, 1844, the first President to make extensive use of the veto. He used it more than twice as many times as the six previous Presidents. Not one of his vetoes was overridden. *Mathew Brady photograph.*

The House of Representatives committee for the impeachment of Andrew Johnson, 1868: left to right, Benjamin F. Butler (Massachusetts), James Wilson (Iowa), Thaddeus Stevens (Pennsylvania), George Boutwell (Massachusetts), Thomas Williams (Pennsylvania), John A. Logan (Illinois), and John A. Bingham (Ohio). *Mathew Brady photograph.*

In his trial before the Senate, Johnson was acquitted by one vote. But the failure to convict in Johnson's case did not negate the power of Congress to remove the President for cause through the impeachment process. In 1974 the threat of impeachment coupled with the power of public opinion brought about the first resignation of a President in U.S. history, that of Richard M. Nixon.

The veto power assigned to the President by the Constitution was only a "qualified negative." A veto can be overridden by a two-thirds vote of both Houses of Congress, but the threat of its use can influence the content of legislation or prevent its enactment. Andrew Jackson, the first President to use the veto extensively, employed it to define his interpretation of the Constitution. He vetoed 19 bills, more than twice the number that the 6 previous Presidents had struck down, and not one of his vetoes was overridden. Jackson's use of the veto immeasurably strengthened the Office of the Presidency. However, the veto was not widely used by other Chief Executives in the first half of the 19th century. Not until after the Civil War did it become the formidable check that it has been throughout the 20th century.

"The Constitution of the United States," said Woodrow Wilson, "was not made to fit us like a strait jacket. In its elasticity lies its chief greatness." The often-praised wisdom of the authors of the Constitution consisted largely of their restraint. They resisted the temptation to write too many specifics into the basic document. They contented themselves with establishing a framework of government that included safeguards against the abuse of power. When the Marshall decision in *Marbury* v. *Madison* completed the system of checks and balances, the United States had a government in which laws could be enacted, interpreted, and executed to meet changing circumstances.

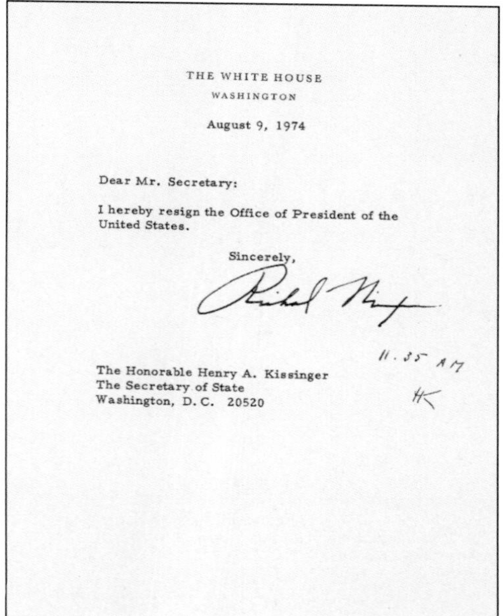
THE WHITE HOUSE
WASHINGTON

August 9, 1974

Dear Mr. Secretary:

I hereby resign the Office of President of the United States.

Sincerely,

Richard Nixon

The Honorable Henry A. Kissinger
The Secretary of State
Washington, D.C. 20520

11.35 AM
HK

President Richard Nixon's letter of resignation, 1974, is the first Presidential resignation in U.S. history. An act of March 1, 1792, provides that a President or Vice President shall tender his resignation to the Secretary of State. *8 by 10 inches.*

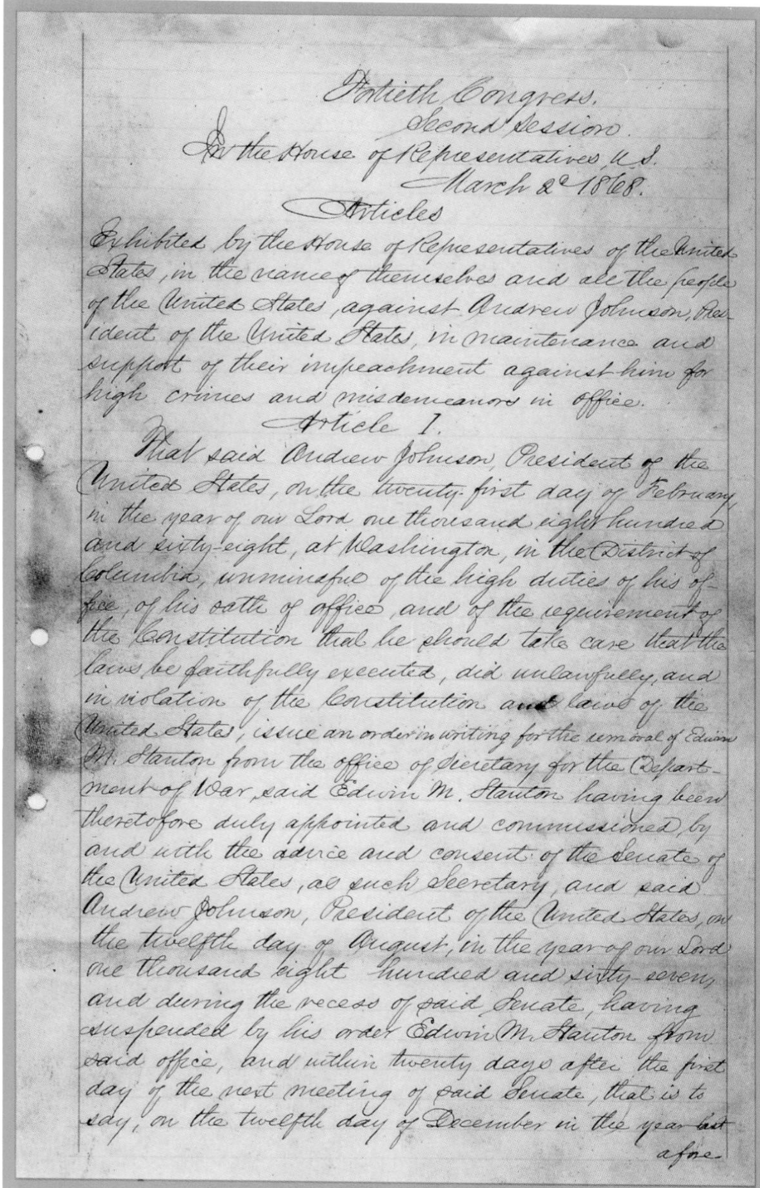
Fortieth Congress,
Second Session.
In the House of Representatives, U.S.
March 2d 1868.

Articles

Exhibited by the House of Representatives of the United States, in the name of themselves and all the people of the United States, against Andrew Johnson, President of the United States, in maintenance and support of their impeachment against him for high crimes and misdemeanors in office.

Article I.

That said Andrew Johnson, President of the United States, on the twenty-first day of February in the year of our Lord one thousand eight hundred and sixty-eight, at Washington, in the District of Columbia, unmindful of the high duties of his office, of his oath of office, and of the requirement of the Constitution that he should take care that the laws be faithfully executed, did unlawfully, and in violation of the Constitution and laws of the United States, issue an order in writing for the removal of Edwin M. Stanton from the office of Secretary for the Department of War, said Edwin M. Stanton having been theretofore duly appointed and commissioned, by and with the advice and consent of the Senate of the United States, as such Secretary, and said Andrew Johnson, President of the United States, on the twelfth day of August, in the year of our Lord one thousand eight hundred and sixty-seven, and during the recess of said Senate, having suspended by his order Edwin M. Stanton from said office, and within twenty days after the first day of the next meeting of said Senate, that is to say, on the twelfth day of December in the year last afore-

The articles of impeachment of Andrew Johnson, 1868. *Records of the U.S. Senate, National Archives; 21 pages plus endorsement, 8 1/2 by 13 5/8 inches.*

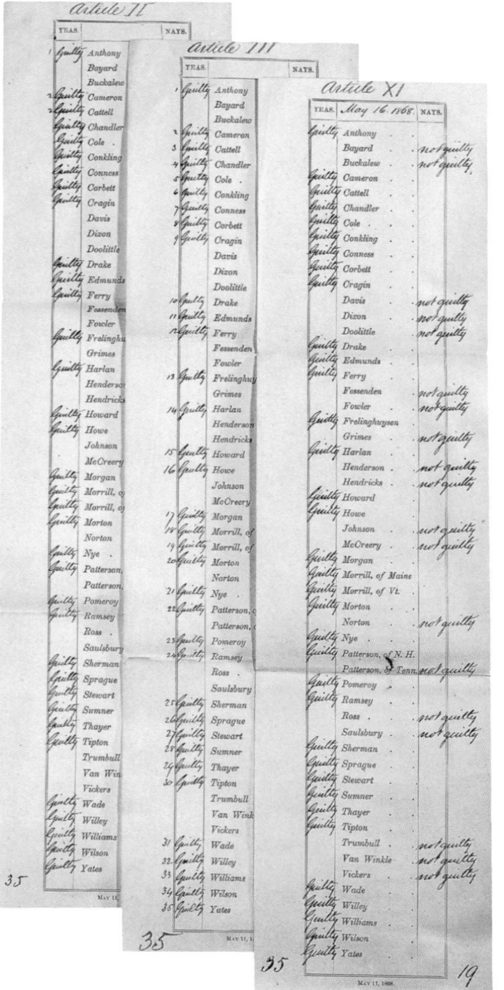
Article II
Article III
Article XI May 16. 1868.

Three ballots used in the impeachment trial of President Andrew Johnson, March–May 1868. Johnson was acquitted by one vote. *Records of the U.S. Senate, National Archives; 4 1/2 by 18 inches.*

Admission ticket to the U.S. Senate proceedings in the trial of President Andrew Johnson, 1868, after his impeachment by the House of Representatives. The right of Congress to impeach and remove a Chief Executive is the ultimate check on a President. *3 1/2 by 3 inches.*

6.

Government. In the discussions to which this interest has given rise, and in the arrangements by which they may terminate, the occasion has been judged proper, for asserting as a principle in which the rights and interests of the United States are involved, that the American Continents, by the free and independent condition which they have assumed and maintain, are henceforth not to be considered as subjects for future colonization by any European Power.

Since the close of the last Session of Congress, the Commissioners and Arbitrators for ascertaining and determining the amount of indemnification which may be due to Citizens of the United States under the decision of His Imperial Majesty the Emperor of Russia, in conformity to the Convention concluded at St. Petersburg on the 12th of July 1822, have assembled in this City, and organized themselves as a Board for the performance of the duties assigned to them by that Treaty. The Commission constituted under the 11th Article of the Treaty of the 22nd of February 1819 between the United States and Spain, is also in session here; and, as the term of three years limited by the Treaty, for the execution of the trust, will expire before the period of the next regular meeting of Congress, the attention of the Legislature will

President James Monroe's 1823 annual message to Congress contained the Monroe Doctrine, which warned European powers not to interfere in the affairs of the Western Hemisphere. *Records of the U.S. Senate, National Archives; in the handwriting of a clerk or clerks and signed by Monroe, page 6 of 36 pages. 7 3/4 by 12 3/4 inches.*

Understandably, the United States has always taken a particular interest in its closest neighbors—the nations of the Western Hemisphere. Equally understandably, expressions of this concern have not always been favorably regarded by other American nations.

The Monroe Doctrine is the best known U.S. policy toward the Western Hemisphere. Buried in a routine annual message delivered to Congress by President James Monroe in December 1823, the doctrine warns European nations that the United States would not tolerate further colonization or puppet monarchs. The doctrine was conceived to meet major concerns of the moment, but it soon became a watchword of U.S. policy in the Western Hemisphere.

The Monroe Doctrine was invoked in 1865 when the U.S. government exerted diplomatic and military pressure in support of Mexican President Benito Juárez. This support enabled Juárez to lead a successful revolt against the Emperor Maximilian, who had been placed on the throne by the French government.

Almost 40 years later, in 1904, European creditors of a number of Latin American countries threatened armed intervention to collect debts. President Theodore Roosevelt promptly proclaimed the right of the United States to exercise an "international police power" to curb such "chronic wrongdoing." As a result, U.S. Marines were sent into Santo Domingo in 1904, Nicaragua in 1911, and Haiti in 1915, ostensibly to keep the Europeans out. Other Latin American nations viewed these interventions with misgiving, and relations between the "great Colossus of the North" and its southern neighbors remained strained for many years.

A new policy began to take shape in the late 1920s, when the Department of State emphasized the fact that the Monroe Doctrine represented "a case of the United States *v.* Europe, and not of the United States *v.* Latin America." President-elect Herbert Hoover undertook an extensive goodwill tour in late 1928 to 11 Latin American countries and later removed the last American troops from Nicaragua. President Franklin D. Roosevelt pledged continuation of the Good Neighbor Policy in his first inaugural address.

In the early days of World War II, based on the Monroe Doctrine, the 21 republics of the Pan-American Union agreed that 1 or more of them could occupy any colony in the New World owned by a European nation that had been conquered

Benito Juárez, President of Mexico during the French attempt to maintain Emperor Maximilian on the Mexican throne in the 1860s. Vigorously opposed to this violation of the Monroe Doctrine, the United States supported Juárez with diplomatic pressure and military aid. *Mathew Brady photograph.*

President Theodore Roosevelt, ca. 1912. Roosevelt's policy extended the Monroe Doctrine to permit armed intervention by the United States in any Latin American state threatened by a European power or guilty of national "wrongdoing or impotence."

by Germany. Thus the defense of the hemisphere became a shared responsibility.

In a March 31, 1961, speech to Latin American ambassadors, President John F. Kennedy announced his 10-point Alliance for Progress, a reinstatement of Roosevelt's Good Neighbor Policy. Kennedy emphasized the need for Latin American countries and the United States to work toward a common goal of "economic progress and social justice," thereby "transform[ing] the [Western Hemisphere] into a vast crucible of revolutionary ideas and efforts."

Since the end of World War II, there have been several notable exceptions to the U.S. policy of assistance to and cooperation with its Latin American neighbors. In 1958–59, after Fidel Castro led a successful revolt against Cuba's Batista government, he began to cultivate relations with the U.S.S.R., and in January 1961, confronted by the presence of a Communist government in the Western Hemisphere, the United States broke off diplomatic relations with Cuba. In April about 1,500 Cuban exiles who had been trained and equipped by the Central Intelligence Agency invaded Cuba at the Bay of Pigs. Castro's forces easily stopped the invasion and forced the troops to surrender. Then in the fall of 1962, the U.S. government discovered that the Soviet Union had begun to build medium-range missile launching sites in Cuba. With the support of the Organization of American States (successor to the Pan-American Union), President John F. Kennedy threw a naval and air quarantine around the island. After several tense days, the Soviet Union agreed to withdraw the missiles and dismantle the sites, and the United States pledged not to invade Cuba and to lift the blockade. Subsequently, the United States dismantled several of its obsolete air and missile bases in Turkey.

During the 1980s, President Ronald Reagan's policy toward Latin America was one that essentially rejected compromise and negotiation. Throughout the decade, amid congressional and public debate, Reagan supported arms sales and military aid to counterinsurgency forces in El Salvador and to rebel forces in Nicaragua. Meanwhile, the Reagan administration refused to negotiate with the Salvadoran rebels or the Nicaraguan Sandanista government, claiming that the Soviets were supplying them with arms.

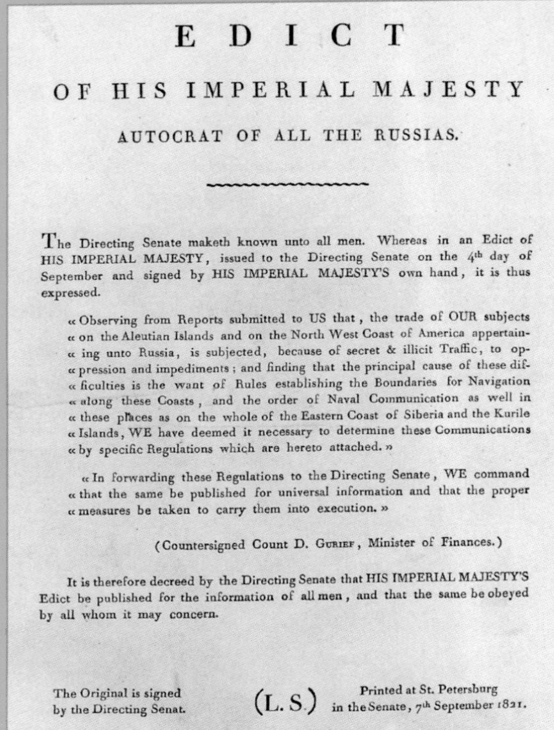

EDICT

OF HIS IMPERIAL MAJESTY

AUTOCRAT OF ALL THE RUSSIAS.

The Directing Senate maketh known unto all men. Whereas in an Edict of HIS IMPERIAL MAJESTY, issued to the Directing Senate on the 4th day of September and signed by HIS IMPERIAL MAJESTY'S own hand, it is thus expressed.

« Observing from Reports submitted to US that, the trade of OUR subjects « on the Aleutian Islands and on the North West Coast of America appertain- « ing unto Russia, is subjected, because of secret & illicit Traffic, to op- « pression and impediments; and finding that the principal cause of these dif- « ficulties is the want of Rules establishing the Boundaries for Navigation « along these Coasts, and the order of Naval Communication as well in « these places as on the whole of the Eastern Coast of Siberia and the Kurile « Islands, WE have deemed it necessary to determine these Communications « by specific Regulations which are hereto attached. »

« In forwarding these Regulations to the Directing Senate, WE command « that the same be published for universal information and that the proper « measures be taken to carry them into execution. »

(Countersigned Count D. Gurief, Minister of Finances.)

It is therefore decreed by the Directing Senate that HIS IMPERIAL MAJESTY'S Edict be published for the information of all men, and that the same be obeyed by all whom it may concern.

The Original is signed by the Directing Senat. (L. S.) Printed at St. Petersburg in the Senate, 7th September 1821.

Tsar Alexander II's 1821 ukase (edict) extending Russia's control over Alaskan waters. The fear that Russia intended further expansion in western America hastened the formulation of the Monroe Doctrine. *Printed English translation, 7 5/8 by 12 5/8 inches.*

The Cuban government under Fidel Castro supported both the Salvadoran rebels and the Sandanistas, particularly by offering political advice, and the Soviets supplied direct aid to the Sandanistas once they were in power in Nicaragua.

In December 1989, after reports that Panamanian dictator Manuel Noriega planned to attack U.S. citizens in Panama, President George Bush sent U.S. military forces into that country, where they engaged in a brief conflict with Panamanian forces. Noriega took refuge in the Vatican's diplomatic mission in Panama City and eventually surrendered to U.S. forces. He was flown to Florida and arraigned on drug trafficking charges on January 4, 1990. U.S. troops were withdrawn from Panama a few weeks later. Although crowds of Panamanians celebrated Noriega's capture, the U.S. actions in other Central American countries in the 1980s were not so well received by the citizens themselves. As the United States moved into the 1990s, the tone of its future relations with Latin America, particularly with Central America, was still uncertain.

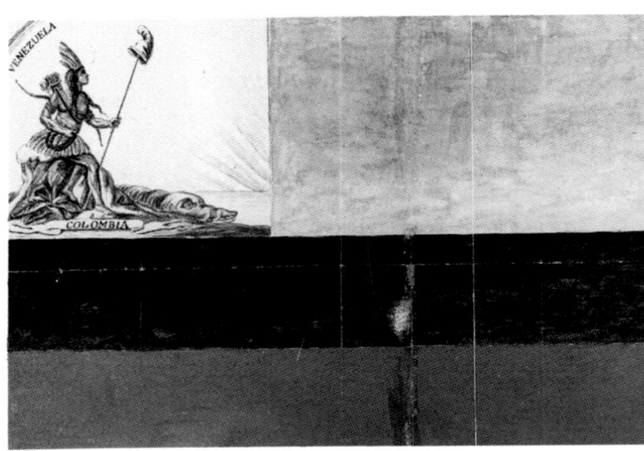

The design for the flag of Gran Colombia (present-day Venezuela, Colombia, Ecuador, and Panama), a federation established in 1819 by Simón Bolívar. *13 1/8 by 11 7/8 inches.*

Souvenir album presented to President-elect Herbert Hoover in Lima, Peru, on December 2, 1928. The tour marked the beginning of what President Franklin D. Roosevelt later called the Good Neighbor Policy. *From the Herbert Hoover Library; tooled and gold-stamped red leather covers; pages adorned with woodcuts, photographs, and signatures; 14 ½ by 10 ½ inches.*

F. Behrendt cartoon that appeared in a Dutch newspaper during the Cuban missile crisis, 1962. *From the John F. Kennedy Library; printed copy with artist's handwritten caption, 9 ⅛ by 8 inches.*

Coat of arms of the independent Republic of Cuba, 1906. The Spanish-American War of 1898 freed Cuba from Spanish control. *8 ¾ by 12 ½ inches.*

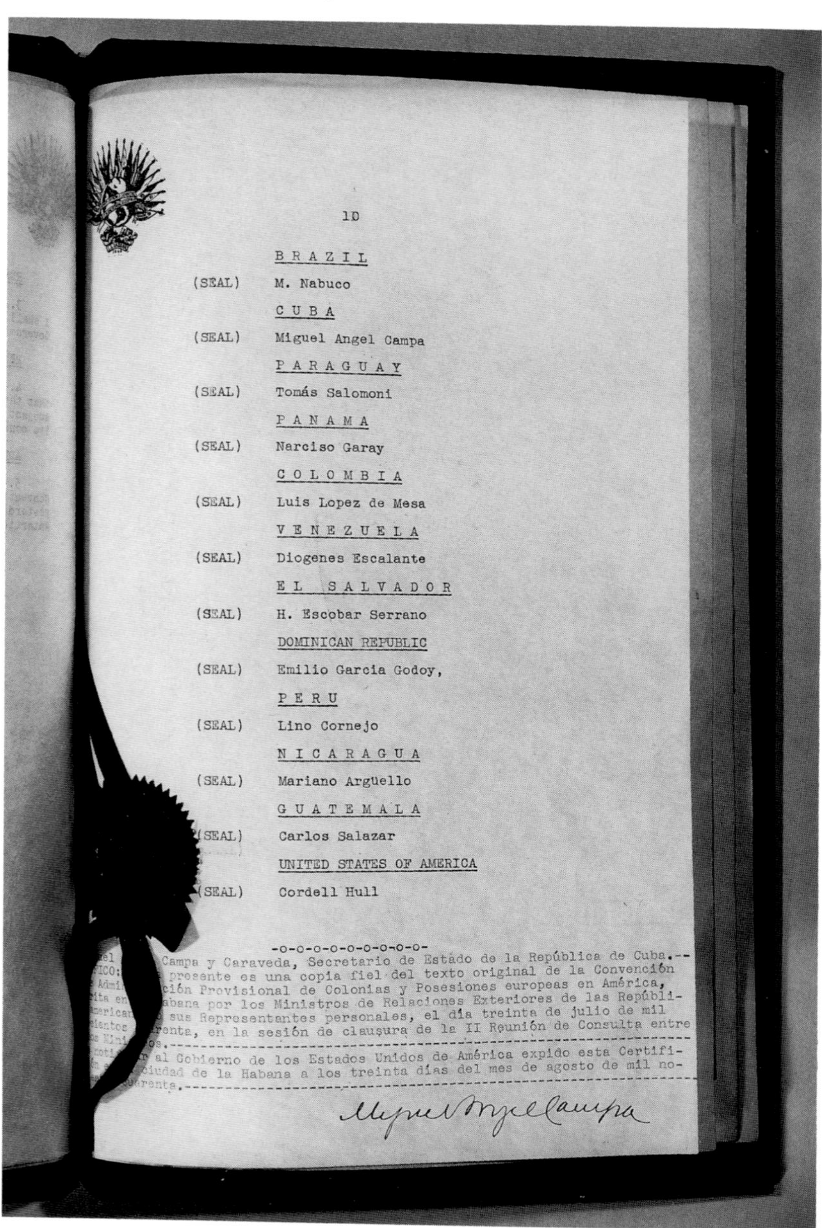

10

B R A Z I L

(SEAL) M. Nabuco

C U B A

(SEAL) Miguel Angel Campa

P A R A G U A Y

(SEAL) Tomás Salomoni

P A N A M A

(SEAL) Narciso Garay

C O L O M B I A

(SEAL) Luis Lopez de Mesa

V E N E Z U E L A

(SEAL) Diogenes Escalante

E L S A L V A D O R

(SEAL) H. Escobar Serrano

DOMINICAN REPUBLIC

(SEAL) Emilio Garcia Godoy,

P E R U

(SEAL) Lino Cornejo

N I C A R A G U A

(SEAL) Mariano Argüello

G U A T E M A L A

(SEAL) Carlos Salazar

UNITED STATES OF AMERICA

(SEAL) Cordell Hull

-o-o-o-o-o-o-o-o-o-

...Campa y Caraveda, Secretario de Estádo de la República de Cuba.-- ...presente es una copia fiel del texto original de la Convención ...ción Provisional de Colonias y Posesiones europeas en América, ...abana por los Ministros de Relaciones Exteriores de las Repúbli... ...sus Representantes personales, el día treinta de julio de mil ...renta, en la sesión de clausura de la II Reunión de Consulta entre ...os.--
...r al Gobierno de los Estados Unidos de América expido esta Certifi... ...ciudad de la Habana a los treinta días del mes de agosto de mil no... ...uarenta.---

Miguel Angel Campa

The Act of Havana, 1940. The governments of the American republics warned the Axis powers against taking over territory in the Americas owned by European nations conquered by Germany. *Convention, page 10 of 10 pages, 9 ¼ by 14 ¼ inches.*

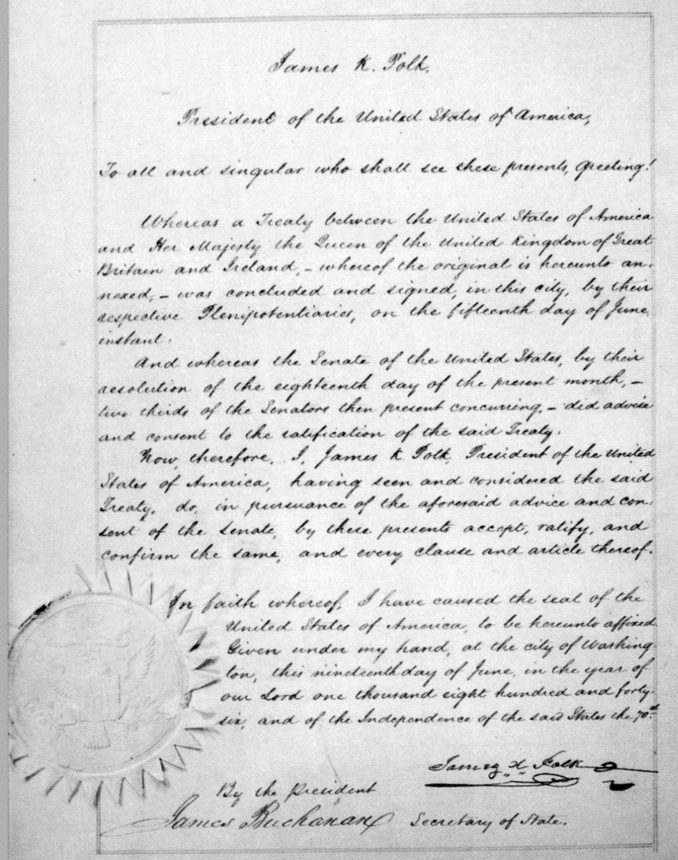

James K. Polk,

President of the United States of America,

To all and singular who shall see these presents, Greeting!

Whereas a Treaty between the United States of America and Her Majesty the Queen of the United Kingdom of Great Britain and Ireland, – whereof the original is hereunto annexed, – was concluded and signed, in this city, by their respective Plenipotentiaries, on the fifteenth day of June, instant:

And whereas the Senate of the United States, by their resolution of the eighteenth day of the present month, – two thirds of the Senators then present concurring, – did advise and consent to the ratification of the said Treaty,

Now, therefore, I, James K. Polk, President of the United States of America, having seen and considered the said Treaty, do, in pursuance of the aforesaid advice and consent of the Senate, by these presents accept, ratify, and confirm the same, and every clause and article thereof.

In faith whereof, I have caused the seal of the United States of America, to be hereunto affixed. Given under my hand, at the city of Washington, this nineteenth day of June, in the year of our Lord one thousand eight hundred and forty-six, and of the Independence of the said States the 70th.

James K. Polk

By the President

James Buchanan Secretary of State.

thereof, may be observed and fulfilled with good faith by the United States and the citizens thereof.

In witness whereof, I have hereunto set my [illegible] and caused the seal [illegible]nited States to be [illegible]. Done at the [illegible] of Washington, this fifth day of August, [illegible] the year of our Lord one thousand eight hundred and forty-six, and of the Independence of the United States the seventy-first.

James K. Polk

By the President:

James Buchanan

Secretary of State.

The Oregon Treaty, 1846; proclamation, left; ratification, right. This treaty divided the Oregon country between the United States and Canada at the 49th parallel and added Oregon, Washington, Idaho, and parts of Montana and Wyoming to the United States. *American original, 8 pages, 10 by 13 3/4 inches.*

"Sweet land of liberty," a line from a patriotic hymn written in the 1830s, expresses the sense of mission that gripped the American people as they dreamed of the land west of their boundaries. It was their "Manifest Destiny," they felt, to settle and bring the blessings of democracy to a continent stretching from the Atlantic to the Pacific. Despite the territorial claims of Great Britain, Oregon, especially its verdant Willamette Valley, attracted land-hungry emigrants from the East.

American claims to this area began with the 1791 voyage of Capt. Robert Gray, who discovered the river that still bears the name of his ship, the *Columbia.* Although tough American traders followed Gray to the west coast, the Hudson's Bay Company's fur traders held most of the interior for Great Britain.

As early as 1820, Americans became concerned about British occupation of the region, and efforts were made to promote immigration to the area. Private citizens, Congressmen, and businessmen developed ambitious plans for settlement and described the wonders of the country in speeches, pamphlets, and letters. Oregon was extolled as "the most valuable of all the unoccupied parts of the earth." In the 1830s missionaries such as Dr. Marcus Whitman established stations in Oregon and continued propagandizing for settlement. In the spring of 1843 the great overland migration began; "Oregon fever" broke out like an epidemic. That year more than 100 covered wagons and nearly 1,000 men, women, and children braved the elements, hostile Indians, and other hardships to begin the difficult and tedious 2,000-mile journey from Independence, MO, over the Oregon Trail. In 1845 an estimated 3,000 emigrants traveled to Oregon. By 1846, the U.S. government felt it necessary to provide military escort for the wagon trains, and by 1847 the number of people using the trail had increased to nearly 5,000.

During the 1840s Oregon fever turned into war fever. Citizens' groups adopted resolutions urging the immediate eviction of the British from the Oregon country. Calling for "54° 40′ or fight," they would accept nothing short of the entire area up to the chosen latitude.

When James K. Polk was elected President in 1844 on a platform calling for the "reoccupation

A petition by citizens of the Mississippi Valley, Cincinnati, OH, 1843, for the immediate occupation of Oregon. Many Americans opposed to the British presence in Oregon adopted the bellicose slogan "54°40′ or fight" in the 1844 Presidential election campaign. A shrewd compromise by President James K. Polk averted war between Britain and the United States over the Canadian boundary dispute. *8 by 35 ½ inches.*

COLUMBUS, JULY 28, 1843.

SIR:—The undersigned were appointed Commissioners, by the Oregon Convention, to extend and urge forward its principles and determinations. In the performance of that duty they do themselves the honor of forwarding to you a copy of the Declaration which consummated the labors of the Convention, requesting that it may be read for information before the Regiments of your Brigade. We, also, append a memorial which it is hoped may have a favorable reception by yourself and your fellow citizens. It may be filled so as to be signed by officers and members of the Brigade as such, or as citizens of the Republic.

The measures proposed, and principles declared, are entirely American, divested of all shade or suspicion of party influence or effort, by the fact that equal numbers of the Commissioners are of opposite political parties. The failure of Senator Linn's bill, last winter, for the occupation of Oregon, was the moving cause of the Oregon Convention. Our great object is the defence and assertion of national interests and principles, and of American dignity and honor, and the extension of free institutions over regions about to be, if not now, unjustly subjected to the dominion of British arrogance and power.

Very Respectfully,

T. WORTHINGTON, of Ohio,
W. W. SOUTHGATE, of Ky.
E. D. MANSFIELD, of Ohio,

S. MEDARY, } of Ohio.
WM. PARRY,
THOS. M'GUIRE,

A Declaration of the Citizens of the Mississippi Valley, in Convention assembled, at Cincinnati, July 5, 1843, for the purpose of adopting such measures as may induce the immediate occupation of the Oregon Territory by the arms and laws of the United States of North America.

WE, the undersigned, citizens of the Mississippi Valley, do hereby declare to our fellow citizens of the whole Republic, that, in urging forward measures for the immediate occupation of the Oregon Territory and the Northeast coast of the Pacific, from 42 to 54 degs. 40 min. North latitude, we are but performing a duty to ourselves, to the Republic, to the commercial nations of the world, to posterity and to the people of Great Britain and Ireland, not, as we believe, to be benefitted by the further extension of their empire.

Duty to ourselves requires that we should urge the immediate occupation of Oregon, not only for the increase and extension of the West, but for the security of our peace and safety, perpetually threatened by the savage tribes of the Northwest. That this duty is required of us as due to the whole Republic, all parts of which may not appreciate, as they seem not to have appreciated, the value of the Territory in question, and its political importance to the honor, prosperity and power of the Union, to say nothing of our commercial interests and naval predominance, threatened as they are with injury or diminution should the N. E. coast of that ocean pass into the possession of a great naval power. That, as an independent member of the great family of nations, it is due from us to the whole commercial world that the ports of both coasts of this continent should be held by a liberal government, able and willing to extend and facilitate that social and commercial intercourse which an all-wise Providence has made necessary for the intellectual improvement, the social happiness and the moral culture of the human race.

That we owe the entire and absolute occupation of the Oregon to that posterity, which, without such occupation by the citizens and free institutions of our great Republic, could not perfect or make available to themselves or to the world the important considerations above set forth.

That however indignant at the avarice, pride and ambition of Great Britain, so frequently, lawlessly, and so lately evinced, we yet believe that it is for the benefit of all civilized nations that she should fulfil a legitimate destiny, but that she should be checked in her career of *aggression with impunity* and *dominion without right.*

That for the independence and neutrality of the western coasts of the American continents and the islands of the Pacific Ocean, it is important that she should be restrained in the further extension of her power on those coasts, and in the middle and eastern portions of that ocean.

That so far as regards our rights to the Territory in question, we are assured of their perfect integrity, based as they are on discovery and exploration by our own citizens and government, and on purchase and cession from those powers having the pretence or the reality of any right to the same.

That beyond these rights so perfectly established, we would feel compelled to retain the whole Territory, in accordance with Mr. Monroe's universally approved declaration of 1823, that the American continents were not thenceforth to be considered subjects for future colonization by any foreign powers.

Influenced by these reasons and considerations, so important to us and the whole Republic, to liberty to justice and to free governments, we do subscribe our names to this declaration, with the firm, just, and matured determination, never to cease our exertions till its intentions and principles are perfected, and the North American Republic, whose citizens we are, shall have established its laws, its arms, and its free institutions from the shores of the Pacific to the Rocky Mountains, throughout the limits above specified.

And we do hereby protest, as we shall continue to protest, against any act or negociation, past, in process, or hereafter to be perfected, which shall yield possession of any portion of the same to any foreign power, and above all do we remonstrate against the possession of any part of the N. E. coast of the Pacific Ocean by the power of Great Britain.

RICHARD M. JOHNSON, *President.*

W. W. SOUTHGATE, Kentucky. } *Vice Presidents.*
SAMUEL MEDARY, Ohio.
W. B. EWING, Iowa Ter.
JOHN CAIN, Indiana.

Wm. Parry, } Secretaries.
Rufus King,

MEMORIAL FOR THE IMMEDIATE OCCUPATION OF THE OREGON.

The undersigned, Citizens of the County of Pickaway and State of Ohio

respectfully urge upon Congress the expedience, necessity, and propriety of asserting and maintaining the principles and policy set forth in the resolutions and declaration of the Oregon Convention held in Cincinnati, July 3d, 4th and 5th, 1843.

NAMES.	NAMES.

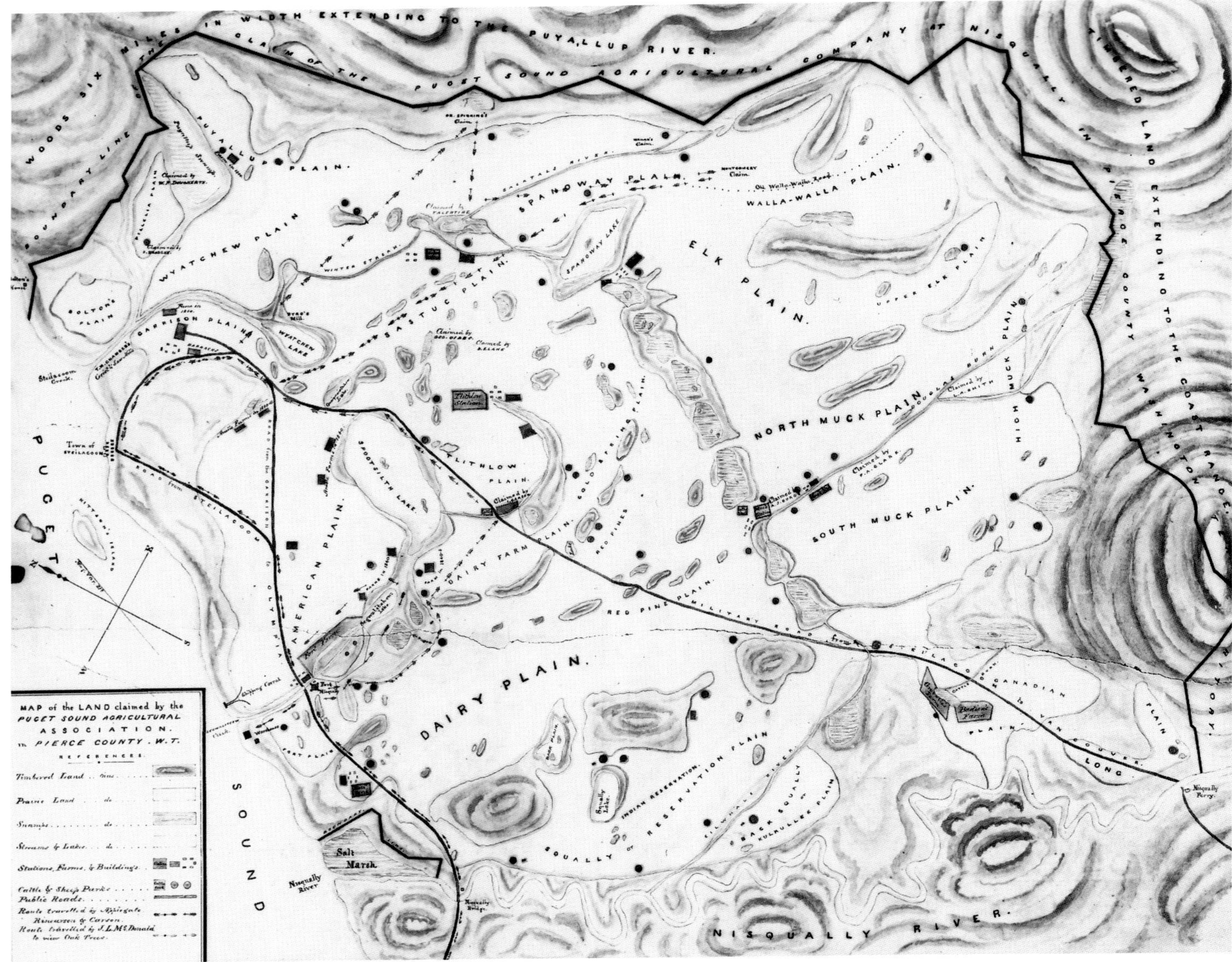

Map of claims by the British Puget Sound Agricultural Association in Pierce County, Washington Territory. After the Oregon Treaty, these lands were occupied by Americans. *23 7/8 by 19 1/2 inches.*

of Oregon and the re-annexation of Texas," war with both England and Mexico seemed imminent. But Polk's diplomacy helped avoid war with Great Britain. Unwilling to risk a conflict, Britain ceded all lands except Vancouver Island below the 49th parallel. The Oregon Treaty was concluded June 15, 1846, and the future states of Oregon, Washington, and Idaho and parts of what were to become Montana and Wyoming were added to the Union. The Oregon country became Oregon Territory in 1849, and the federal population census of 1850 counted over 12,000 inhabitants within the territory's boundaries.

Nauvoo (Ill.) Dec. 17. 1845

Sir

As there is a recommend to Congress in the President Message for a suitable number of Stockades and block houses to be erected between our western frontier, and the Rocky Mountains. If some one of our people could be favored with the Agency, for that purpose we would build them cheaper, than in any otherwise could be done, as we expect to emigrate West of the mountains next season. If we should eventually settle on Vancouver's Island, according to our calculation we shall greatly desire to have a mail route, established between here, and Oregon, we would like to contract for the same through the summer month, when we arrive at the place of our destination we fondly anticipate, we shall have no old settler to find fault with us and if Oregon should be annexed to the United States which in all probability will be, and Vancouver's Island incorporated in the same, by our promptly paying the national revenue, and taxes, we can live in peace with all men.

Yours &c
Most Obediently
Brigham Young
President of the Church of Jesus Christ of Latter Day Saints

Hon. W. L. Marcy
Sec of War
Washington D.C.

Letter from Brigham Young to Secretary of War William Marcy, December 17, 1845. Forced from their homes in Nauvoo, IL, the Mormons briefly contemplated a move to Vancouver Island and offered to build blockhouses along the trail to Oregon. *7 3/4 by 9 3/4 inches.*

Landscape entitled "Active Passage, Saturna Group, looking west," a view of the area of the Northwest boundary. The artist was sent along with the 1857–62 survey of the 49th parallel to record the terrain. *Watercolor by James Madsion Alden, 13 ¾ by 9 ¾ inches.*

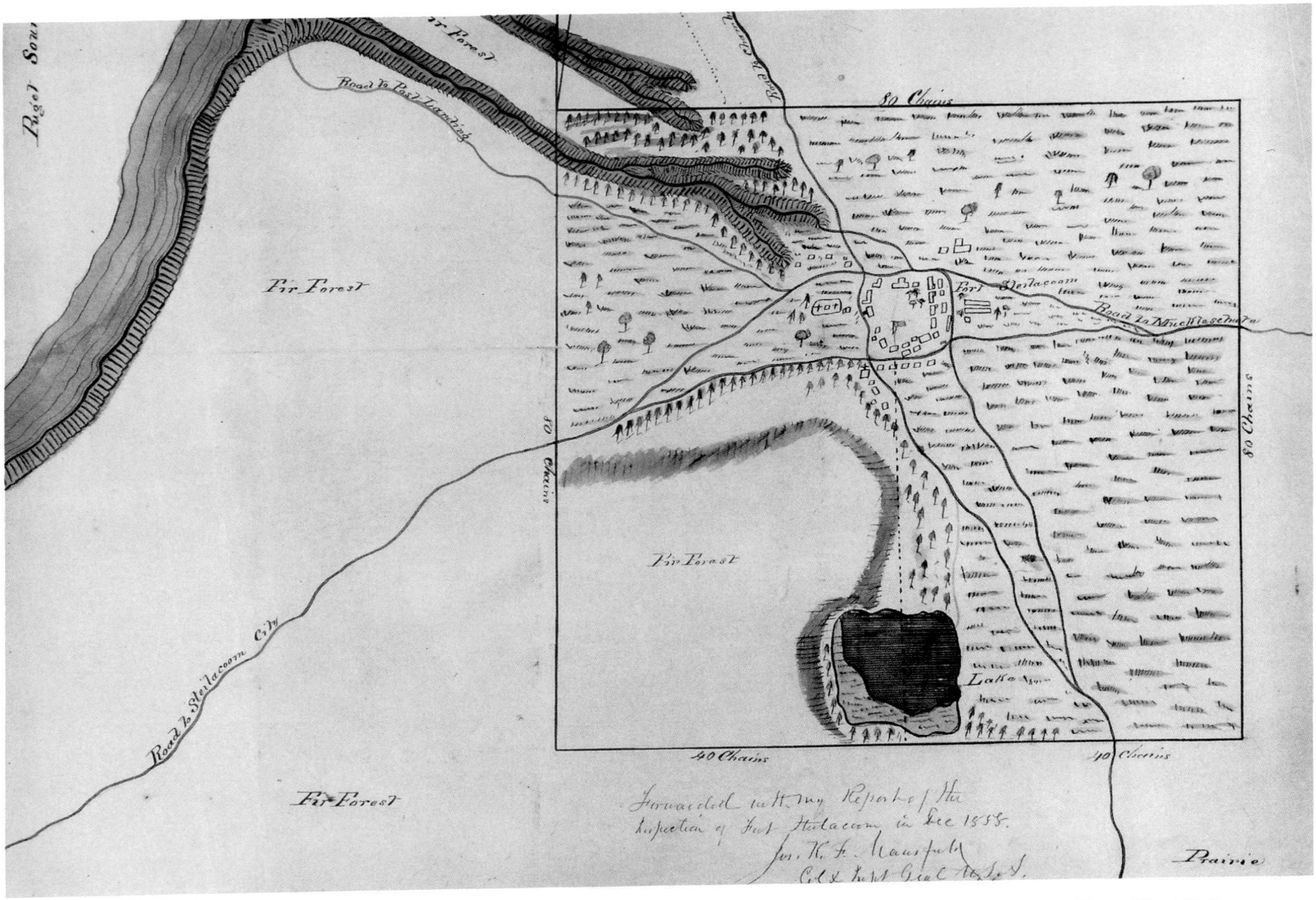

Map of Fort Steilacoom, Washington Territory, 1858. This post and others like it supported the rapid American settlement of the region. *22 by 16 ¼ inches, detail.*

Wagons were rolling west in large numbers when this family paused in Loup Valley, NE, in 1886. *Solomon D. Butcher photograph.*

The interior of a covered wagon used by John Bemmerly in 1849 to travel from Cincinnati, OH, to Yolo County, CA. For weeks on end, such wagons served as homes on wheels for westward-moving pioneers.

Account of supplies purchased by Capt. Henry E. Maynadier, 10th Infantry, who escorted immigrants on the Oregon Trail, 1861. The federal government financed such escorts and expected a detailed accounting, including the number of cartridges used.
Pages 1, 3, and 4 of 4 pages, 8 by 12 ½ inches.

General Return of the Property purchased by Captain Henry E. Maynadier 10th Infantry for the expedition for the Protection of Emigrants to Oregon &c (Act of March 2nd 1861), showing the use and disposition made of each Article.

No. of Vou.	Kind of Property	How accounted for
1861 2nd Qr.	20 Colts Revolving Rifles	Sold at Walla Walla see a/c of Sale
" "	1000 Cartridges	Used by guards & hunters
" "	50 Colt's Pistols	Sold at Walla Walla
" "	150 prs (300) Blankets correct	230 sold to men of the party and proceeds accounted for in a/c current 4th Qr. 1861. 70 given as presents to Indians, by authority of instructions of Secretary of War.
" "	1 piece Scarlet Cloth 21½ yds	Given to the Sioux, Cheyenne, Snake, Bannack, Arapahoe, Cayuse and Nez Percé Indians as presents under authority of instructions of the Secretary of War.
	2 " Blue " 44 "	
	4 " Red prints 153¼ "	
	2 " Fancy prints 100 "	
	2 " Blue Denims 130 "	
	2 " Cotton Bed tick 103 "	
	5 doz Printed Hdkfs	" "
	4 gross Worsted Binding	" "
	24 lbs Patent Thread	" "
	1 gross Blue Steel Thimbles	" "
	2000 Victoria Needles	" "
	2 doz Leather Belts	" "
	16 doz Rings	" "
	5 doz Bracelets	" "
	60 lbs Assorted Beads	" "
	3 gross Barley Corn Beads	" "

No. of Vou.	Kind of Property	How accounted for
10. 2nd Qr. 1861	2 Spring Wagons	Sold at Walla Walla
11. " "	1 Medecine Chest	" " " "
	1 Sett Surgical Instruments	" " " "
	1 lot of Medecines	" " " "
12. 14. 15. 16. 17. 18	48 Horses ?	39 horses sold at Walla Walla
19. 20. 22. 23. 24	27 Mules	24 Mules " " " "
25. 26. 27. 29	140 Oxen	96 Oxen " " " "
34. 36. 37 2nd	3 Beeves — (143 head)	9 horses and 3 mules died strayed & stolen. 18 Oxen died and broken down as per affidavit of Wm. Mc Browne Wagon Master. 29 Killed for Beef; see Provision Return.
Qr. 1861, and 3. 3rd Qr. 1861	10 Wagons	3 Wagons broken & abandoned - see affidavit. 7 Wagons sold at Walla Walla
	How 96 sold 18 died 29 killed 143	
30. 2nd Qr. '61	6 doz Emigrant Cups	Partly worn out on the journey and sold at Walla Walla, in one lot (see A/c of Sale)
	6 " Tin Plates	
	2 " Camp Kettles	
	2 " Fry Pans	
	2 " Ovens & lids	" "
	2 " 10 qt Pans	" "
	6 " Coffee Boilers	" "
	2 " Coffee Mills	" "
	6 10 qt Cov'd Buckets	" "
	6 Wash Basins	" "
	6 Lanterns	" "
	2 doz Tin Cups	" "
	2 " Pepper & Salt Boxes	" "
	6 " Pressed Pint pans	" "
	6 Gridirons	" "

No. of Vou.	Kind of Property	How accounted for
30. 2nd Qr. 1861	2 lb Canister	Partly worn out and sold at Walla Walla.
	6 Extra Candle stands for lamps	
	4 Tar Buckets	
32. " "	17 Grey Blankets	Sold at Walla Walla with the Saddles.
	31 Saddle Blankets	
	200 yds Heavy Duck	Used for making Wagon Covers, and sold with the wagons at Walla Walla
	1 lb Linen Thread	
	5½ lbs Cotton Rope	
	1 doz Sacking Needles	Worn out by use.
33. " "	Provisions	See Return of Provisions and Abstract of Issues.
1. 3. & 4 3rd Qr.	Do Do	
33. 2nd Qr.	1 gross Matches	Used on the journey from Omaha to Walla Walla
	100 lbs Lead	
	20 lbs Powder	" " "
	6 Mc Eley's Caps	" " "
	140 lbs Picket Rope	" " "
	10 Water Kegs	Sold with the Wagons.
	1 doz Water Pails	Worn out in service
	12 Lanterns	" " " "
	4 doz Axe handles	" " " "
	6 Spades	" " " "
	12 Cans Patent Grease	Used on the journey
	1 Keg Tar	" " " "
38. 2nd Qr. 61	584 lbs Ox chain	Sold at Walla Walla
	50 Swivels	" " " "
	50 Ox Yoke and Bows	Partly worn out, and sold with the wagons at Walla Walla.

I certify that the above Return is correct and just.
Henry E. Maynadier
Capt 10th Infy.

Manuel de la Peña y Peña Presidente
interino de los Estados Unidos Mexicanos

A todos los que las presentes vieren sabed:

Que en la Ciudad de Guadalupe Hidalgo se concluyó y firmó el día dos de Febrero del presente año, un tratado de paz, amistad, límites y arreglo definitivo entre los Estados Unidos Mexicanos y los Estados Unidos de América por medio de Plenipotenciarios de ambos Gob[...] debida y respectivamente para este efecto. cuyo tratado y [...] cional son en la forma y tenor siguiente.

En el nombre de Dios Todo poderoso:

Los Estados-Unidos Mexicanos y los Estados-Unidos de América, animados de un sincero deseo de poner término á las calamidades de la guerra que desgraciadamente existe entre ambas repúblicas, y de establecer sobre bases sólidas relaciones de paz y buena amistad, que procuren recíprocas ventajas á los ciudadanos de uno y otro pais, y afiancen la concordia, armonía

In the name o[...] God:

The United-S[...] and the United [...] animated by a sinc[...] an end to the cala[...] which unhappily e[...] two republics, and [...] a solid basis relati[...] friendship, which [...] procal benefits upo[...] both, and assure th[...] mony, and mutual confidence

The treaty of Guadalupe Hidalgo, signed February 2, 1848, added nearly 2 million square miles to the United States, including present-day California, Arizona, Nevada, Utah, New Mexico, and parts of Colorado and Wyoming. *Mexican exchange copy, text in Spanish and English, 72 pages, 10 ½ by 14 ½ inches.*

Inset: **Maj. Gen. Winfield Scott at Vera Cruz. Scott took the city of Vera Cruz on March 26, 1847, and marched into Mexico City on September 14 of that year.** *Copy of lithograph by Nathaniel Currier.*

Down the Santa Fe Trail on horseback, in caravans with bushwhackers and muleskinners, and around the Horn in square-rigged ships, the Americans went. They searched for trade and adventure in Taos, Santa Fe, Yerba Buena (later to become San Francisco), and El Pueblo de Nuestra Señora la Reina de los Angeles de Porciuncula. In all these places, amid low adobe buildings on open plazas, they traded pots, pans, and cloth for fur and silver and then labored back to Independence or St. Joseph, MO, or Boston, MA. But ultimately trade was not enough. The Americans' sense of "Manifest Destiny" led them to seek the Mexicans' lands for their own.

The first step in the process was the annexation of Texas. Under Sam Houston, Americans in Texas staged a successful revolt against Mexico in 1836 and proclaimed an independent republic. Southerners were anxious to bring Texas into the Union as a slave state, while others feared that an independent republic would ally itself with Great Britain and block further westward expansion. Most Texans favored joining the United States, and in 1845 the "Lone Star State" was admitted to the Union.

Second Lt. Bezaleel Wells Armstrong, 2d Dragoons, an 1841 West Point graduate, ca. 1856. He served with the Army in Mexico in 1847–48 and died 2 years later at his home in New Lisbon, OH, of disease contracted in Mexico. *Mathew Brady photograph.*

Watercolor sketches of camels used from 1857 to 1860 by the U.S. Army in an experiment to supply Army posts in the West. The outbreak of the Civil War ended the experiment. The camels were dispersed throughout the region, where they became part of western legends. These sketches were used by the artist, Anne Glidden, as part of her 1858 claim for compensation from Congress for services rendered by her late husband in obtaining the camels. George Glidden had been American consul in Cairo, Egypt. *Records of the U.S. House of Representatives, National Archives; 10 by 7 ½ inches.*

Mexican lancers charging American troops under the overall command of Gen. Stephen Watts Kearny in the Battle of the Plains of Mesa, January 9, 1847. The site is now part of the Los Angeles suburb of Vernon. *From the Franklin D. Roosevelt Library; watercolor by William Meyers, 16 ¼ by 10 ¼ inches.*

After the Oregon Treaty settled the dispute with Great Britain, President James K. Polk turned his attention to acquiring the Mexican lands to the west of Texas by peaceful means. He attempted to purchase California from Mexico, but the Mexicans refused to meet his minister. Polk ordered the American army under the command of Gen. Zachary Taylor to advance to the Rio Grande. Sixteen American soldiers were killed in territory on the Texas border that was claimed by both Mexico and the United States, and Polk called for war. "Mexico has shed American blood on American soil," he said in his war message of May 11, 1846. Congress declared war on May 13.

Support for "Polk's war" was not universal: Many Whigs opposed the war for political reasons, and northern and eastern abolitionists regarded it as a means of strengthening and extending the institution of slavery. In his "Spot Resolution" of December 22, 1847, Abraham Lincoln of Illinois, who had been elected to the House of Representatives after the declaration of war, demanded to know the exact spot "on American soil" where blood had been shed. In fact, Lincoln emphasized, the "American soil" was claimed by both Texas and Mexico. The House of Representatives passed a declaration that Polk had started the war "unnecessarily and unconstitutionally."

Outside Congress, other public figures denounced the war. Writer Henry David Thoreau was jailed for refusing to pay a tax that he contended would support an unjust war. Some were able to reconcile their opposition to the origins of the war to their obligation to serve the nation. "It is rather late," wrote Robert E. Lee, ". . . to discuss the origin of the war; that ought to have been understood before we engaged in it." Lee joined in the fighting as an officer in the U.S. Army, as did Ulysses S. Grant.

Some eager volunteers were simply anxious to join the Army before the fighting ended, and these men rushed to the colors. Patriotic women handstitched battle flags. Many Members of Congress who had not supported the declaration of war voted for men and supplies to prosecute it once it was under way. While two American armies fought south of the Rio Grande, soldiers under Gen. Stephen Watts Kearny marched west to take Taos and Santa Fe and crossed the desert to California. There they defeated Mexican lancers at the Battle of the Plains of Mesa and elsewhere and conquered the region.

Following Mexico's military defeat in 1847, negotiations began over the spoils. Some Americans favored annexing all of Mexico, while a small number fearing the expansion of slavery opposed taking any of Mexico's possessions. The peace treaty signed at Guadalupe Hidalgo on February 2, 1848, represented a compromise between the two positions.

The United States received California and the region known as New Mexico, which included present-day Arizona, Utah, and Nevada and parts of New Mexico, Colorado, and Wyoming. The question of slavery in the new territory was tem-

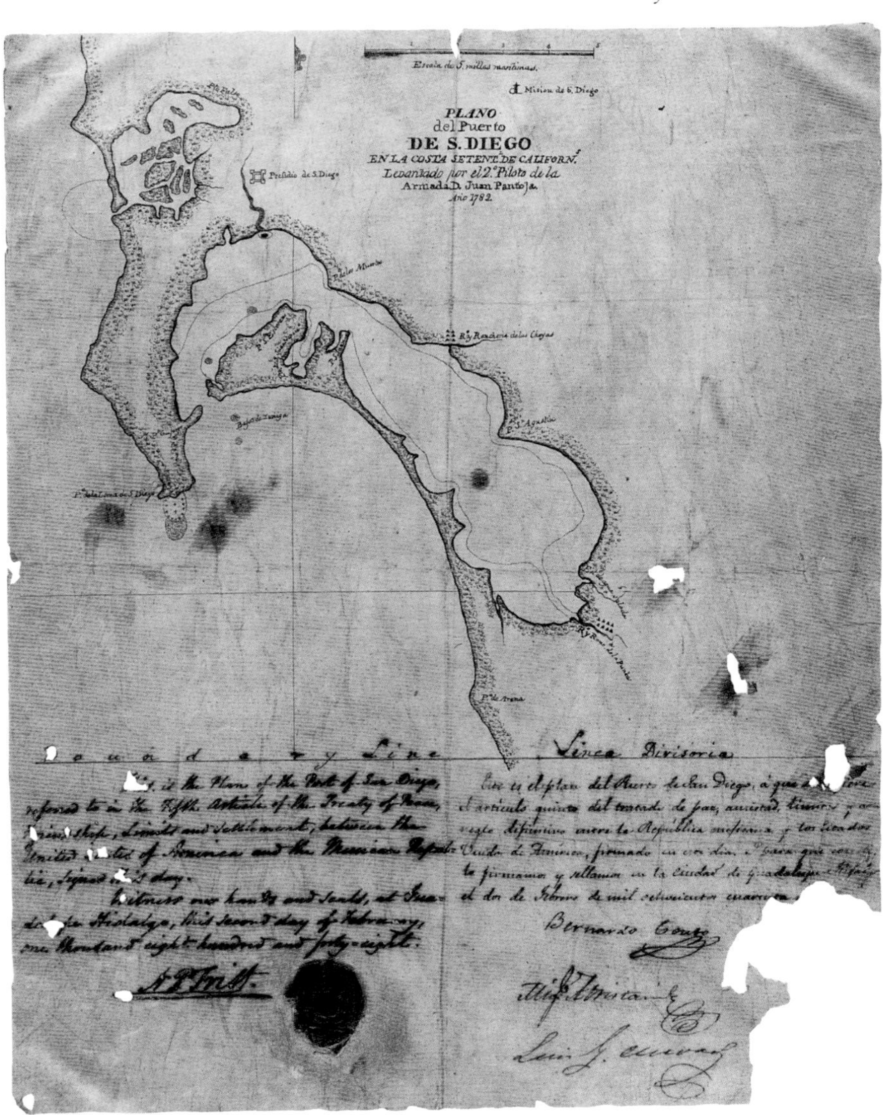

Map of the port of San Diego, 1847. This was used by President Polk's envoy, Nicholas Trist, in negotiating part of the Treaty of Guadalupe Hidalgo.
11 by 13 3/4 inches.

porarily resolved by the Compromise of 1850, which admitted California as a free state and indefinitely postponed a decision on the status of the rest of the region.

Americans in the new territories were separated from the settled areas of the Mississippi Valley by hundreds of miles, and the federal government was forced to grapple with the problem of defending the area and supplying its outposts. Railroads provided one answer, and James Gadsden of South Carolina was authorized by President Franklin Pierce to purchase from Mexico the Gila River Valley, now in southern Arizona and New Mexico, so that tracks might be laid over the shortest and most practical route to California. With the Gadsden Purchase in 1853, the United States completed its transcontinental expansion.

"Panning out" for gold, ca. 1871. *William Henry Jackson photograph.*

Tonto Apache woman and child at the edge of the Salt River reservoir in Arizona, 1910.

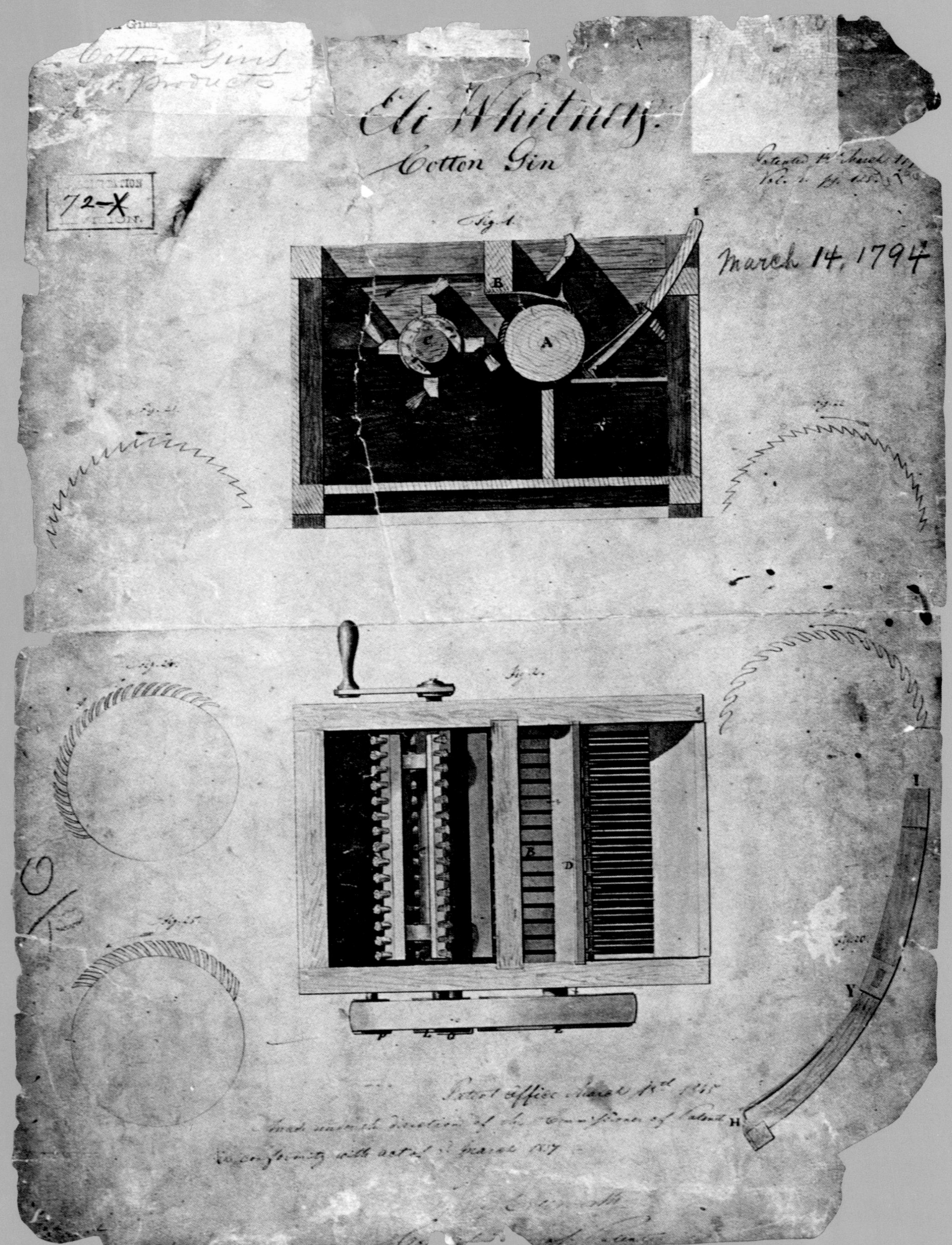
Eli Whitney.
Cotton Gin
March 14, 1794

An ingenious device patented by Eli Whitney on March 14, 1794, to separate cotton fiber from seed helped set in motion a series of events that culminated in the Civil War. The cotton gin expanded the cotton culture and greatly encouraged the growth of slavery in the South. Production rose from 100,000 bales in 1801 to over 5 million bales in 1859. "King Cotton" reigned in the South, and its production required the labor of more than half of the slaves in the United States. The southern economy and much of America's prosperity became dependent on slavery. This increasing dependence on slave labor contributed greatly to the deepening political and moral struggle between slave and free states.

Each new acquisition of territory created a crisis over the extension of cotton culture and with it the extension of slavery. The Mexican Cession after the Treaty of Guadalupe Hidalgo was no exception. During the Mexican War, Ralph Waldo Emerson predicted that, because of the slavery question, annexing any Mexican territory "will be as the man swallows the arsenic, it will poison us." He proved to be tragically accurate.

California's application for admission to the Union as a free state drew threats of secession from the South, and the dissolution of the nation seemed imminent. Kentucky Senator Henry Clay, who had helped draw the 36° 30′ line dividing slave from free states in the Missouri Compromise of 1820, joined Senator Stephen A. Douglas of Illinois to devise a new compromise in 1850. The dying Senator John C. Calhoun of South Carolina, chief defender of the status quo, was carried into the Senate to oppose the compromise.

Daniel Webster defended the compromise, declaring, "I speak today for the preservation of the Union." After 9 months of speeches and debates, five of Clay's seven original resolutions were drafted into law and came to be known as

Confederate $10 bill, 1861 issue, showing slave picking cotton. *6 ¾ by 3 ⅛ inches.*

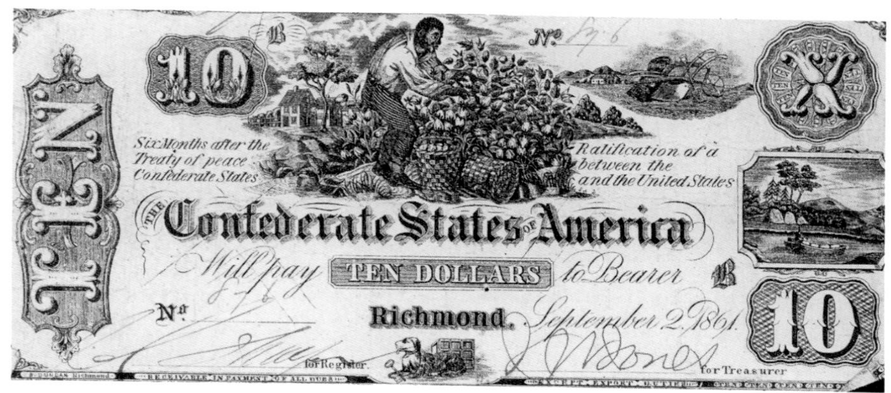

Cotton gin, Madison County, AL, 1923.

Patent drawing of Eli Whitney's cotton gin, 1794. Designed to separate cotton fiber from seed, the machine made a cotton economy profitable, thereby encouraging slavery in the South. *16 ¾ by 22 inches.*

the Compromise of 1850. It admitted California as a free state, provided for "popular sovereignty" in admitting new states from the Mexican Cession, adjusted the Texas-New Mexico boundary, ended the slave trade in the District of Columbia, and enacted a stronger fugitive slave law. The prosperous country was in a compromising mood, and economic interests sought an end to sectional disputes and an emphasis on territorial expansion. But the Compromise of 1850 proved to be an uneasy truce of short duration.

In 1856 popular sovereignty and sporadic guerrilla warfare in "Bleeding Kansas" rekindled sectional fires. In the following year the Supreme Court ruled on the case of Dred Scott, a slave who had sought his freedom after his master took him into territory where slavery was forbidden by the Missouri Compromise of 1820. The majority opinion, handed down by Chief Justice Roger C. Taney, stated that slaves were property and that Dred Scott's sojourn in the Minnesota Territory had not freed him. Most important, the Dred Scott decision nullified the Missouri Compromise and hardened the lines between proslavery and antislavery factions.

Thereafter, events seemed to move inexorably toward what William H. Seward called "the irrepressible conflict." All the fears of the South were confirmed in 1859 when John Brown led a raid on a federal arsenal at Harpers Ferry, VA, as the first step toward a slave insurrection. The election of Abraham Lincoln, who called slavery "a moral, a social, and a political wrong," brought the Southern states to the brink of secession. When Senator John J. Crittenden of Kentucky attempted yet another compromise, he found that the issues were beyond negotiation. Thomas Jefferson's apprehension that the debate over slavery in 1820 seemed like a "fire bell in the night" had proven true.

Petition in support of the Crittenden Compromise, 1861. The compromise included a constitutional amendment ensuring the existence of slavery unless prohibited by state law and extending the Missouri Compromise line dividing free and slaveholding states to the Pacific Ocean. The compromise did not receive Lincoln's support and failed in Congress.
Records of the U.S. Senate, National Archives; 38 7/8 by 25 3/8 inches.

Seal of the Knights of the Golden Circle. This was a pre–Civil War organization of southerners dedicated to the expansion of slavery in the so-called golden circle—the lands bordering the Caribbean. *Brass, 1 7/8 inches in diameter.*

Henry Clay's resolutions of January 29, 1850, that became the Compromise of 1850. The compromise temporarily settled the issue of slavery in the newly acquired territories of the Mexican Cession and included a stringent fugitive slave law. *Page 1 of 3 pages, 7 3/4 by 9 7/8 inches.*

It being desirable, for the peace, concord and harmony of the Union of these States, to settle and adjust amicably all existing questions of controversy ~~which they now~~ between them, arising out of the institution of Slavery, upon a fair equitable and just basis: Therefore

1st Resolved that California, with suitable boundaries, ought upon her application to be admitted as one of the States of this Union, without the imposition by Congress of any restriction in respect to the exclusion or introduction of Slavery within those boundaries.

2. Resolved that as Slavery does not exist by law, and is not likely to be introduced into any of the Territory acquired by the United States from the Republic of Mexico, it is inexpedient for Congress to provide by law either for its introduction into or exclusion from any part of the said Territory; and that appropriate Territorial Governments ought to be established by Congress in all of the said territory, not assigned as the boundaries of the proposed State of California, without the adoption of any restriction or condition on the subject of Slavery.

3. Resolved that the Western boundary of the State of Texas ought to be fixed on the Rio del Norte, commencing one Marine League from its mouth, and running up that river to the Southern line of New Mexico, thence with that line Eastwardly, and so continuing in the same direction to the line as established between the U. S. and Spain, excluding any portion of New Mexico, whether

lying

Dred Scott, ca. 1857.

The Dred Scott case, 1856–57. This Supreme Court decision denied Dred Scott, a former slave, his claim to freedom on the basis of previous residence in free territories. The decision, which also voided the Missouri Compromise of 1820, aroused a storm of protest in the North. *43 pages, 7 7/8 by 12 inches.*

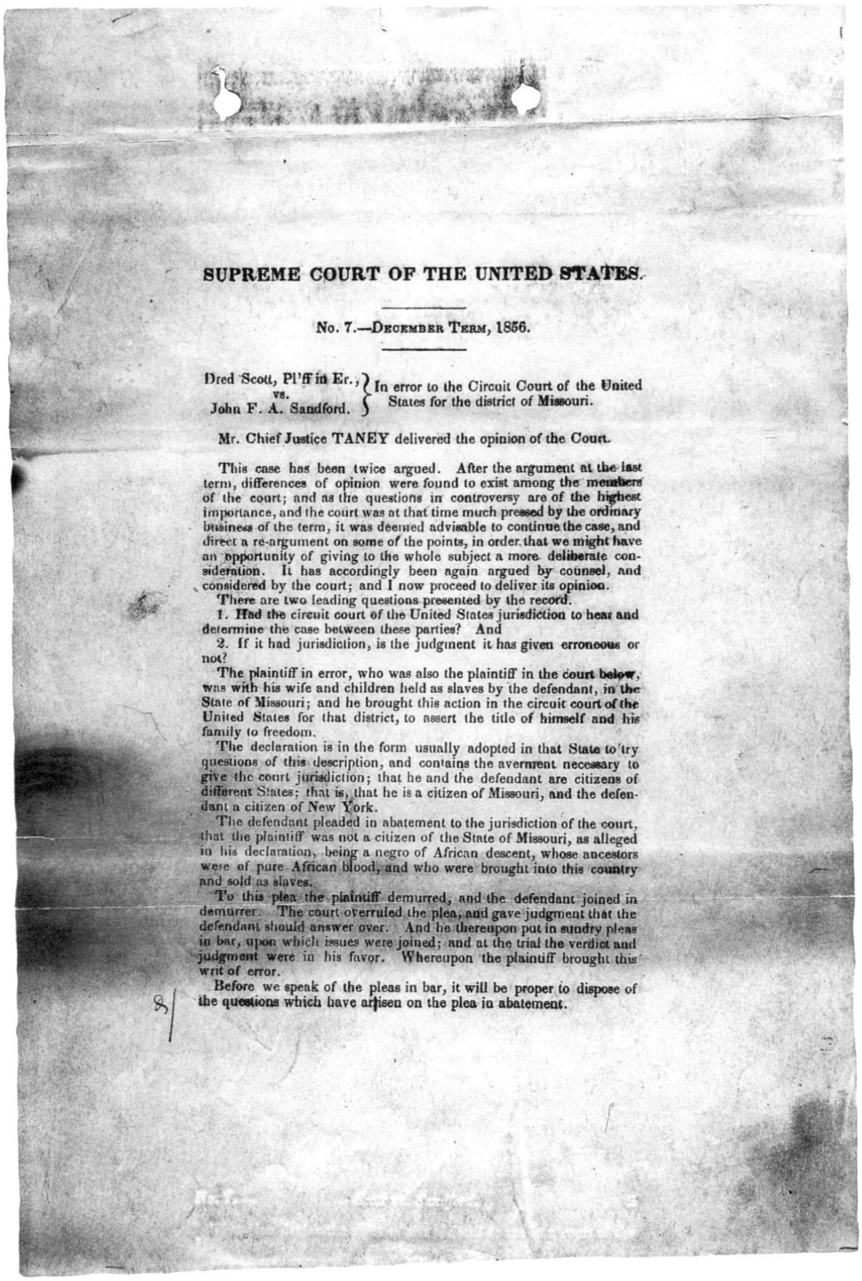

SUPREME COURT OF THE UNITED STATES.

No. 7.—December Term, 1856.

Dred Scott, Pl'ff in Er., vs. John F. A. Sandford. } In error to the Circuit Court of the United States for the district of Missouri.

Mr. Chief Justice TANEY delivered the opinion of the Court.

This case has been twice argued. After the argument at the last term, differences of opinion were found to exist among the members of the court; and as the questions in controversy are of the highest importance, and the court was at that time much pressed by the ordinary business of the term, it was deemed advisable to continue the case, and direct a re-argument on some of the points, in order that we might have an opportunity of giving to the whole subject a more deliberate consideration. It has accordingly been again argued by counsel, and considered by the court; and I now proceed to deliver its opinion.

There are two leading questions presented by the record.

1. Had the circuit court of the United States jurisdiction to hear and determine the case between these parties? And

2. If it had jurisdiction, is the judgment it has given erroneous or not?

The plaintiff in error, who was also the plaintiff in the court below, was with his wife and children held as slaves by the defendant, in the State of Missouri; and he brought this action in the circuit court of the United States for that district, to assert the title of himself and his family to freedom.

The declaration is in the form usually adopted in that State to try questions of this description, and contains the averment necessary to give the court jurisdiction; that he and the defendant are citizens of different States; that is, that he is a citizen of Missouri, and the defendant a citizen of New York.

The defendant pleaded in abatement to the jurisdiction of the court, that the plaintiff was not a citizen of the State of Missouri, as alleged in his declaration, being a negro of African descent, whose ancestors were of pure African blood, and who were brought into this country and sold as slaves.

To this plea the plaintiff demurred, and the defendant joined in demurrer. The court overruled the plea, and gave judgment that the defendant should answer over. And he thereupon put in sundry pleas in bar, upon which issues were joined; and at the trial the verdict and judgment were in his favor. Whereupon the plaintiff brought this writ of error.

Before we speak of the pleas in bar, it will be proper to dispose of the questions which have arisen on the plea in abatement.

8|

John Brown, ca. 1859.

A provisional constitution drawn up by John Brown for blacks, "People Degraded by the Laws," and others, 1858. It would have governed his proposed state until the Constitution was amended to prohibit slavery. *15 pages, 4 3/8 by 7 inches.*

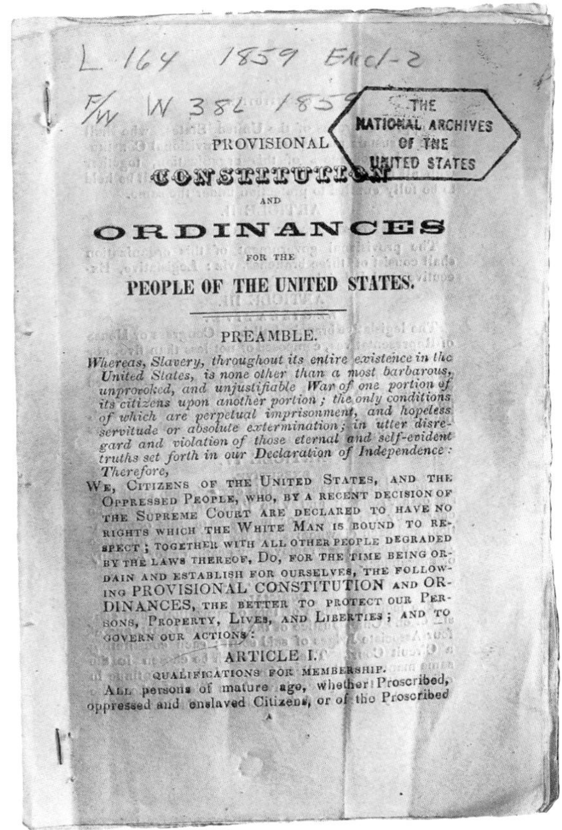

PROVISIONAL

CONSTITUTION

AND

ORDINANCES

FOR THE

PEOPLE OF THE UNITED STATES.

PREAMBLE.

Whereas, Slavery, throughout its entire existence in the United States, is none other than a most barbarous, unprovoked, and unjustifiable War of one portion of its citizens upon another portion; the only conditions of which are perpetual imprisonment, and hopeless servitude or absolute extermination; in utter disregard and violation of those eternal and self-evident truths set forth in our Declaration of Independence: Therefore,

We, Citizens of the United States, and the Oppressed People, who, by a recent decision of the Supreme Court are declared to have no rights which the White Man is bound to respect; together with all other people degraded by the laws thereof, Do, for the time being ordain and establish for ourselves, the following PROVISIONAL CONSTITUTION and ORDINANCES, the better to protect our Persons, Property, Lives, and Liberties; and to govern our actions:

ARTICLE I.

QUALIFICATIONS FOR MEMBERSHIP.

All persons of mature age, whether Proscribed, oppressed and enslaved Citizens, or of the Proscribed

John Brown
Harpers Ferry
Invasion
Papers Pertaining
to.
1st Sess 36 Cong

Slave pen of Price, Birch & Co., slave merchants, Alexandria, VA, ca. 1861. Buying and selling slaves aroused widespread indignation in the North. *William R. Pywell photograph.*

Opposite, bottom right:
Wrapper for documents of the Senate select committee investigating John Brown's raid on Harpers Ferry, VA, in 1859. As much as any other incident, John Brown's abortive insurrection convinced the South of its precarious position in the Union. *Records of the U.S. Senate, National Archives; 10 ¾ by 15 inches.*

President Abraham Lincoln's Emancipation Proclamation, January 1, 1863. The Proclamation freed slaves in areas "still in rebellion" and changed the character of the Civil War from a struggle to preserve the Union to a crusade for human liberty.
Pages 1 and 5 of 5 pages, 10 3/4 by 16 3/4 inches.

one thousand eight hundred and sixty three, and of the Independence of the United States of America the eighty-seventh.

Abraham Lincoln

By the President:
William H. Seward
Secretary of State

By the President of the United States of America:

A Proclamation.

Whereas, on the twenty-second day of September, in the year of our Lord one thousand eight hundred and sixty-two, a proclamation was issued by the President of the United States, containing, among other things, the following, to wit:

"That on the first day of January, in the "year of our Lord one thousand eight hundred "and sixty-three, all persons held as slaves within "any State or designated part of a State, the people "whereof shall then be in rebellion against the "United States, shall be then, thenceforward, and "forever free; and the Executive Government of the "United States, including the military and naval "authority thereof, will recognize and maintain "the freedom of such persons, and will do no act "or acts to repress such persons, or any of them, "in any efforts they may make for their actual "freedom.

"That the Executive will, on the first day

Issued in the midst of the Civil War, the Emancipation Proclamation became a universal symbol of liberation from bondage. Its immediate effect was to change the character of the Civil War from a struggle to preserve the Union to a crusade for human liberty.

President Abraham Lincoln had hesitated to take a firm stand against slavery early in the Civil War because of the need to defer to opinion in the border states so precariously bound to Union. But by 1862 the danger of European support for Southern independence outweighed other considerations. On September 22, 5 days after the Union forces stopped the Confederate invasion of Maryland at Antietam Creek, President Lincoln issued the Emancipation Proclamation, warning the Confederate states that slaves would be freed in all areas still in rebellion in January 1863.

The announcement of the Emancipation Proclamation brought an immediate emotional response in western Europe, where workers gathered at large meetings to applaud the launching of the crusade in America. In such an atmosphere, European governments abandoned ideas of intervening in support of the Confederacy.

African Americans all over the country, even those in border states and in Union-occupied territory where the document specifically did not apply, believed the Proclamation's words, "thenceforward and forever free." They celebrated a great day of liberation in 1863 and flocked to Union lines. Yet only a total Union victory could give the Proclamation full effect in the South.

In 1861 Americans in both the North and South had entered into the Civil War in high spirits, each side expecting a quick victory. Recruiting posters aroused patriotism and helped fill the ranks of the army and navy, and volunteer units adopted romantic uniforms. But the Civil War

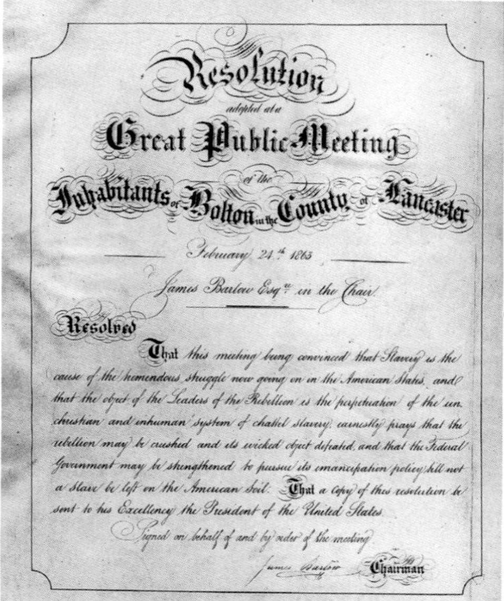

Resolution
adopted at a
Great Public Meeting
of the
Inhabitants of Bolton in the County of Lancaster

February 24th 1863

James Barlow Esqr. in the Chair

Resolved

That this meeting being convinced that Slavery is the cause of the tremendous struggle now going on in the American States, and that the object of the Leaders of the Rebellion is the perpetuation of the unchristian and inhuman system of chattel slavery, earnestly prays that the rebellion may be crushed and its wicked object defeated, and that the Federal Government may be strengthened to pursue its emancipation policy till not a Slave be left on the American Soil. That a copy of this resolution be sent to his Excellency the President of the United States.

Signed on behalf of and by order of the meeting

James Barlow Chairman

Resolution presented by the inhabitants of Bolton, England, on February 24, 1863, in support of emancipation and the Union. News of the Emancipation Proclamation was received joyously by the working people in Europe, and expressions of good will flowed to President Lincoln. *16 ½ by 20 ¾ inches.*

Flag design for the Confederacy, 1861. When the Confederacy was formed, a flag committee was flooded with design suggestions. This submission represents the eye of both God and Jefferson Davis watching over the South. *15 ¾ by 11 inches.*

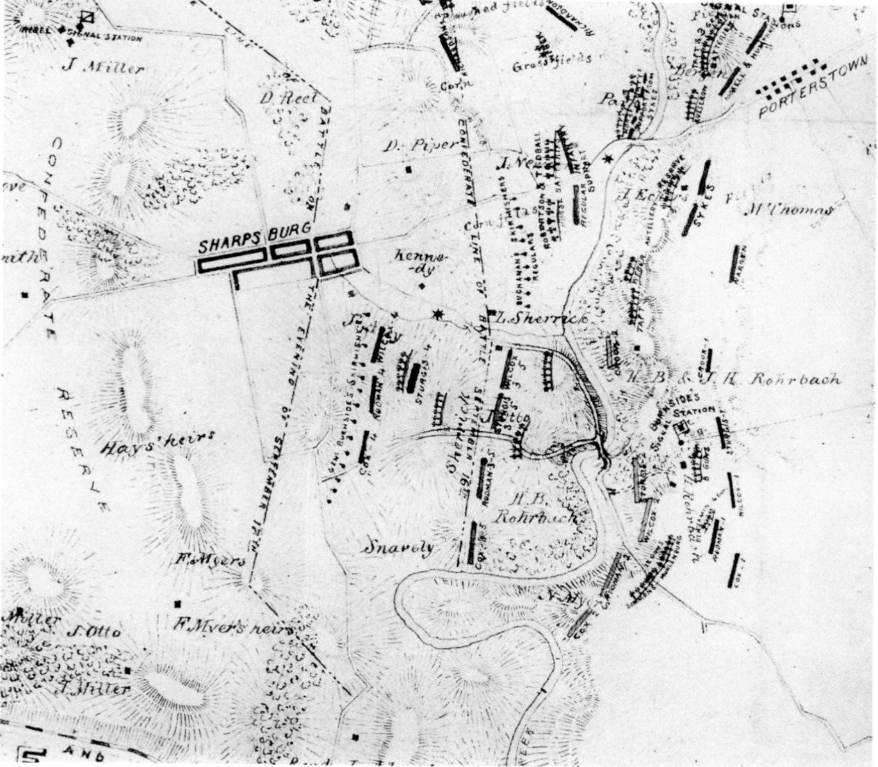

Map of the Battle of Antietam, September 17, 1862. Called the bloodiest single day of the war, this battle resulted in a Union victory that staved off foreign recognition of the Confederacy and enabled President Lincoln to issue the Emancipation Proclamation from a position of strength. *21 ½ by 17 ⅜ inches, detail.*

proved not to be a short conflict; as it dragged on, enthusiasm flagged. Both sides had to resort to conscription by 1863.

After the Emancipation Proclamation, black troops were also recruited for the Union despite the misgivings of many in the North. The performance of the 1st and 3d Louisiana Negro Regiments at Port Hudson, LA, on May 27, 1863, however, laid to rest the question of the African-American suitability for military service. After the battle of New Market Heights, VA, on September 29, 1864, Maj. Gen. Benjamin F. Butler authorized a medal for gallantry for black members of the Army of the James.

For nearly 2½ years after the issuance of the Proclamation, the fighting continued. Chancellorsville, Vicksburg, Gettysburg, the Wilderness campaign, Sherman's march through Georgia, Petersburg—battle followed battle in weary succession with mounting death tolls unequaled in U.S. history to date until the Confederacy was finally exhausted. In April 1865, at Appomattox Court House in Virginia, Confederate general Robert E. Lee and Union general Ulysses S. Grant agreed to terms of surrender. The war was over.

The slaves emancipated by the great Proclamation were now free in fact. Indeed, all the slaves in the country were freed by the ratification of the 13th amendment to the Constitution later that year.

Immediately after the war, General Lee, along with many other former Confederate soldiers, gave his oath of loyalty to the United States and applied for amnesty and the restoration of his U.S. citizenship. By accident, the oath did not accompany his submitted application. The application was not acted upon, and Lee died on October 12, 1870, without having his citizenship restored. In 1975, as a united nation embarked on the celebration of its Bicentennial, Congress restored Lee's citizenship posthumously retroactive to June 18, 1865.

Former slave family, one of many fleeing north to Union lines after the Emancipation Proclamation was issued in 1863. *Stereograph, 7 by 4 inches.*

Butler Medal, 1864. Maj. Gen. Benjamin F. Butler authorized a special medal for gallantry for black troops under his command in the Battle of New Market Heights, VA, in 1864. *Silver, 1 5/8 inches in diameter.*

CIRCULAR.

Office Provo. Mar., 2d Sub Dist., Mo.,
Hannibal, Dec. 17th, 1863.

By the terms set forth in General Order No. 135, dated Nov. 14th 1863, it is made the duty of Provost Marshals and Assistants to enlist all able-bodied Colored men, of suitable age, into the U. S. Service, &c. I desire to call attention of the citizens of the District to the necessity of using their best efforts in bringing in such as desire to enlist and in making it known through the District that I am fully prepared to enlist and send forward all able-bodied Colored volunteers that may be offered.

By orders from Provost Marshal General Col. Fry, all persons who bring in an accepted recruit, will be entitled to a fee of $2.00.

The people of the District should be energetic in this matter, as every Colored recruit furnished the Government will leave us one white man, free from the coming draft. All parties or persons found recruiting or persuading Colored men for Regiments out of the State, will be arrested and imprisoned, and their cases submitted to Head Quarters of the Department of Missouri.

A. B. COHEN, Major,
and Ass't Provost Marshal.

Recruiting poster for black troops, 1863. The Emancipation Proclamation authorized the acceptance of former slaves and free blacks into the military. *12 ¼ by 9 ¼ inches.*

A fierce assault on Port Hudson, LA, 1863. *From an engraving, ca. 1899.*

Part of the military service record of Daniel Thatcher, 77th Ohio Infantry, Company "D." *4 1/2 by 9 1/4 inches.*

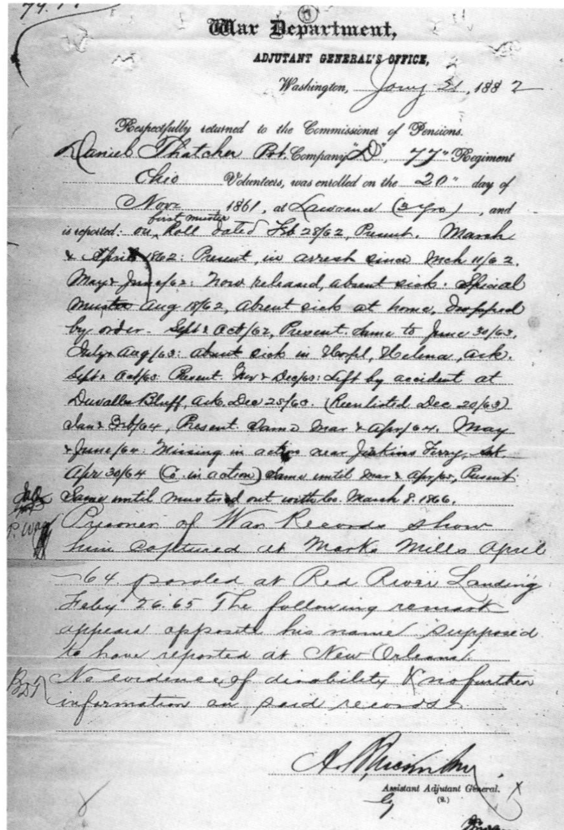

War Department,

ADJUTANT GENERAL'S OFFICE,

Washington, Jany 31, 1882

Respectfully returned to the Commissioner of Pensions.

Daniel Thatcher Pvt. Company "D", 77th Regiment Ohio Volunteers, was enrolled on the 20th day of Nov. 1861, at Lawrence (3 yrs.), and is reported: on first muster Roll dated Feb 28/62, Present. March & April 1862: Present, in arrest since Mch 11/62. May & June/62: Now released, absent sick. Special Muster Aug 18/62, absent sick at home, dropped by order. Sept & Oct/62, Present. Same to June 30/63. July & Aug/63: absent sick in Hospl, Helena, Ark. Sept & Oct/63: Present. Nov & Dec/63: Left by accident at Duvalls Bluff, Ark. Dec 25/63. (Reenlisted Dec 20/63) Jan & Feb/64, Present. Same Mar & Apr/64. May & June/64: Missing in action near Jenkins Ferry, Ark. Apr 30/64 (Co. in action) Same until Mar & Apr/65, Present. Same until mustered out with Co. March 8. 1866.

Prisoner of War Records show him captured at Marks Mills April 64 paroled at Red River Landing Feby 26.65 The following remark appears opposite his name "Supposed to have reported at New Orleans".

No evidence of disability & no further information on said records.

Assistant Adjutant General.

Union Navy recruiting poster, ca. 1862. Although the Navy was weak at the war's beginning, it later played a major role in bringing about a Union victory. *19 3/8 by 24 inches.*

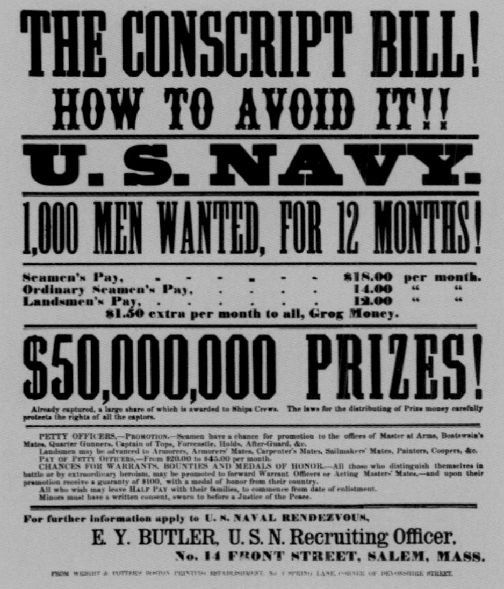

Kearny Cross, 1863. This cross was struck for officers of the command of Maj. Gen. Philip Kearny, who had been killed at Chantilly, VA, in September 1862. A similar medal in bronze was made for noncommissioned officers and privates. *Gold, 1 inch in diameter.*

Michigan Infantry, U.S. Army, ca. 1862, from the Mathew Brady Collection. Brady's photographs provide the most extensive visual record of the Civil War. He died penniless in 1896, and part of his collection was purchased at auction by the federal government. *Glass negative, 10 by 4 inches.*

Col. Abram Duryee's Zouaves (5th Regiment, New York Volunteers) at Camp Federal Hill, MD, 1861, wearing uniforms similar to those of French North African regiments. Many Southern as well as Northern volunteer units adopted similar uniforms in the early years of the war. *Watercolor by William McIlvaine, a member of the regiment; 16 by 13 inches.*

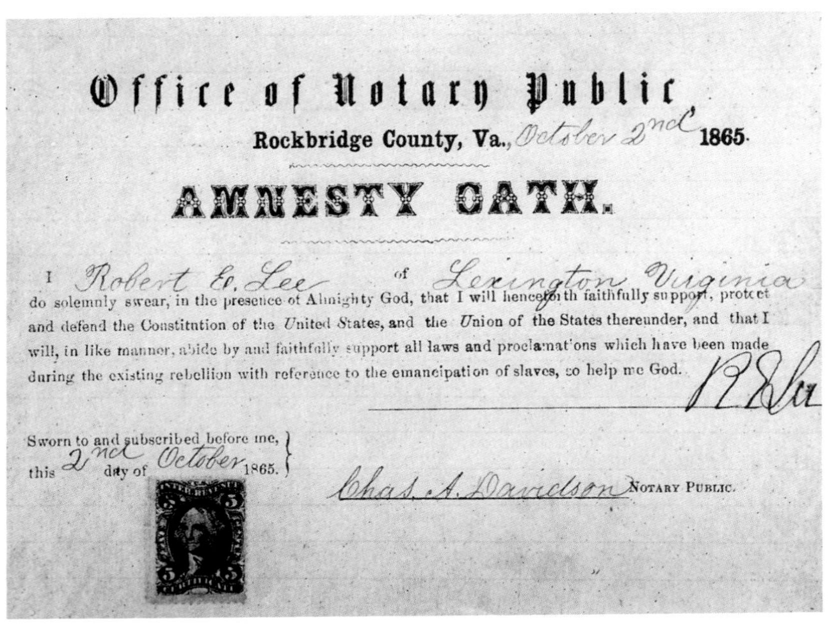

Office of Notary Public

Rockbridge County, Va., October 2nd 1865.

AMNESTY OATH.

I Robert E. Lee of Lexington Virginia do solemnly swear, in the presence of Almighty God, that I will henceforth faithfully support, protect and defend the Constitution of the United States, and the Union of the States thereunder, and that I will, in like manner, abide by and faithfully support all laws and proclamations which have been made during the existing rebellion with reference to the emancipation of slaves, so help me God.

R E Lee

Sworn to and subscribed before me, this 2nd day of October 1865.

Chas. A. Davidson Notary Public.

Gen. Robert E. Lee's amnesty oath, 1865. Lee's loyalty to the state of Virginia led him to use his West Point training in the service of the Confederacy. Following the end of the war, he applied to the President for amnesty and the restoration of his citizenship, which was not granted until 1975. *7 ¾ by 6 ¾ inches.*

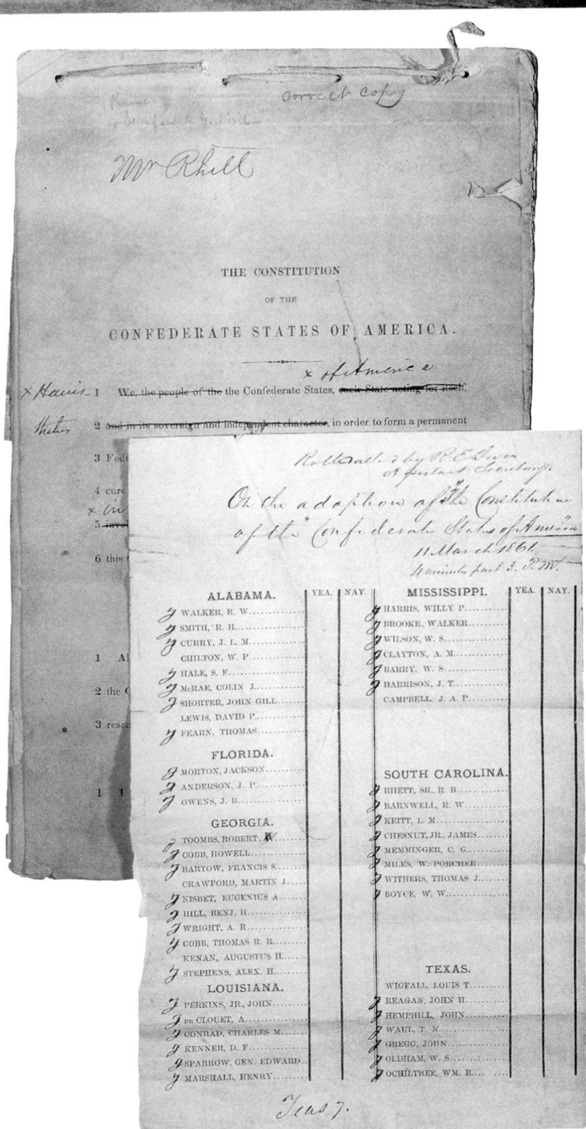

THE CONSTITUTION

OF THE

CONFEDERATE STATES OF AMERICA.

1 We, the people of the Confederate States, ~~each State acting for itself~~

2 ~~and in its sovereign and independent character~~, in order to form a permanent

On the adoption of the Constitution of the Confederate States of America
11 March 1861.

ALABAMA.
WALKER, R. W.
SMITH, R. H.
CURRY, J. L. M.
CHILTON, W. P.
HALE, S. F.
McRAE, COLIN J.
SHORTER, JOHN GILL.
LEWIS, DAVID P.
FEARN, THOMAS.

FLORIDA.
MORTON, JACKSON.
ANDERSON, J. P.
OWENS, J. B.

GEORGIA.
TOOMBS, ROBERT.
COBB, HOWELL.
BARTOW, FRANCIS S.
CRAWFORD, MARTIN J.
NISBET, EUGENIUS A.
HILL, BENJ. H.
WRIGHT, A. R.
COBB, THOMAS R. R.
KENAN, AUGUSTUS H.
STEPHENS, ALEX. H.

LOUISIANA.
PERKINS, JR., JOHN.
DE CLOUET, A.
CONRAD, CHARLES M.
KENNER, D. F.
SPARROW, GEN. EDWARD.
MARSHALL, HENRY.

MISSISSIPPI.
HARRIS, WILLY P.
BROOKE, WALKER.
WILSON, W. S.
CLAYTON, A. M.
BARRY, W. S.
HARRISON, J. T.
CAMPBELL, J. A. P.

SOUTH CAROLINA.
RHETT, SR., R. B.
BARNWELL, R. W.
KEITT, L. M.
CHESNUT, JR., JAMES.
MEMMINGER, C. G.
MILES, W. PORCHER.
WITHERS, THOMAS J.
BOYCE, W. W.

TEXAS.
WIGFALL, LOUIS T.
REAGAN, JOHN H.
HEMPHILL, JOHN.
WAUL, T. N.
GREGG, JOHN.
OLDHAM, W. S.
OCHILTREE, WM. B.

Galley proof of the Constitution of the Confederate States of America, with handwritten corrections (probably by an anonymous clerk), and the tally sheet of the vote on the motion before the Confederate congress to adopt the constitution, March 11, 1861. *Constitution, 27 pages, 8 ¼ by 14 inches; tally sheet, 7 ½ by 11 ⅞ inches.*

President Abraham Lincoln, 1864. Just before he signed the Emancipation Proclamation, Lincoln said, "I never, in my life, felt more certain that I was doing right than I do in signing this paper." *Mathew Brady photograph.*

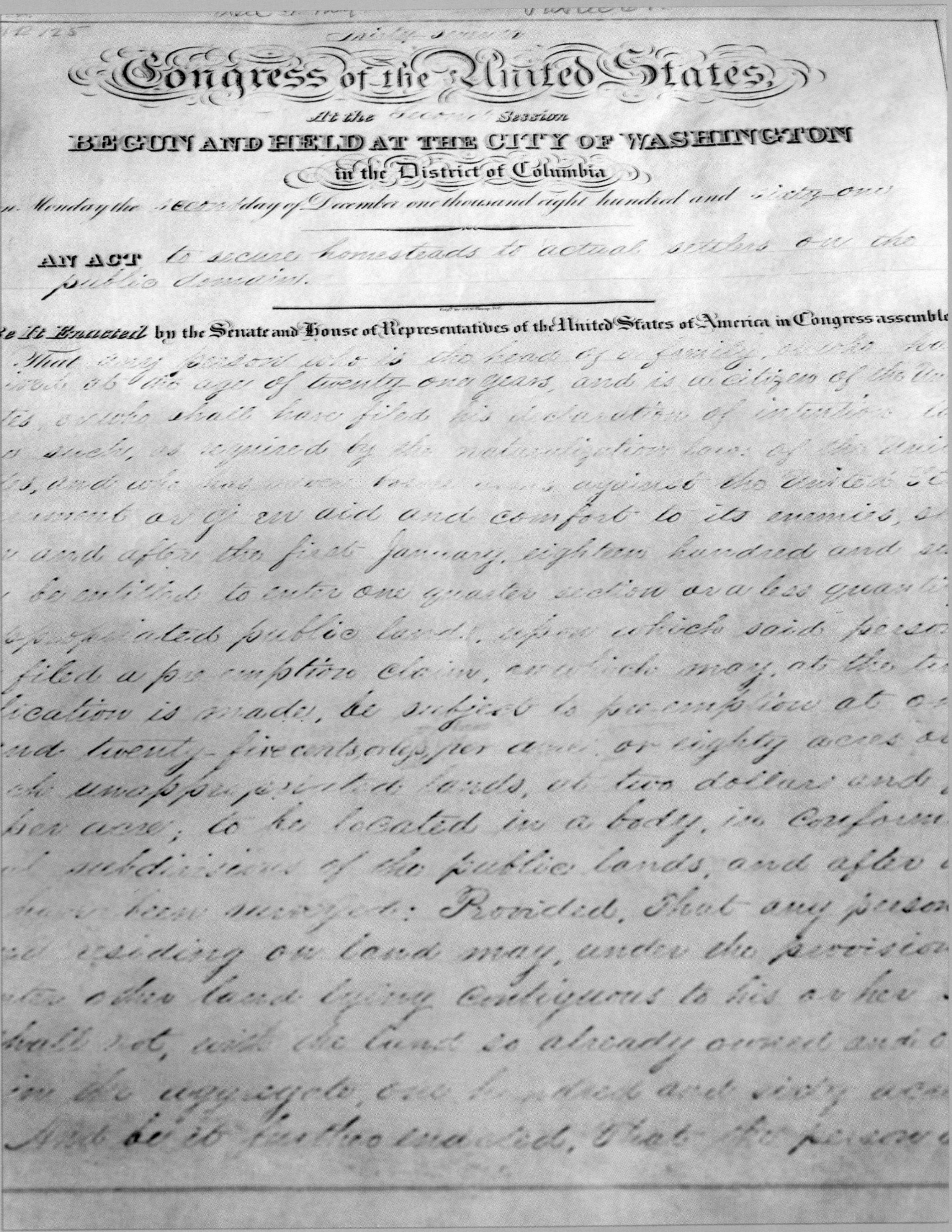

Thirty-seventh

Congress of the United States,

At the Second Session

BEGUN AND HELD AT THE CITY OF WASHINGTON

in the District of Columbia

on Monday the second day of December one thousand eight hundred and sixty-one

AN ACT to secure homesteads to actual settlers on the public domain.

Be It Enacted by the Senate and House of Representatives of the United States of America in Congress assembled

That any person who is the head of a family, or who has
rived at the age of twenty-one years, and is a citizen of the Un
tes, or who shall have filed his declaration of intention to
a such, as required by the naturalization laws of the Uni
tes, and who has never borne arms against the United St
rnment or given aid and comfort to its enemies, sh
and after the first January, eighteen hundred and si
be entitled to enter one quarter section or a less quanti
appropriated public lands, upon which said person
filed a preemption claim, or which may, at the ti
lication is made, be subject to preemption at o
and twenty-five cents, or less, per acre; or eighty acres o
ch unappropriated lands, at two dollars and
per acre; to be located in a body, in conform
l subdivisions of the public lands, and after
have been surveyed: Provided, That any person
and residing on land may, under the provision
nter other land lying contiguous to his or her
shall not, with the land so already owned and o
in the aggregate, one hundred and sixty acr
And be it further enacted, That the person a

Land, for centuries the main source of civilized wealth, was the magnet that drew people westward. They came to America in search of abundant, cheap virgin land; they moved into the wilderness to obtain it; they worked it, raised their families on it, and speculated with it. But buying new land was expensive. The government, the nation's largest landowner, sold only in sizable tracts, and as a result, vast acreage ended up in the hands of speculators. Then, too, many in the North came to fear a plantation agriculture, which would expand slavery into these lands. Some frustrated citizens tried to obtain free land simply by occupying it, a practice called "squatting." Others sought a new federal land law and in the 1840s adopted the ringing slogan "Free soil, free speech, free labor, free men."

Powerful interests opposed the easy sale of new lands. Before the great tide of emigration from Europe began in the 1840s, eastern factory owners feared that they would lose their supply of laborers. At the same time, southerners saw the settlement of western land by small freeholders as a threat to their "peculiar institution"—slavery. Southern representatives in the Congress successfully blocked the passage of any homestead legislation prior to the Civil War.

The Homestead Act, finally enacted during the war in 1862, provided that any adult citizen or alien who had filed an intent to become a citizen could obtain 160 acres of public land by paying small registration fees and farming the land for 5 years.

The act, however, proved to be no panacea for poverty. Comparatively few laborers and farmers could afford to move long distances, build a farm, or acquire the necessary tools, seed, and livestock. In the end, most of those who purchased land under the act came from areas quite close to their new homesteads (Iowans moved to Nebraska, Minnesotans to South Dakota, and so on). Unfortunately, the act was framed so ambiguously that it seemed to invite fraud, and early modifications by Congress only compounded the problem. Most of the land went to speculators,

Opposite: **The Homestead Act, 1862. The act provided for the distribution of federal lands to qualified settlers. The availability of land was a driving force behind the westward movement.** *4 pages, 15 1/2 by 21 1/8 inches.*

Sod house owned by C. B. Purdy near Minatare, NE. Purdy's home, which he called "Sans Souci," was similar to many other farm dwellings in the Great Plains.

Stretching wire for a new fence. Barbed wire played a major role in the farmers' conquest of the plains and contributed to the decline of the cattlemen's open range.

The Dan Lohr ranch, Custer County, NE, 1888. With a combination of perseverance and luck, settlers could achieve considerable prosperity. *Solomon D. Butcher photograph.*

cattlemen, miners, lumbermen, and railroads. Of some 500 million acres dispensed by the General Land Office between 1862 and 1904, only 80 million acres went to homesteaders. Indeed, small farmers acquired more land under the Homestead Act in the 20th century than in the 19th.

The Indians took the brunt of the relentless westward expansion. Sometimes they ceded their land, sometimes they were forced onto reservations, and sometimes they were even driven off these lands onto smaller and poorer parcels. The Plains Indians were particularly hard hit by the wanton slaughter of the buffalo. They resisted as long as possible, and occasionally, as at the Battle of the Little Big Horn, they won a temporary victory. For the most part, however, the Indians were killed or driven from their patrimony. From the Red River in Texas in 1874–75 to Rosebud Creek in Montana in 1876 and finally at Wounded Knee in South Dakota in 1890, the Indians succumbed to the numbers, the technology, and the land hunger of the white man.

Cattlemen often preceded farmers (sodbusters) to the Great Plains and gave the cowboy—and the "long drive," Abilene, Dodge City, the Lincoln County War, Billy the Kid, and Wyatt Earp—a place in American legend and folklore. When farmers came, they stretched their barbed wire across the open range and battled wind, drought, other harsh weather, and loneliness. The mail-order catalog became important, for it enabled the men to order the seed and equipment they needed and kept the women in touch with the outside world. Some settlers viewed their hard life sardonically, as voiced in the ballad "The Lane County Bachelor":

How happy I am on my government claim,
Where I've nothing to lose and nothing to gain,

Application for land under the Homestead Act, 1863. Daniel Freeman of Gage County, Nebraska Territory, was one of the first settlers to apply. Settlers received their land patents after presenting the application form and proof of occupancy and citizenship and paying a nominal fee. *7 3/4 by 9 3/4, 8 1/4 by 10 1/8, and 7 5/8 by 5 1/2 inches, respectively.*

Application No. 1 } Homestead Land Office Brownville N.T. January 1st 1863

I Daniel Freeman of Gage County Nebraska Territory Do hereby apply to Enter under the Provisions of the act of Congress approved May 20th 1862 Entitled, an act to secure Homesteads to actual Settlers on the Public Domain The South half of N.W.¼ & N.E.¼ of N.W.¼ & S.W.¼ of N.E.¼ Sec. 26. in Township Four (4) N. in Range Five East. containing 160 acres Having filed my Pre-Emption Declaration thereto on the Eighth day of September 1862

Daniel Freeman

Land office at Brownville N.T. January 1st 1863

I Richard F. Barret, Register of the Land office do hereby certify that the above application is for Surveyed Lands of the Class which the applicant is legally Entitled to Enter under the Homestead act. of May 20th 1862 and that there is No Prior valid adverse Right to the Same

Richard F. Barret
Register

HOMESTEAD.

Land Office at Brownville Neb
January 20th 1868.

CERTIFICATE, No. 1 — APPLICATION, No. 1

It is hereby certified, That pursuant to the provisions of the act of Congress, approved May 20, 1862, entitled "An act to secure homesteads to actual settlers on the public domain," Daniel Freeman has made payment in full for S½ of NW¼ & NE¼ of NW¼ & SW¼ of NE¼ of Section Twenty six (26) in Township four (4) N of Range five (5) E containing 160 acres.

Now, therefore, be it known, That on presentation of this Certificate to the COMMISSIONER OF THE GENERAL LAND OFFICE, the said Daniel Freeman shall be entitled to a Patent for the Tract of Land above described.

Henry M. Atkinson Register.

PROOF REQUIRED UNDER HOMESTEAD ACTS MAY 20, 1862, AND JUNE 21, 1866.

WE, Joseph Graff and Samuel Kilpatrick do solemnly swear that we have known Daniel Freeman for over five years last past; that he is the head of a family consisting of wife and two children and is — a citizen of the United States; that he is an inhabitant of the S½ of NW¼ & NE¼ of NW¼ and SW¼ of NE¼ of section No. 26 in Township No. 4 N of Range No. 5 E and that no other person resided upon the said land entitled to the right of Homestead or Pre-emption.

That the said Daniel Freeman — entered upon and made settlement on said land on the 1st day of January, 1863, and has built a house thereon part log & part frame 14 by 20 feet one story. with two doors two windows. shingle roof. board floors and is a comfortable house to live in

and has lived in the said house and made it his exclusive home from the 1st day of January, 1863, to the present time, and that he has since said settlement ploughed, fenced, and cultivated about 35 — acres of said land, and has made the following improvements thereon, to wit: built a Stable. a Sheep Shed 100 feet long Corn Crib. and has 40 apple and about 400 peach trees set out.

Joseph Graff
Samuel Kilpatrick

I, Henry M. Atkinson Register do hereby certify that the above affidavit was taken and subscribed before me this 20th day of January, 1868.

Henry M. Atkinson
Register

WE CERTIFY that Joseph Graff and Samuel Kilpatrick whose names are subscribed to the foregoing affidavit, are persons of respectability.

Henry M. Atkinson, Register.
Jno. L. Carson, Receiver.

Nothing to eat and nothing to wear,
Nothing from nothing is honest and square.
But here I am stuck and here I must stay.
My money's all gone and I can't get away:
There's nothing will make a man hard and profane
Like starving to death on a government claim.

But for those who toughed it out, that life was not without its rewards. There was the satisfaction of owning one's own parcel of land and working it with one's hands, and there was always the promise that in a good year the earth could be bountiful beyond measure.

By 1890 the Director of the Census could announce that so much westward settlement had taken place that "there can hardly be said to be a frontier line." A milestone in American history had been passed. Henceforth, American expansion would be beyond the nation's continental borders and into urban areas that became the home of the great majority of Americans by the end of the next century.

Medal of Honor awarded to 1st Sgt. John Henry, Company "I," 3d Cavalry, for valor at Rosebud Creek, Montana Territory, on June 17, 1876. Eight days after this battle, another cavalry unit under Gen. George A. Custer was wiped out by Sioux Indians at the Little Big Horn River. *Bronze, 2 inches in diameter.*

Stereoscope with stereographs: a Blackfoot Indian, 1879; Fort Garland, CO, 1872; cattle roundup, ca. 1902. Through such pictures the American public learned about the West. *Each stereograph, 7 by 3 ½ inches.*

Farm machinery catalog, 1895. American agricultural technology turned the United States into the world's foremost granary. *40 pages, 9 ⅝ by 7 inches.*

Thirty-Seventh Congress of the United States of America;

At the Second Session,

Begun and held at the city of Washington, on Monday, the Second day of December, one thousand eight hundred and sixty-one

AN ACT

Donating public lands to the several States and Territories which may provide colleges for the benefit of agriculture and the Mechanic arts.

Be it enacted *by the Senate and House of Representatives of the United States of America in Congress assembled,* **That** there be granted to the several States for the purposes hereinafter mentioned an amount of public land to be apportioned to each State a quantity equal to thirty thousand acres for each Senator and representative in Congress to which the States are respectively entitled by the apportionment under the census of eighteen hundred and sixty: Provided, That no mineral lands shall be selected or purchased under the provisions of this act. Sec. 2 And be it further enacted, That the land aforesaid, after being surveyed, shall be apportioned to the several States in sections or subdivisions of sections, not less than one quarter of a section; and whenever there are public lands in a State, subject to sale at private entry at one dollar and twenty-five cents per acre the quantity to which said State shall be entitled shall be selected from such lands within the limits of such State, and the Secretary of the Interior is hereby directed to issue to each of the states in which there is not the quantity of public lands subject to sale at private entry at one dollar and twenty-five cents per acre to which said State may be entitled under the provisions of this act, land scrip to the amount in acres for the deficiency of its distributive share: said scrip to be sold by said States and the proceeds thereof applied to the uses and purposes prescribed in this act and for no other use or purpose whatsoever: Provided That in no case shall any State to which land scrip may thus be issued, be allowed to locate the same within the limits of any other State, or of any Territory of the United States, but their assignees may thus locate said land scrip upon any of the unappropriated lands of the United States subject to sale at private entry at one dollar and twenty-five cents or less per acre. And provided further, that not more than one million acres shall be located by such assignees in any one of the States, And provided further that no such location shall be made before

...

Sec. 8. And be it further enacted, That the Governors of the several States to which scrip shall be issued under this act shall be required to report annually to Congress all sales made of such scrip until the whole shall be disposed of, the amount received for the same and what appropriation has been made of the proceeds.

Galusha A. Grow
Speaker of the House of Representatives.

Solomon Foot
President of the Senate pro tempore

Approved, July 2. 1862.
Abraham Lincoln

The Morrill Act, 1862. The act granted public land to states for the establishment of colleges of agricultural and mechanical arts. These state colleges brought higher education within the reach of increasing numbers of students. *3 pages, 15 5/8 by 21 5/8 inches.*

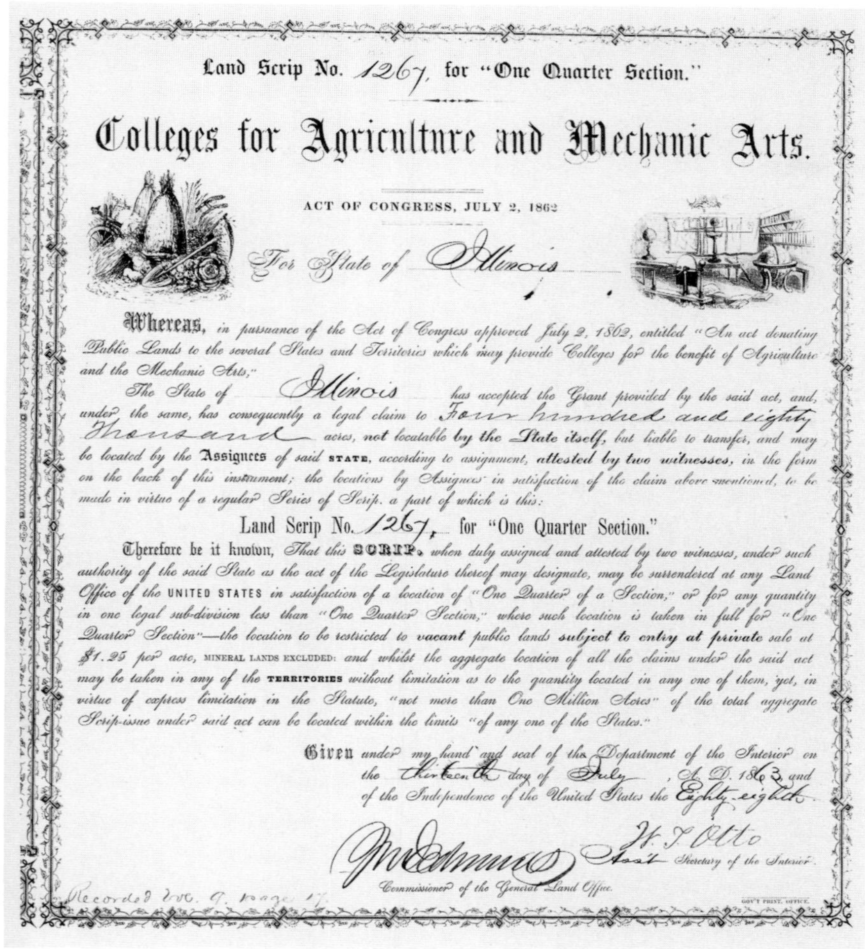

Land Scrip No. 1267, for "One Quarter Section."

Colleges for Agriculture and Mechanic Arts.

ACT OF CONGRESS, JULY 2, 1862

For State of Illinois.

Whereas, in pursuance of the Act of Congress approved July 2, 1862, entitled "An act donating Public Lands to the several States and Territories which may provide Colleges for the benefit of Agriculture and the Mechanic Arts,"

The State of Illinois has accepted the Grant provided by the said act, and, under the same, has consequently a legal claim to Four hundred and eighty Thousand acres, not locatable by the State itself, but liable to transfer, and may be located by the Assignees of said STATE, according to assignment, attested by two witnesses, in the form on the back of this instrument; the locations by Assignees in satisfaction of the claim above mentioned, to be made in virtue of a regular Series of Scrip. a part of which is this:

Land Scrip No. 1267, for "One Quarter Section."

Therefore be it known, That this SCRIP, when duly assigned and attested by two witnesses, under such authority of the said State as the act of the Legislature thereof may designate, may be surrendered at any Land Office of the UNITED STATES in satisfaction of a location of "One Quarter of a Section," or for any quantity in one legal sub-division less than "One Quarter Section," where such location is taken in full for "One Quarter Section"—the location to be restricted to vacant public lands subject to entry at private sale at $1.25 per acre, MINERAL LANDS EXCLUDED: and whilst the aggregate location of all the claims under the said act may be taken in any of the TERRITORIES without limitation as to the quantity located in any one of them, yet, in virtue of express limitation in the Statute, "not more than One Million Acres" of the total aggregate Scrip-issue under said act can be located within the limits "of any one of the States."

Given under my hand and seal of the Department of the Interior on the thirteenth day of July, A. D. 1863, and of the Independence of the United States the Eighty-eighth.

W. T. Otto
Asst Secretary of the Interior.

J M Edmunds
Commissioner of the General Land Office.

Recorded Vol. 9. page 17.

GOV'T PRINT. OFFICE.

Federal land scrip certificate issued to the state of Illinois under the Morrill Act for the promotion of higher education, 1862. *13 by 15 5/8 inches.*

Sponsored by Senator Justin Morrill of Vermont, "An Act Donating public lands to the several States and Territoris [sic] which may provide colleges for the benefit of agriculture and the Mechanic arts" marked the first federal aid to higher education. But the government's recognition of its obligation to provide schools for its future citizens dates from the beginning of the republic.

"Knowledge, being necessary to good government and the happiness of mankind, schools and the means of education shall forever be encouraged." So wrote the Continental Congress in the Northwest Ordinance of 1787. With this ordinance, Congress established a precedent for the support of public education that would grow to substantial commitments in later years.

Land was the key to the federal government's early involvement, for this was the most readily available resource in the unopened continent. As public lands were surveyed into 6-mile-square townships, a 1-square-mile section in each township was reserved for the support of public schools. The land itself was rarely used for school construction but rather was sold off, with proceeds used for funding the school program. The system invited misuse by opportunists, and substantial portions of the educational land grants never benefited education. Nevertheless, land-grant support became a substantial factor in providing education to most American children who could never hope to attend private or charity-supported schools.

The Morrill Act committed the federal government to grant to each state 30,000 acres of public land issued in the form of "land scrip" certificates for each of its Representatives and Senators in Congress. Although many states squandered the revenue from this endowment, which grew to an allocation of over 100 million acres, the Morrill land

Teacher and students in front of sod schoolhouse, Woods County, Oklahoma Territory, ca. 1895.

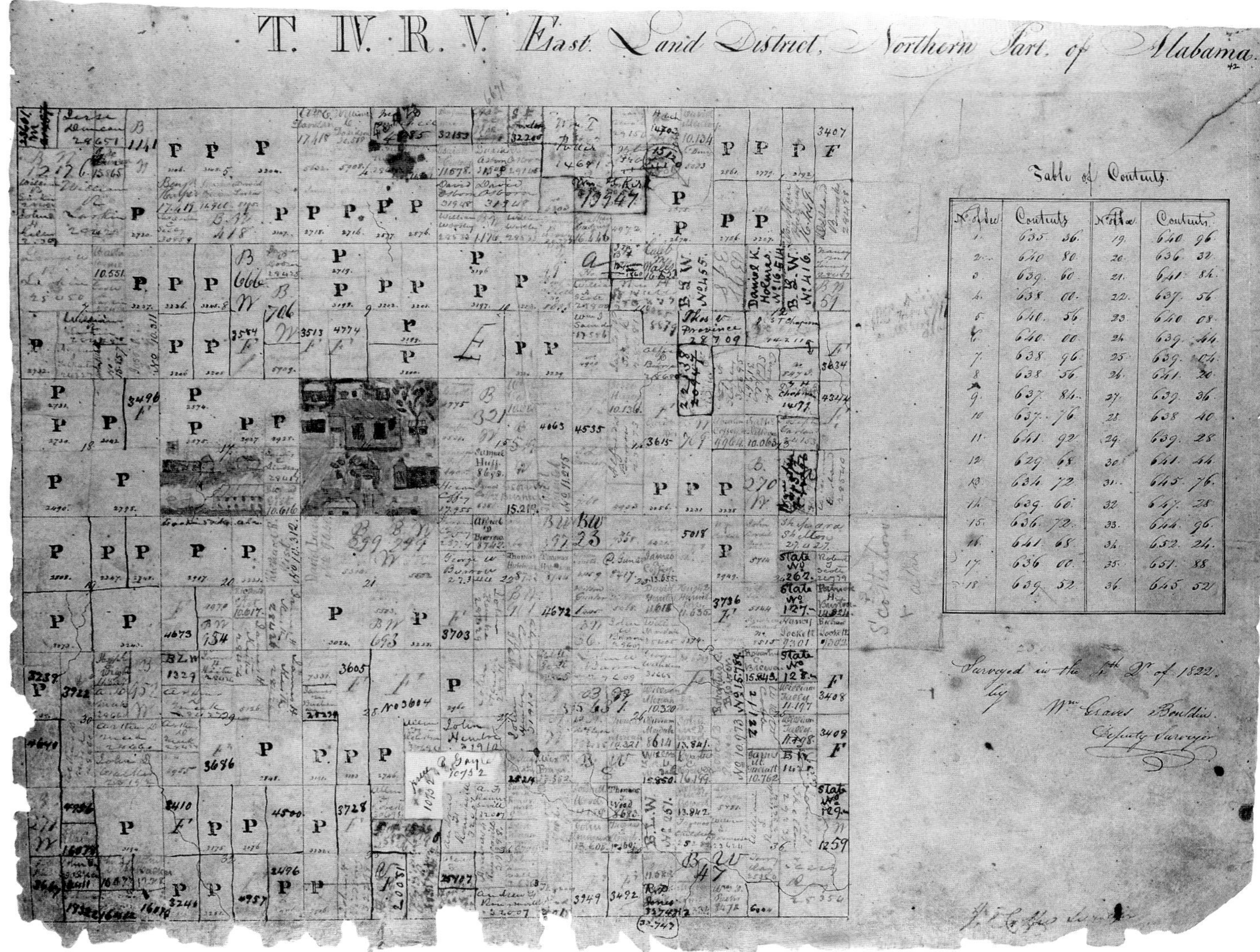

grants laid the foundation for a national system of state colleges and universities. In some cases, the land sales financed existing institutions; in others, new schools were chartered by the states. Major universities such as Nebraska, Washington State, Clemson, and Cornell were chartered as land-grant schools. State colleges brought higher education within reach of millions of students, a development that could not help but reshape the nation's social and economic fabric.

Some 80 years after the Morrill Act, Congress passed another piece of legislation that greatly expanded educational opportunity: the Servicemen's Readjustment Act of 1944, known as the GI bill of rights. Under the terms of the act, any honorably discharged GI from World War II was entitled to a maximum of 4 years of tuition-free college or technical training with a monthly subsistence payment. Some 12 million men and women took advantage of the GI bill. The legislation was notable in that it made a higher education possible for tens of thousands of men and women who would otherwise have been unable to afford one. Similar legislation benefited veterans of later wars.

Alabama plat of land grants, showing schoolhouse drawn into section 16. The Land Ordinance of 1785 provided that proceeds from the sale of one section of public land in each township were to be allotted for public schools.
17 5/8 by 13 5/8 inches.

Class in tractor repair at South Dakota State College, a land-grant institution, 1949.

Mass examination at Michigan State College (now University), 1950. As a result of the GI bill, more students graduated from college in 1950 than in any previous year in American history.

Seventy-eighth Congress of the United States of America;
At the Second Session

Begun and held at the City of Washington on Monday, the tenth day of January, one thousand nine hundred and forty-four

AN ACT

To provide Federal Government aid for the readjustment in civilian life of returning World War II veterans.

Be it enacted by the Senate and House of Representatives of the United States of America in Congress assembled, That this Act may be cited as the "Servicemen's Readjustment Act of 1944".

TITLE I

CHAPTER I—HOSPITALIZATION, CLAIMS, AND PROCEDURES

SEC. 100. The Veterans' Administration is hereby declared to be an essential war agency and entitled, second only to the War and Navy Departments, to priorities in personnel, equipment, supplies, and material under any laws, Executive orders, and regulations pertaining to priorities, and in appointments of personnel from civil-service registers the Administrator of Veterans' Affairs is hereby granted the same authority and discretion as the War and Navy Departments and the United States Public Health Service: *Provided*, That the provisions of this section as to priorities for materials shall apply to any State institution to be built for the care or hospitalization of veterans.

SEC. 101. The Administrator of Veterans' Affairs and the Federal Board of Hospitalization are hereby authorized and directed to expedite and complete the construction of additional hospital facilities for war veterans, and to enter into agreements and contracts for the use by or transfer to the Veterans' Administration of suitable Army and Navy hospitals after termination of hostilities in the present war or after such institutions are no longer needed by the armed services; and the Administrator of Veterans' Affairs is hereby authorized and directed to establish necessary regional offices, sub-offices, branch offices, contact units, or other subordinate offices in centers of population where there is no Veterans' Administration facility, or where such a facility is not readily available or accessible: *Provided*, That there is hereby authorized to be appropriated the sum of $500,000,000 for the construction of additional hospital facilities.

SEC. 102. The Administrator of Veterans' Affairs and the Secretary of War and Secretary of the Navy are hereby granted authority to enter into agreements and contracts for the mutual use or exchange

The Servicemen's Readjustment Act, 1944, popularly known as the GI bill. The act put higher education within the reach of millions of veterans of World War II and later military conflicts. *3 pages, 10 by 14 ¾ inches.*

S.R. 8.

Pub. Res. 10

Fortieth Congress of the United States of America;

At the third Session,

Begun and held at the city of Washington, on Monday, the seventh day of December, one thousand eight hundred and sixty-eight.

A RESOLUTION

Proposing an amendment to the Constitution of the United States.

Resolved *by the Senate and House of Representatives of the United States of America in Congress assembled,* (two-thirds of both Houses concurring) That the following article be proposed to the legislatures of the several States as an amendment to the Constitution of the United States, which, when ratified by three-fourths of said legislatures shall be valid as part of the Constitution, namely:

Article XV.

Section 1. The right of citizens of the United States to vote shall not be denied or abridged by the United States or by any State on account of race, color, or previous condition of servitude —

Section 2. The Congress shall have power to enforce this article by appropriate legislation —

Schuyler Colfax

Speaker of the House of Representatives.

B. F. Wade

President of the Senate pro tempore.

Attest:

Edw. McPherson

Clerk of House of Representatives.

Geo. C. Gorham

Secy of Senate U.S.

To former abolitionists and to the Radical Republicans in Congress who fashioned Reconstruction after the Civil War, the 15th amendment, enacted in 1870, appeared to signify the fulfillment of all promises to African Americans. Set free by the 13th amendment, with citizenship guaranteed by the 14th amendment, black males were given the vote by the 15th amendment. From that point on, the freedmen were generally expected to fend for themselves. In retrospect, it can be seen that the 15th amendment was in reality only the beginning of a struggle for equality that would continue for more than a century before African Americans could begin to participate fully in American public and civic life.

African Americans exercised the franchise and held office in many Southern states through the 1880s, but in the early 1890s, steps were taken to ensure subsequent "white supremacy." Literacy tests for the vote, "grandfather clauses" excluding from the franchise all whose ancestors had not voted in the 1860s, and other devices to disfranchise African Americans were written into the constitutions of the former Confederate states. Social and economic segregation were added to black America's loss of political power. In 1896 the Supreme Court decision *Plessy* v. *Ferguson* legalized "separate but equal" facilities for the races. For more than 50 years, the overwhelming majority of African-American citizens were reduced to second-class citizenship under the "Jim Crow" segregation system. During that time African Americans sought to secure their rights and improve their position through organizations such as the National Association for the Advancement of Colored People and the National Urban League and through the individual efforts of reformers like Booker T. Washington, W.E.B. DuBois, and A. Philip Randolph.

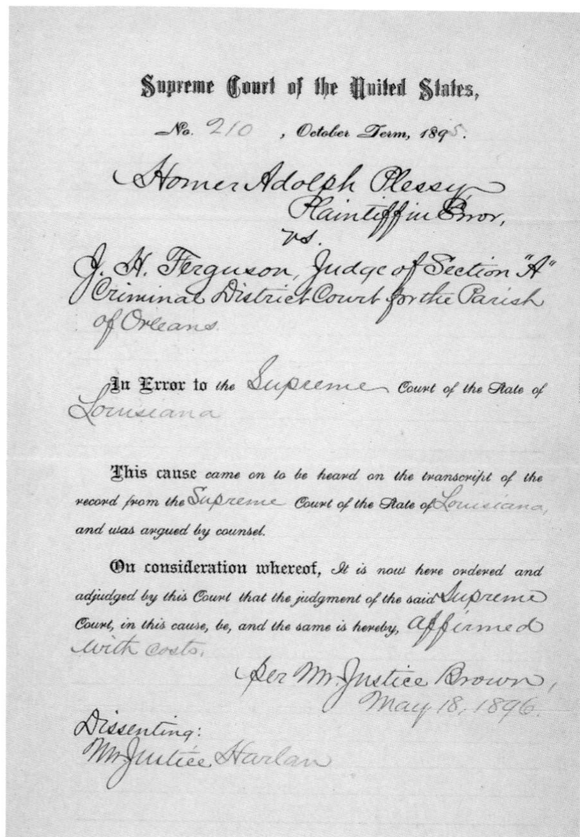

Supreme Court of the United States,

No. 210, October Term, 1895.

Homer Adolph Plessy, Plaintiff in Error,

vs.

J. H. Ferguson, Judge of Section "A" Criminal District Court for the Parish of Orleans.

In Error to the Supreme Court of the State of Louisiana.

This cause came on to be heard on the transcript of the record from the Supreme Court of the State of Louisiana, and was argued by counsel.

On consideration whereof, It is now here ordered and adjudged by this Court that the judgment of the said Supreme Court, in this cause, be, and the same is hereby, affirmed with costs.

Per Mr. Justice Brown, May 18, 1896.

Dissenting: Mr. Justice Harlan

***Plessy* v. *Ferguson*, 1896. This Supreme Court decision gave legal sanction to segregation by calling for "separate but equal" public facilities.** *97 pages, 8 3/8 by 13 3/4 inches.*

"Separate but equal" schools, illustrated in *Racial Inequalities in Education*, a 1938 National Association for the Advancement of Colored People (NAACP) publication. *6 by 8 3/4 inches.*

Opposite: **The 15th amendment, 1870. Freed by the 13th amendment and guaranteed citizenship by the 14th amendment, former slaves and free blacks were ostensibly given the vote by the 15th amendment. In actuality, however, it marked only the beginning of a long struggle for equality by black Americans.** *15 3/4 by 21 3/4 inches.*

World War II brought a new opportunity for advancement within the dominant white social structure. African Americans were drafted into the armed services and fought as effective soldiers to preserve Western democracy. In 1946 President Harry S. Truman established the Committee on Civil Rights, whose report "To Secure These Rights" led him in 1948 to deliver a ringing civil rights message to Congress. In July 1948 Truman's executive order to end segregation in the armed services began a historic change that would be completed by the early 1950s.

In 1954 the Supreme Court struck down the principle of "separate but equal" in the landmark decision *Brown* v. *The Board of Education of Topeka.* "In the field of public education," wrote Chief Justice Earl Warren, "the doctrine of 'separate but equal' has no place. Separate facilities are inherently unequal." The Court directed that schools should be desegregated "with all deliberate speed."

This initial victory for racial equality was actually only the beginning of a yet another new struggle. To implement the court's order, President Dwight D. Eisenhower in 1957 dispatched federal troops and placed the Arkansas National Guard under federal command to desegregate Central High School in Little Rock, AR. Although many communities achieved school integration peaceably, those that resisted made headlines. While the National Association for the Advancement of Colored People worked through the federal courts to secure equal rights for African Americans, the Southern Christian Leadership Conference, led by Martin Luther King, Jr., engaged in nonviolent demonstrations that reached a climax in the 1963 March on Washington for Jobs and Freedom.

During this time, the Civil Rights Acts of 1957, 1960, 1964, 1965, and 1968 provided for broader protection of equality under the law for all races, nationalities, and religious groups. The 1964 act was amended by the 1972 Equal Employment Opportunity Act, the 1978 Pregnancy Discrimination Act, and the 1991 Civil Rights Act. The Civil Rights Commission, established by the 1957 act, investigates charges that the vote and equal protection of the law have been denied. The Civil Rights Division of the Department of Justice prosecutes violations of the Civil Rights Acts; and the Equal Employment Opportunity Commission, established by the 1964 act, has responsibility for ensuring the government's policy of nondiscriminatory federal employment. In 1962 President John F. Kennedy issued an Executive order prohibiting racial or religious discrimination in federal housing, and in 1968, Congress barred discrimination in all housing in the Open Housing Act and the less-publicized National Housing Act.

The most direct attack on the problem of African-American disfranchisement came in 1965. Prompted by reports of continuing discriminatory voting practices in many Southern states, President Lyndon B. Johnson, himself a southerner, urged Congress on March 15, 1965, to pass legislation "which will make it impossible to thwart the Fifteenth Amendment." He reminded Congress that "we cannot have government for all the people until we first make certain it is government of and by all the people." The Voting Rights Act of 1965, extended in 1970, 1975, and 1982, abolished all remaining deterrents to exercising the franchise and authorized federal supervision of voter registration where necessary.

"All men are created equal," wrote Thomas Jefferson in the Declaration of Independence. Transforming this concept into a reality for all citizens has been and continues to be one of the central challenges of our national existence.

Brown v. _The Board of Education of Topeka_, 1954. In overturning the _Plessy_ decision, Chief Justice Earl Warren wrote: "In the field of public education, the doctrine of 'separate but equal' has no place. Separate educational facilities are inherently unequal."
Opinion, 4 pages, 6 by 9 ¼ inches.

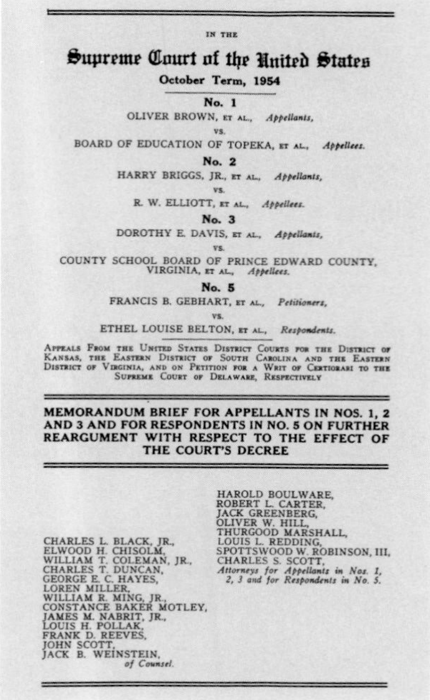

IN THE

Supreme Court of the United States

October Term, 1954

No. 1
OLIVER BROWN, ET AL., *Appellants,*
VS.
BOARD OF EDUCATION OF TOPEKA, ET AL., *Appellees.*

No. 2
HARRY BRIGGS, JR., ET AL., *Appellants,*
VS.
R. W. ELLIOTT, ET AL., *Appellees.*

No. 3
DOROTHY E. DAVIS, ET AL., *Appellants,*
VS.
COUNTY SCHOOL BOARD OF PRINCE EDWARD COUNTY, VIRGINIA, ET AL., *Appellees.*

No. 5
FRANCIS B. GEBHART, ET AL., *Petitioners,*
VS.
ETHEL LOUISE BELTON, ET AL., *Respondents.*

APPEALS FROM THE UNITED STATES DISTRICT COURTS FOR THE DISTRICT OF KANSAS, THE EASTERN DISTRICT OF SOUTH CAROLINA AND THE EASTERN DISTRICT OF VIRGINIA, AND ON PETITION FOR A WRIT OF CERTIORARI TO THE SUPREME COURT OF DELAWARE, RESPECTIVELY

MEMORANDUM BRIEF FOR APPELLANTS IN NOS. 1, 2 AND 3 AND FOR RESPONDENTS IN NO. 5 ON FURTHER REARGUMENT WITH RESPECT TO THE EFFECT OF THE COURT'S DECREE

HAROLD BOULWARE,
ROBERT L. CARTER,
JACK GREENBERG,
OLIVER W. HILL,
THURGOOD MARSHALL,
LOUIS L. REDDING,
SPOTTSWOOD W. ROBINSON, III,
CHARLES S. SCOTT,
Attorneys for Appellants in Nos. 1, 2, 3 and for Respondents in No. 5.

CHARLES L. BLACK, JR.,
ELWOOD H. CHISOLM,
WILLIAM T. COLEMAN, JR.,
CHARLES T. DUNCAN,
GEORGE E. C. HAYES,
LOREN MILLER,
WILLIAM R. MING, JR.,
CONSTANCE BAKER MOTLEY,
JAMES M. NABRIT, JR.,
LOUIS H. POLLAK,
FRANK D. REEVES,
JOHN SCOTT,
JACK B. WEINSTEIN,
of Counsel.

The 1963 March on Washington for Jobs and Freedom was the culmination of 5 years of intense civil rights activity. A huge gathering heard the Reverend Martin Luther King, Jr., sound the keynote with his stirring "I have a dream" speech, delivered from the steps of the Lincoln Memorial.

Civil rights leaders meeting with President John F. Kennedy on the day of the 1963 March on Washington: left to right, Secretary of Labor W. Willard Wirtz; Floyd McKissick, Congress of Racial Equality (CORE); Matthew Ahmann, National Catholic Conference for Interracial Justice; Whitney Young, National Urban League; the Reverend Martin Luther King, Jr., Southern Christian Leadership Conference (SCLC); John Lewis, Student Nonviolent Coordinating Committee (SNCC); Rabbi Joachim Prinz, American Jewish Congress; the Reverend Eugene Carson Blake, Commission on Race Relations for the National Council of Churches; A. Philip Randolph, AFL-CIO; the President; Vice President Lyndon B. Johnson; Walter Reuther, United Auto Workers; and Roy Wilkins, National Association for the Advancement of Colored People (NAACP). *Abbie Rowe photograph.*

PUBLIC LAW 89-110

S. 1564

THE WHITE HOUSE AUG 5 1965 RECEIVED

AUG 6 1965

Eighty-ninth Congress of the United States of America

AT THE FIRST SESSION

Begun and held at the City of Washington on Monday, the fourth day of January, one thousand nine hundred and sixty-five

An Act

To enforce the fifteenth amendment to the Constitution of the United States, and for other purposes.

Be it enacted by the Senate and House of Representatives of the United States of America in Congress assembled, That this Act shall be known as the "Voting Rights Act of 1965".

Sec. 2. No voting qualification or prerequisite to voting, or standard, practice, or procedure shall be imposed or applied by any State or political subdivision to deny or abridge the right of any citizen of the United States to vote on account of race or color.

Sec. 3. (a) Whenever the Attorney General institutes a proceeding under any statute to enforce the guarantees of the fifteenth amendment in any State or political subdivision the court shall authorize the appointment of Federal examiners by the United States Civil Service Commission in accordance with section 6 to serve for such period of time and for such political subdivisions as the court shall determine is appropriate to enforce the guarantees of the fifteenth amendment (1) as part of any interlocutory order if the court determines that the appointment of such examiners is necessary to enforce such guarantees or (2) as part of any final judgment if the court finds that violations of the fifteenth amendment justifying equitable relief have occurred in such State or subdivision: *Provided*, That the court need not authorize the appointment of examiners if any incidents of denial or abridgement of the right to vote on account of race or color (1) have been few in number and have been promptly and effectively corrected by State or local action, (2) the continuing effect of such incidents has been eliminated, and (3) there is no reasonable probability of their recurrence in the future.

(b) If in a proceeding instituted by the Attorney General under any statute to enforce the guarantees of the fifteenth amendment in any State or political subdivision the court finds that a test or device has been used for the purpose or with the effect of denying or abridging the right of any citizen of the United States to vote on account of race or color, it shall suspend the use of tests and devices in such State or political subdivisions as the court shall determine is appropriate and for such period as it deems necessary.

(c) If in any proceeding instituted by the Attorney General under any statute to enforce the guarantees of the fifteenth amendment in any State or political subdivision the court finds that violations of the fifteenth amendment justifying equitable relief have occurred within the territory of such State or political subdivision, the court, in addition to such relief as it may grant, shall retain jurisdiction for such period as it may deem appropriate and during such period no voting qualification or prerequisite to voting, or standard, practice, or procedure with respect to voting different from that in force or effect at the time the proceeding was commenced shall be enforced unless and until the court finds that such qualification, prerequisite, standard, practice, or procedure does not have the purpose and will not have the effect of denying or abridging the right to vote on account of race or color: *Provided*, That such qualification, prerequisite, standard, practice, or procedure may be enforced if the qualification, prerequisite, standard, practice, or procedure has been submitted by the chief legal officer or other appropriate official of such State or subdivision to the Attorney General and the Attorney General has not interposed an objection within sixty days after such

The Voting Rights Act of 1965. Prompted by protest demonstrations against discriminatory voting practices in many Southern states, President Lyndon B. Johnson on March 15, 1965, urged Congress to pass legislation "which will make it impossible to thwart" the voting rights guaranteed by the 15th amendment. *10 pages, 10 by 15 inches.*

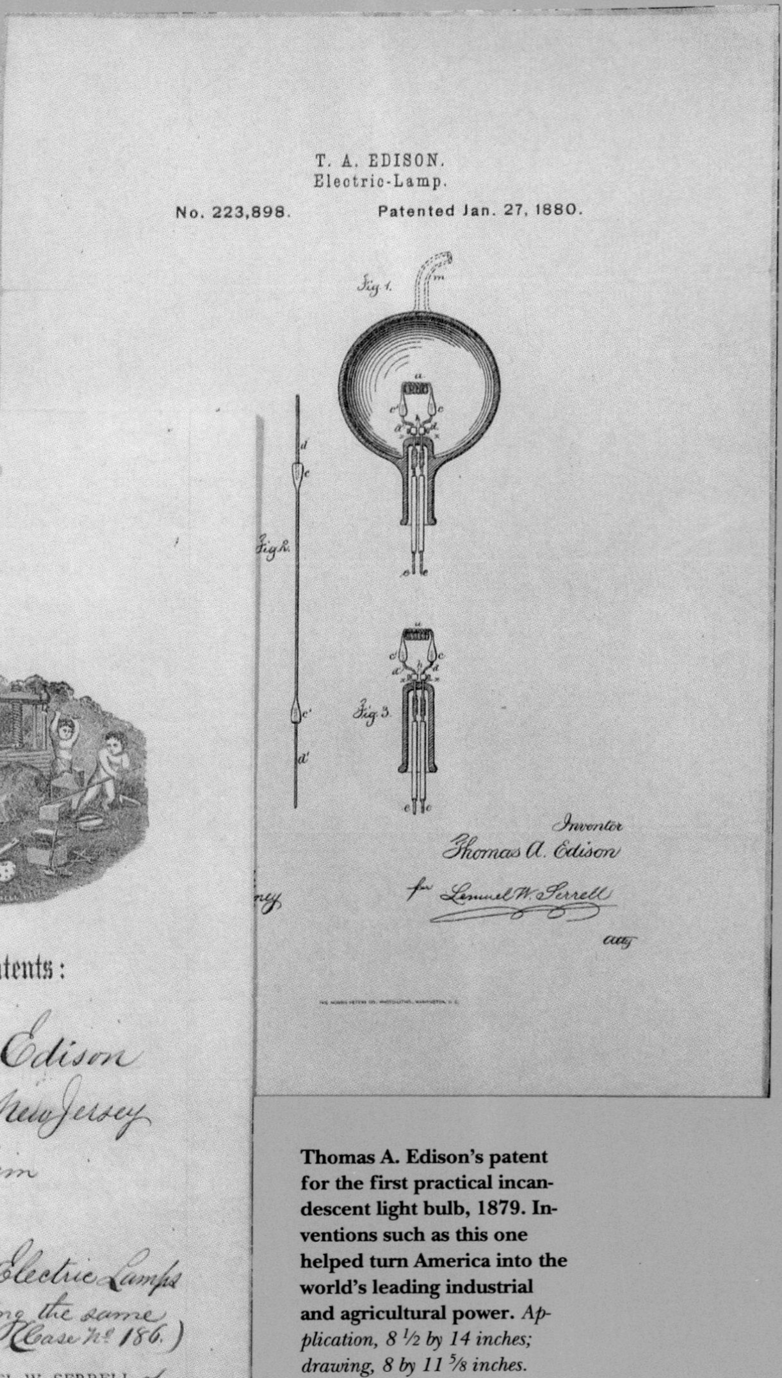

T. A. EDISON.
Electric-Lamp.

No. 223,898. Patented Jan. 27, 1880.

Fig. 1.

Fig. 2.

Fig. 3.

Inventor
Thomas A. Edison
for Lemuel W. Serrell
atty

To the Honorable Commissioner of Patents:

Your Petitioner Thomas A. Edison of Menlo Park in the State of New Jersey prays that LETTERS PATENT may be granted to him

for the invention of an Improvement in Electric Lamps and in the method of manufacturing the same (Case No. 186.) set forth in the annexed specification.

And further pray that you will recognize LEMUEL W. SERRELL, of the City of New York, N. Y., as his Attorney, with full power of substitution and revocation, to prosecute this application, to make alterations and amendments therein, to receive the Patent, and to transact all business in the Patent Office connected therewith.

1879.

Thomas A. Edison's patent for the first practical incandescent light bulb, 1879. Inventions such as this one helped turn America into the world's leading industrial and agricultural power. *Application, 8 1/2 by 14 inches; drawing, 8 by 11 5/8 inches.*

In the United States, as in other industrial countries, a nation of farmers was converted to an urban society through technological innovations that progressively reshaped where and how Americans lived. One factor that encouraged the steady flow of inventions in this country was the federal patent system. Congress established the first patent board in 1790, implementing a provision of the Constitution that the "exclusive right to their respective Writings and Discoveries" should be secured "for limited Times to Authors and Inventors." The patent for Thomas A. Edison's practical incandescent lamp represents the wide-ranging American ingenuity that is documented in patent records in the National Archives.

The list of patents granted to now-famous inventors during the early years can barely convey their lasting significance: Eli Whitney's cotton gin, 1794: Samuel Colt's revolving handgun, 1836; Charles Goodyear's rubber process, 1844; William Kelly's process for making steel, 1851; and Elisha Otis's elevator, 1861. These inventions and others would combine with one another to change the pace and pattern of industrial and agricultural growth and, eventually, the style of American life.

Power station mechanic, 1925. *Lewis Hine photograph.*

Inventors often made revolutionary discoveries without recognizing their importance. Alexander Graham Bell patented his telephone in 1876 as "Improvements in Telegraphy." Although he realized that the new device carried human voices as well as telegraph signals, he did not anticipate the major way in which it would be used. Significant applications of an invention often appeared only over a long period of time and were then buttressed by supporting devices, each carrying its own federal patent.

The federal patent system was intended to guarantee inventors the profit from the initial development of their creation. The expense in-

Elias Howe's sewing machine patent drawing, 1846. Howe's invention was the basis of the inexpensive readymade clothing industry. *20 ¾ by 16 inches.*

volved in exploiting new machines and processes, coupled with the cost of maintaining exclusivity over existing patents, often encouraged the formation of huge corporations that dominated their field. Eventually a series of antitrust laws challenged these corporate monopolies.

If the use of new inventions was difficult to anticipate, equally hard to foresee were the massive consequences on the environment and on what Americans came to call the "quality of life." One invention spawned another, creating new industries based upon seemingly unlimited natural resources. The mass-produced fruits of American inventiveness filled the marketplace, converting masses of citizens into consumers. Vast land areas became covered with shelter, transportation networks, industry, and mining operations. As the wealth of the raw land was converted into consumable abundance, the inheritance of future generations was often sacrificed, and raw materials began to disappear from their ancient depositories. The same industries that supported a high standard of material living created mountains of scrap steel and plastic, rivers of chemical waste, and clouds of soot and smog. Having long equated technological development with progress, Americans began to worry about conserving the nation's resources and to recoil before the grim byproducts of unrestrained or shortsighted industrial activity.

Official recognition that water and air pollution and resource conservation were world problems led to the establishment in 1970 of the Environmental Protection Agency (EPA), charged with administering and enforcing a growing body of pollution-control legislation. Since the creation of the EPA, Congress has passed laws regulating pesticides, ocean dumping, solid waste disposal, and toxic substances, as well as the Clean Air Act, the Clean Water Act, the Noise Control Act, and the Safe Drinking Water Act. The occurrence of large-scale environmental disasters, such as the 1979 accident at the Three Mile Island Nuclear Power Plant and the 1989 Exxon *Valdez* oil spill, and growing public concern over such problems as the depletion of the earth's rain forests and ozone layer and the effects of global warming and acid rain have given the EPA a critical and challenging role to play in the nation's future.

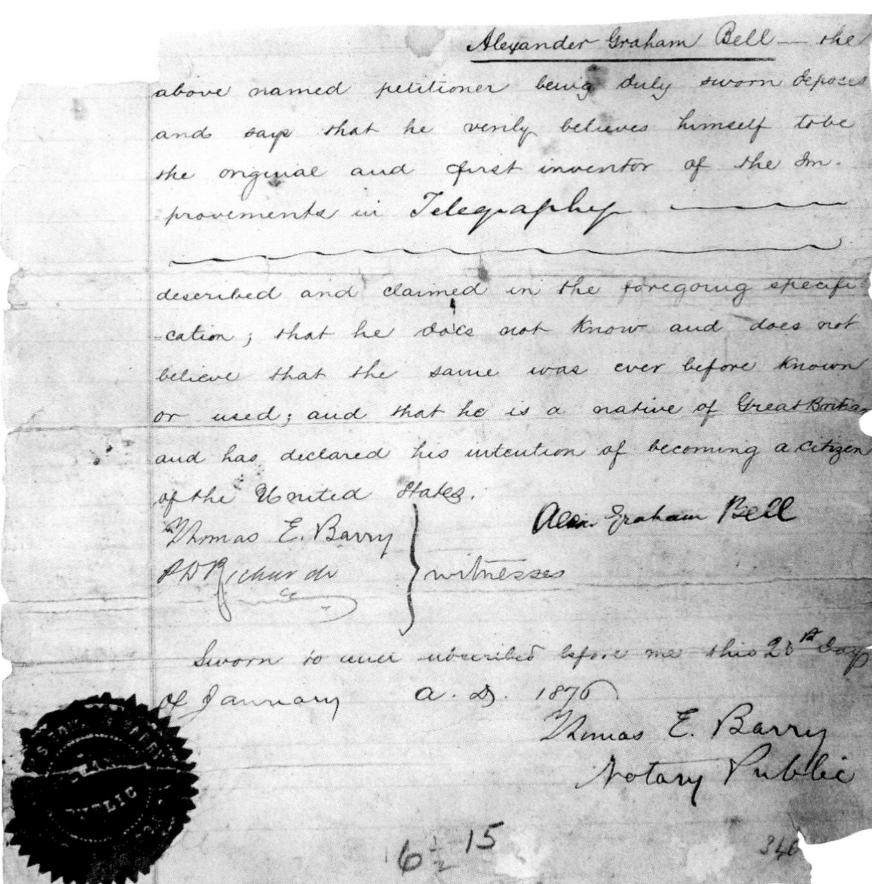

Alexander Graham Bell — the above named petitioner being duly sworn deposes and says that he verily believes himself to be the original and first inventor of the Improvements in Telegraphy — described and claimed in the foregoing specification; that he does not know and does not believe that the same was ever before known or used; and that he is a native of Great Britain and has declared his intention of becoming a citizen of the United States.

Alex. Graham Bell

Thomas E. Barry
P.D. Richards } witnesses

Sworn to and subscribed before me this 20th day of January A.D. 1876
Thomas E. Barry
Notary Public

6 1/2 15 346

Alexander Graham Bell's oath to accompany his patent application for the telephone, 1876. Described as "Improvements in Telegraphy," the device revolutionized voice communication throughout the world. *8 1/4 by 12 3/4 inches, detail.*

Child at a loom in North Carolina, 1912. Textile factories often became sweatshops supported by child labor and characterized by other forms of labor exploitation.
Lewis Hine photograph.

Propaganda sticker issued by the Industrial Workers of the World (IWW). The most radical labor union to emerge in the early 20th century was the IWW, whose members were known as the Wobblies. *1 7/8 by 2 3/8 inches.*

Oil drill bit patented by Howard Hughes, Sr., 1909. This type of bit, still in use today, became a fundamental tool of the petroleum industry and was the foundation of a vast Hughes fortune. *10 by 15 1/8 inches.*

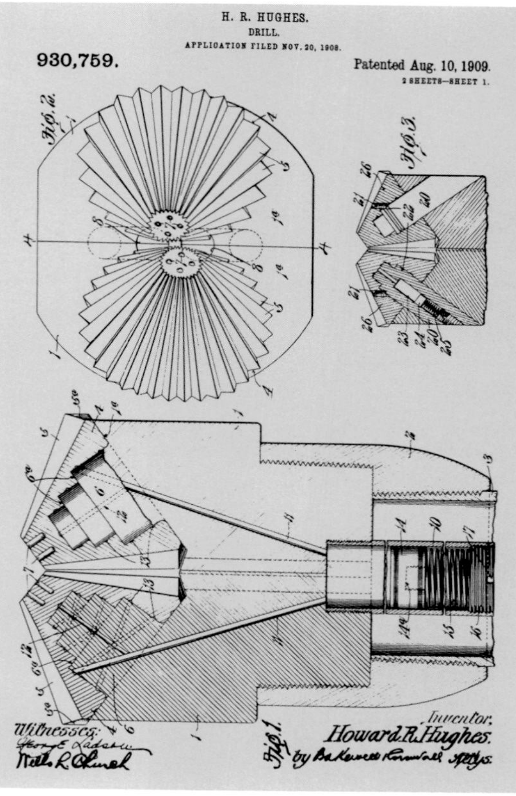

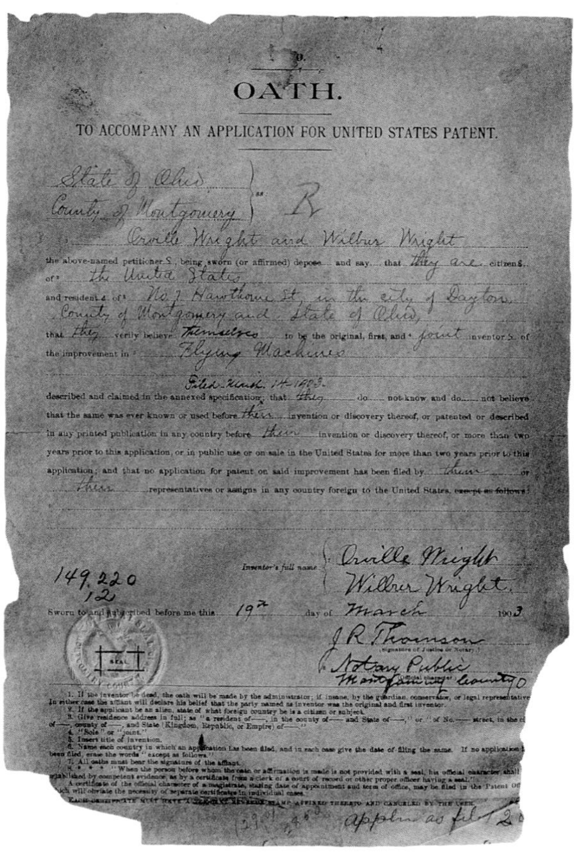

OATH.

TO ACCOMPANY AN APPLICATION FOR UNITED STATES PATENT.

State of Ohio
County of Montgomery } ss: R

Orville Wright and Wilbur Wright the above-named petitioners, being sworn (or affirmed) depose and say that they are citizens of the United States and residents of No. 7 Hawthorne St, in the city of Dayton, County of Montgomery and State of Ohio, that they verily believe themselves to be the original, first, and joint inventors of the improvement in Flying Machines

Filed March 14-1903.

described and claimed in the annexed specification; that they do not know and do not believe that the same was ever known or used before their invention or discovery thereof, or patented or described in any printed publication in any country before their invention or discovery thereof, or more than two years prior to this application, or in public use or on sale in the United States for more than two years prior to this application; and that no application for patent on said improvement has been filed by them or their representatives or assigns in any country foreign to the United States, ~~except as follows:~~

Inventor's full name { Orville Wright
Wilbur Wright.

149,220
12

Sworn to and subscribed before me this 19th day of March 1903

SEAL

J R Thomson
(Signature of Justice or Notary.)
Notary Public
(Official character.) Montgomery County O

1. If the inventor be dead, the oath will be made by the administrator; if insane, by the guardian, conservator, or legal representative. In either case the affiant will declare his belief that the party named as inventor was the original and first inventor.
2. If the applicant be an alien, state of what foreign country he is a citizen or subject.
3. Give residence address in full; as "a resident of —, in the county of — and State of —," or "of No. — street, in the city of —, county of —, and State (Kingdom, Republic, or Empire) of —."
4. "Sole" or "joint."
5. Insert title of invention.
6. Name each country in which an application has been filed, and in each case give the date of filing the same. If no application has been filed, erase the words "except as follows."
7. All oaths must bear the signature of the affiant.
8. * * * "When the person before whom the oath or affirmation is made is not provided with a seal, his official character shall be established by competent evidence, as by a certificate from a clerk of a court of record or other proper officer having a seal."
A certificate of the official character of a magistrate, stating date of appointment and term of office, may be filed in the Patent Office, which will obviate the necessity of separate certificates in individual cases.

EACH CERTIFICATE MUST HAVE A TEN-CENT REVENUE STAMP AFFIXED THERETO AND CANCELED BY THE USER.

Appln as fil

Wilbur and Orville Wright's oath to accompany the patent application for an "improvement in Flying Machines," 1903. Twenty-four years later, Charles A. Lindbergh crossed the Atlantic on a solo flight; 42 years after that, man stood on the moon. Whether Americans liked it or not, their world—even their solar system—was shrinking at a rapid rate. *8 5/8 by 12 1/2 inches.*

Left: Henry Ford's Model-T, 1917. The product of mass production, the Model-T automobile became the key to private transportation for millions of people. *Motion picture frames from the National Archives Ford Film Collection.*

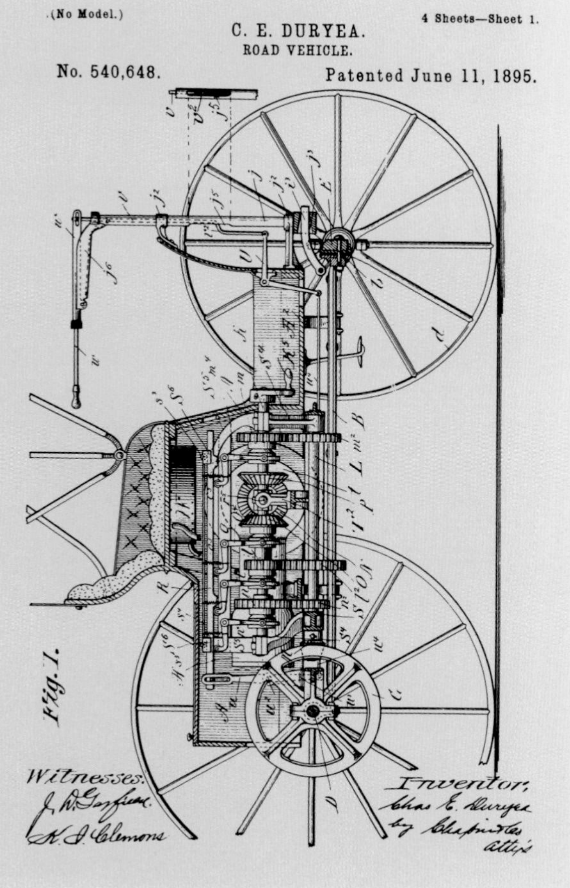

Early automobile design by Charles and Frank Duryea, 1895. The Duryea was the first practical American automobile. *10 by 15 1/8 inches.*

S. J. Res. 40.

Sixty-first Congress of the United States of America;

At the First Session,

Begun and held at the City of Washington on Monday, the fifteenth day of March, one thousand nine hundred and nine.

JOINT RESOLUTION

Proposing an amendment to the Constitution of the United States.

Resolved by the Senate and House of Representatives of the United States of America in Congress assembled (two-thirds of each House concurring therein), That the following article is proposed as an amendment to the Constitution of the United States, which, when ratified by the legislatures of three-fourths of the several States, shall be valid to all intents and purposes as a part of the Constitution:

"ARTICLE XVI. The Congress shall have power to lay and collect taxes on incomes, from whatever source derived, without apportionment among the several States, and without regard to any census or enumeration."

J G Cannon

Speaker of the House of Representatives.

J S Sherman

Vice-President of the United States and President of the Senate.

Attest:

A McDowell
Clerk of the House of Representatives.
Charles G. Bennett
Secretary
By Henry H. Gilfry Chief Clerk

Far-reaching in its social as well as its economic impact, the income tax amendment became part of the Constitution by a curious series of events culminating in a bit of political maneuvering that went awry.

The financial requirements of the Civil War prompted the first American income tax in 1861. At first, Congress placed a flat 3-percent tax on all incomes over $800 and later modified this principle to include a graduated tax. Congress repealed the income tax in 1872, but the concept did not disappear.

After the Civil War, the growing industrial and financial markets of the Eastern United States generally prospered. But the farmers of the South and West suffered from low prices for their farm products, while they were forced to pay high prices for manufactured goods. Throughout the 1860s, 1870s, and 1880s, farmers formed such political organizations as the Grange, the Greenback Party, the National Farmers' Alliance, and the People's (Populist) Party. All of these groups advocated many reforms considered radical for the times, including a graduated income tax.

In 1894, as part of a high tariff bill, Congress enacted a 2-percent tax on income over $4,000. The tax was almost immediately struck down by a five-to-four decision of the Supreme Court, even though the Court had upheld the constitutionality of the Civil War tax as recently as 1881. Although farm organizations denounced the Court's decision as a prime example of the alliance of government and business against the farmer, a general return of prosperity around the turn of the century softened the demand for reform. Democratic Party platforms under the leadership of three-time Presidential candidate William Jennings Bryan, however, consistently included an income tax plank, and the progressive wing of the Republican Party also espoused the concept.

In 1909 progressives in Congress again attached a provision for an income tax to a tariff

Opposite: **The 16th amendment, 1913. This document settled the constitutional question of how to tax income and, by so doing, effected dramatic changes in the American way of life. The signature is that of Joseph Gurney Cannon, Speaker of the House of Representatives from 1903 to 1911, one of the most powerful Speakers in the history of Congress.** *9 ¾ by 14 ¾ inches.*

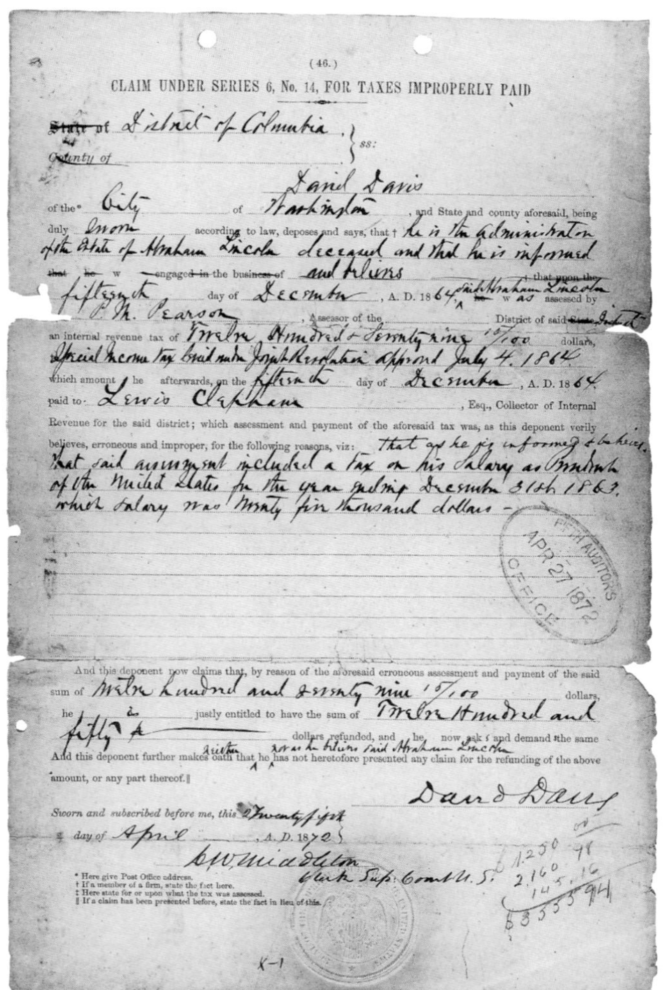

(46.)

CLAIM UNDER SERIES 6, No. 14, FOR TAXES IMPROPERLY PAID

~~State~~ of District of Columbia } ss:
County of

David Davis of the City of Washington, and State and county aforesaid, being duly sworn according to law, deposes and says, that he is the administrator of the Estate of Abraham Lincoln deceased and that he is informed that he w engaged in the business of and heirs that upon the fifteenth day of December, A. D. 1864 said Abraham Lincoln was assessed by J. M. Pearson, Assessor of the District of said District an internal revenue tax of Twelve Hundred & Twenty nine 15/100 dollars, Special Income Tax laid under Joint Resolution approved July 4. 1864 which amount he afterwards, on the fifteenth day of December, A. D. 1864, paid to Lewis Clephane, Esq., Collector of Internal Revenue for the said district; which assessment and payment of the aforesaid tax was, as this deponent verily believes, erroneous and improper; for the following reasons, viz: That as he is informed & believes, that said assessment included a tax on his salary as President of the United States for the year ending December 31st 1863, which salary was twenty five thousand dollars —

FIFTH AUDITOR'S OFFICE APR 27 1872

And this deponent now claims that, by reason of the aforesaid erroneous assessment and payment of the said sum of Twelve hundred and twenty nine 15/100 dollars, he is justly entitled to have the sum of Twelve Hundred and fifty dollars refunded, and he now asks and demands the same. And this deponent further makes oath that he has not heretofore presented any claim for the refunding of the above amount, or any part thereof.

David Davis

Sworn and subscribed before me, this twenty first day of April, A.D. 1872

[illegible] Middleton, Clerk Sup. Court U.S.

* Here give Post Office address.
† If a member of a firm, state the fact here.
‡ Here state for or upon what the tax was assessed.
§ If a claim has been presented before, state the fact in lieu of this.

1,250
2,160
145.16
$3555.94

1872 claim for a refund of taxes unnecessarily paid by Abraham Lincoln in 1863. In 1861 Congress levied a special income tax for the first time, but under the terms of this Internal Revenue Service Act, Presidential salaries were exempt. *8 ½ by 13 inches.*

Warrant for tax refund to the estate of Abraham Lincoln, April 27, 1872. *8 ⅜ by 4 ⅛ inches.*

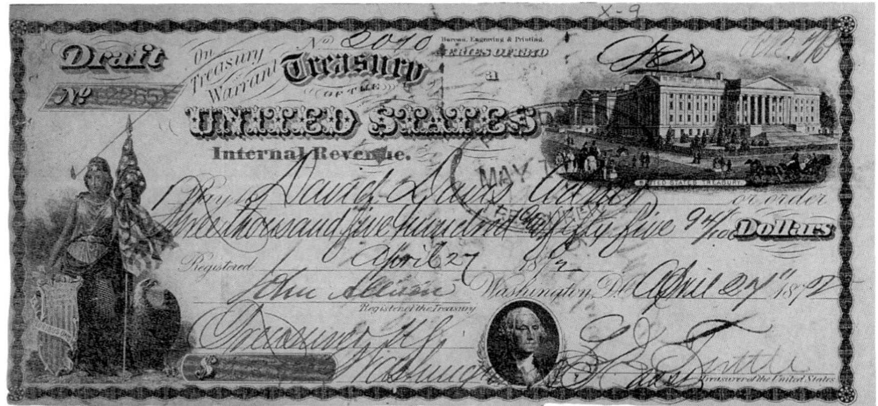

Draft on Treasury Warrant No 2010

Treasury of the United States

Internal Revenue.

Pay to David Davis Admr or order

Three thousand five hundred and fifty five 94/100 Dollars

Registered April 27 1872

John Allison, Register of the Treasury

Washington, D.C. April 27th 1872

Treasurer of the United States

bill. Conservatives, hoping to kill the idea for good, proposed a constitutional amendment enacting such a tax; they believed an amendment would never receive ratification by three-fourths of the states. Much to their surprise, the amendment was ratified by one state legislature after another, and on February 25, 1913, with the certification by Secretary of State Philander C. Knox, the 16th amendment took effect. Yet in 1913, due to generous exemptions and deductions, less than 1 percent of the population paid income taxes at a rate of only 1 percent of net income.

The full potential of the income tax for revenue and for the redistribution of wealth was realized for the first time during the New Deal. President Franklin D. Roosevelt declared that "our revenue laws have operated in many ways to the unfair advantage of the few, and have done little to prevent an unjust concentration of wealth and economic power." The Revenue Act of 1935,

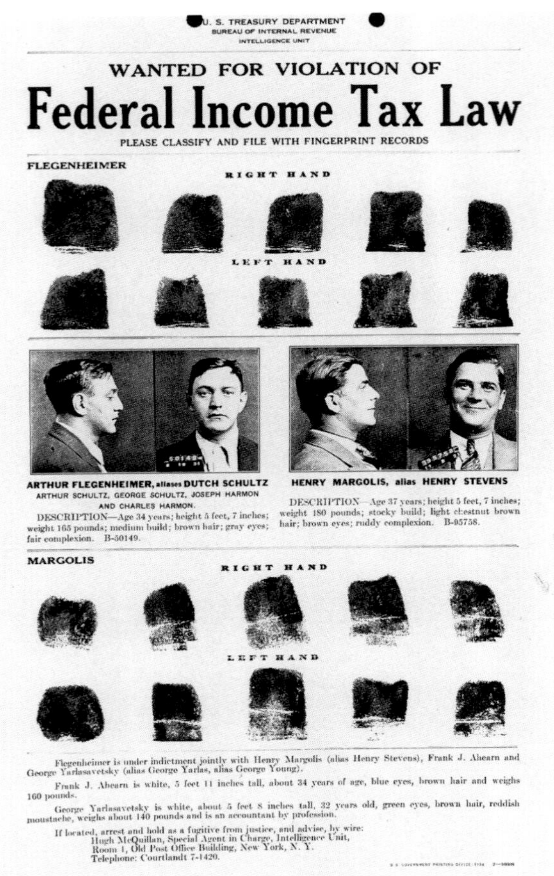

U. S. TREASURY DEPARTMENT
BUREAU OF INTERNAL REVENUE
INTELLIGENCE UNIT

WANTED FOR VIOLATION OF

Federal Income Tax Law

PLEASE CLASSIFY AND FILE WITH FINGERPRINT RECORDS

FLEGENHEIMER

RIGHT HAND

LEFT HAND

ARTHUR FLEGENHEIMER, aliases DUTCH SCHULTZ
ARTHUR SCHULTZ, GEORGE SCHULTZ, JOSEPH HARMON AND CHARLES HARMON.

DESCRIPTION—Age 34 years; height 5 feet, 7 inches; weight 165 pounds; medium build; brown hair; gray eyes; fair complexion. B-50149.

HENRY MARGOLIS, alias HENRY STEVENS

DESCRIPTION—Age 37 years; height 5 feet, 7 inches; weight 180 pounds; stocky build; light chestnut brown hair; brown eyes; ruddy complexion. B-95758.

MARGOLIS

RIGHT HAND

LEFT HAND

Flegenheimer is under indictment jointly with Henry Margolis (alias Henry Stevens), Frank J. Ahearn and George Yarlasavetsky (alias George Yarlas, alias George Young).

Frank J. Ahearn is white, 5 feet 11 inches tall, about 34 years of age, blue eyes, brown hair and weighs 160 pounds.

George Yarlasavetsky is white, about 5 feet 8 inches tall, 32 years old, green eyes, brown hair, reddish moustache, weighs about 140 pounds and is an accountant by profession.

If located, arrest and hold as a fugitive from justice, and advise, by wire:
Hugh McQuillan, Special Agent in Charge, Intelligence Unit,
Room 1, Old Post Office Building, New York, N. Y.
Telephone: Courtlandt 7-1420.

"Wanted" poster, 1934. Arthur Flegenheimer and Henry Margolis were indicted for income tax law violations, a charge commonly used against gangsters and racketeers in the 1930s. Flegenheimer, better known as Dutch Schultz, was a prominent underworld figure. He was fatally wounded in a shoot-out in 1935. *8 ½ by 14 inches.*

Letter of March 8, 1930, about alleged criminal activities of Frank Nitti (referred to as "Nitto" in the letter). Nitti was the so-called enforcer for Al Capone, one of the most notorious criminals of the 1920s and early 1930s. *2 pages, 8 by 10 ½ inches.*

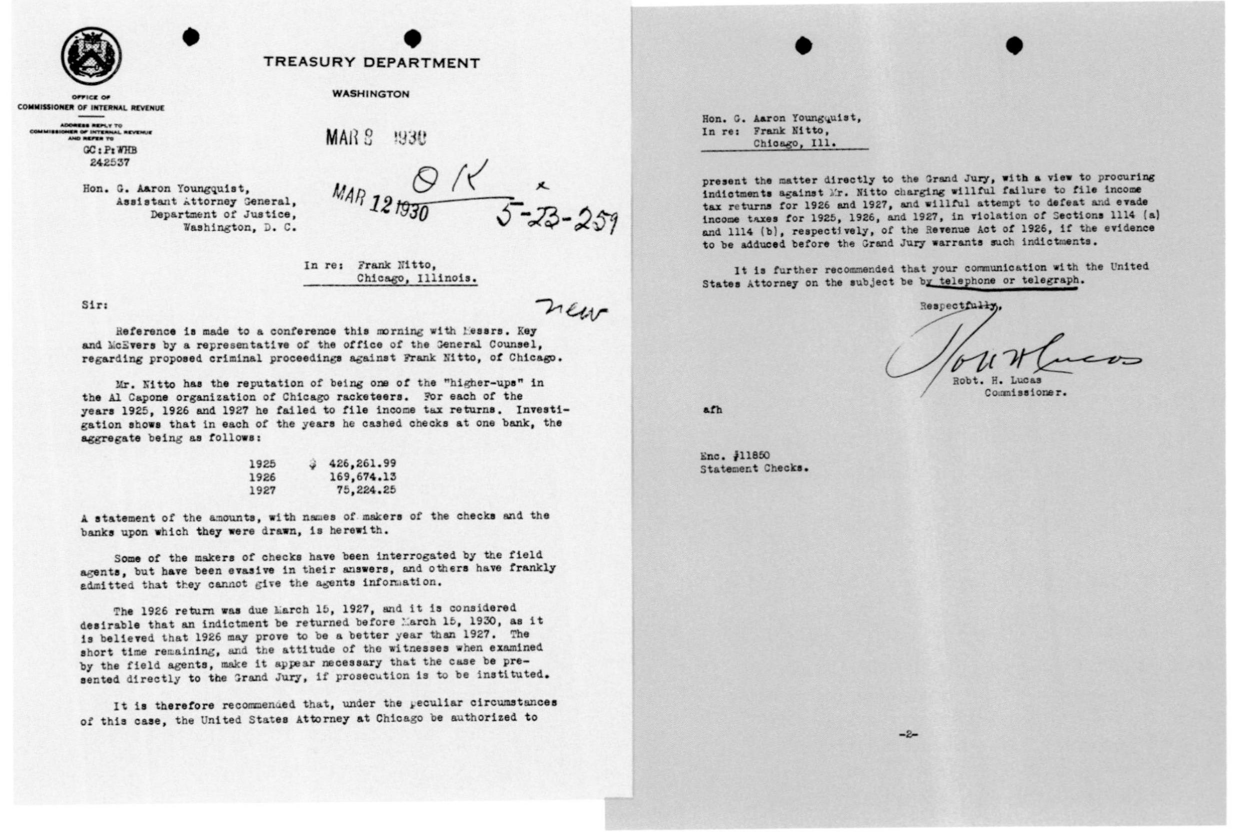

TREASURY DEPARTMENT
WASHINGTON

OFFICE OF
COMMISSIONER OF INTERNAL REVENUE

ADDRESS REPLY TO
COMMISSIONER OF INTERNAL REVENUE
AND REFER TO
GC:P:WHB
242537

MAR 8 1930

MAR 12 1930
OK
5-23-259

Hon. G. Aaron Youngquist,
Assistant Attorney General,
Department of Justice,
Washington, D. C.

In re: Frank Nitto,
Chicago, Illinois.

Sir:

new

Reference is made to a conference this morning with Messrs. Key and McEvers by a representative of the office of the General Counsel, regarding proposed criminal proceedings against Frank Nitto, of Chicago.

Mr. Nitto has the reputation of being one of the "higher-ups" in the Al Capone organization of Chicago racketeers. For each of the years 1925, 1926 and 1927 he failed to file income tax returns. Investigation shows that in each of the years he cashed checks at one bank, the aggregate being as follows:

1925	$ 426,261.99
1926	169,674.13
1927	75,224.25

A statement of the amounts, with names of makers of the checks and the banks upon which they were drawn, is herewith.

Some of the makers of checks have been interrogated by the field agents, but have been evasive in their answers, and others have frankly admitted that they cannot give the agents information.

The 1926 return was due March 15, 1927, and it is considered desirable that an indictment be returned before March 15, 1930, as it is believed that 1926 may prove to be a better year than 1927. The short time remaining, and the attitude of the witnesses when examined by the field agents, make it appear necessary that the case be presented directly to the Grand Jury, if prosecution is to be instituted.

It is therefore recommended that, under the peculiar circumstances of this case, the United States Attorney at Chicago be authorized to

Hon. G. Aaron Youngquist,
In re: Frank Nitto,
Chicago, Ill.

present the matter directly to the Grand Jury, with a view to procuring indictments against Mr. Nitto charging willful failure to file income tax returns for 1926 and 1927, and willful attempt to defeat and evade income taxes for 1925, 1926, and 1927, in violation of Sections 1114 (a) and 1114 (b), respectively, of the Revenue Act of 1926, if the evidence to be adduced before the Grand Jury warrants such indictments.

It is further recommended that your communication with the United States Attorney on the subject be by telephone or telegraph.

Respectfully,

Robt. H. Lucas

Robt. H. Lucas
Commissioner.

afh

Enc. #11850
Statement Checks.

-2-

popularly called the Wealth Tax Act, went a long way toward remedying the evils he described. It provided steeply graduated personal income taxes up to 75 percent on income in excess of $5 million. Wealthy Americans deplored the leveling effect of the graduated income tax and called President Roosevelt "a traitor to his own class." Almost immediately, income tax evasion became an important area of criminal activity.

The income tax did not directly affect most Americans until World War II: In 1939 only 5 percent of Americans paid federal income taxes. But the Revenue Act of 1942 raised tax rates, lowered exemptions, and created the Victory Tax of 5 percent on incomes over $624, broadening the income tax base considerably. The new payroll witholding tax was the greatest change for the majority of Americans. The "Pay-As-You-Go" tax plan, developed by Beardsley Ruml, the treasurer of the R. H. Macy department store, was adopted in the Current Tax Payment Act of 1943. The result of the new tax plan was that over 74 percent of Americans were paying federal income taxes by 1945.

The income tax has become the most important source of federal revenue. Without it, the social reforms of the 1930s, the financial costs of World War II, national defense during the cold war, and the programs of the "Great Society" of the 1960s would have been impossible.

During the 1970s, the U.S. economy suffered from unprecedented peacetime inflation rates. Unemployment rates were also high, and productivity growth lagged behind that of previous post–World War II decades. In the late 1970s, a group of predominantly Republican Congressmen developed new policy ideas that would be known as supply-side economics. They believed that tax reductions would stimulate a rise in savings, investment, and work effort, thereby causing economic

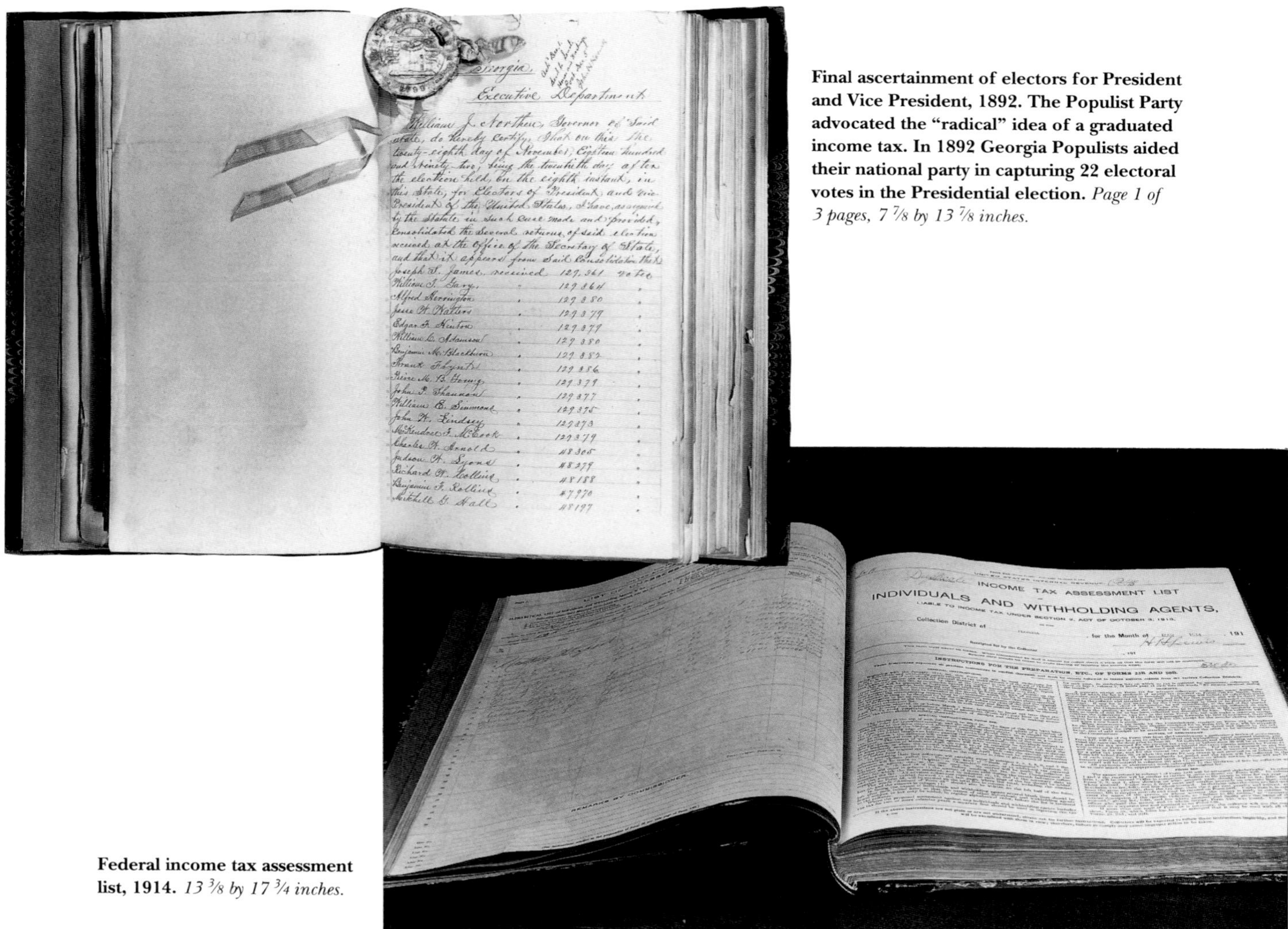

Final ascertainment of electors for President and Vice President, 1892. The Populist Party advocated the "radical" idea of a graduated income tax. In 1892 Georgia Populists aided their national party in capturing 22 electoral votes in the Presidential election. *Page 1 of 3 pages, 7 7/8 by 13 7/8 inches.*

Federal income tax assessment list, 1914. *13 3/8 by 17 3/4 inches.*

growth and increased productivity.

President Ronald Reagan, elected in 1980, incorporated these ideas into his "Program for Economic Recovery." On July 29, 1981, Congress passed Reagan's tax legislation—the largest tax cut in U.S. history for both individuals and corporations. Yet by November 1982, the unemployment rate was at its highest point since 1940, with over 11 million people out of work. In his 1984 State of the Union message, President Reagan called for action on another aspect of supply-side economics—$100 billion in budget cuts over a 3-year period (and no increased taxes).

On December 11, 1985, in an almost desperate effort to end the huge budget deficit, Congress passed the Balanced Budget and Emergency Deficit Control Act, also known by the names of its principal sponsors, Gramm-Rudman-Hollings. This law mandated cuts in the deficit by setting progressively lower federal deficit targets for fiscal years 1986–91 and calling for automatic federal spending cuts if the targets were not met. In July 1986 the Supreme Court ruled that the law's mechanism for enacting the automatic cuts was unconstitutional because it assigned executive branch functions to the Comptroller General, a legislative branch officer. The Court left the law's "fallback" provision intact—Congress would have to legislate the cuts.

In late September 1986 Congress passed the Tax Reform Act, which drastically changed income tax brackets and deductions. The Revenue Act of 1987, signed in December of that year, increased taxes by $23 billion over a 2-year period, but on January 5, 1987, President Reagan had produced the first trillion-dollar budget in U.S. history, and the annual budget deficit in the late 1980s hovered around $150 billion.

Under President George Bush, who continued the policies of "Reaganomics," the economy con-

Women trimming currency at the Treasury Department, 1907. The ratification of the 16th amendment resulted in an increase in work for the Treasury Department, but even before the income tax, the department employed many women as typists, stenographers, file clerks, and currency trimmers.

tinued to decline. Stock prices slowly began to rise after a record 508-point drop on October 19, 1987, but they plummeted again in October 1989. By July 1990, leading economists pronounced that the country was in a recession. Still facing growing budget deficits, Congress passed a budget bill on October 27, 1990, that raised taxes by $140 billion over 5 years. The annual budget deficit reached $269 billion in 1991 and $290 in 1992.

Although the recession officially ended in February 1991, the economy was slow to recover. The 1992 Presidential election campaigns focused primarily on economic issues, and Governor Bill Clinton of Arkansas, who called for a change from the policies of supply-side economics, emerged the winner. He faced the formidable challenge of revitalizing an economy with unprecedented federal budget deficits; stagnating real incomes; intense foreign competition, both in products and over jobs; runaway health care costs; and disagreement over the sources, amount, and use of tax revenues. President Clinton called on Congress and the American people to join his administration in a plan to address these problems for a new and better future.

President Ronald Reagan addresses Congress, 1987. Reagan based his "Program for Economic Recovery" on the principles of supply-side economics. *From the Ronald Reagan Library.*

Beardsley Ruml's idea for a "Pay-As You-Go" tax plan, adopted in the Current Tax Payment Act of 1943, simplified the payment of federal income taxes for many Americans.

PART I.

THE COVENANT OF THE LEAGUE OF NATIONS.

THE HIGH CONTRACTING PARTIES,

In order to promote international co-operation and to achieve international peace and security

by the acceptance of obligations not to resort to war,
by the prescription of open, just and honourable relations between nations,
by the firm establishment of the understandings of international law as the actual rule of conduct among Governments, and
by the maintenance of justice and a scrupulous respect for all treaty obligations in the dealings of organised peoples with one another,

Agree to this Covenant of the League of Nations.

ARTICLE 1.

The original Members of the League of Nations shall be those of the Signatories which are named in the Annex to this Covenant and also such of those other States named in the Annex as shall accede without reservation to this Covenant. Such accession shall be effected by a Declaration deposited with the Secretariat within two months of the coming into force of the Covenant. Notice thereof shall be sent to all other Members of the League.

Any fully self-governing State, Dominion or Colony not named in the Annex may become a Member of the League if its admission is agreed to by two-thirds of the Assembly, provided that it shall give effective guarantees of its sincere intention to observe its international obligations, and shall accept such regulations as may be prescribed by the League inregard to its military, naval and air forces and armaments.

Any Member of the League may, after two years' notice of its intention so to do, withdraw from the League, provided that all its international obligations and all its obligations under this Covenant shall have been fulfilled at the time of its withdrawal.

ARTICLE 2.

The action of the League under this Covenant shall be effected through the instrumentality of an Assembly and of a Council, with a permanent Secretariat,

Senator Henry Cabot Lodge of Massachusetts, 1919. Senator Lodge proposed reservations to American participation in the League of Nations that were unacceptable to President Wilson. Other Senators, called "irreconcilables," opposed all American participation in the organization.

Senate resolution to reject the Treaty of Versailles after President Wilson refused to compromise on American participation in the League of Nations, 1920. Not until 1921 did a joint resolution of Congress officially end the war with Germany. *8 by 10 ½ inches.*

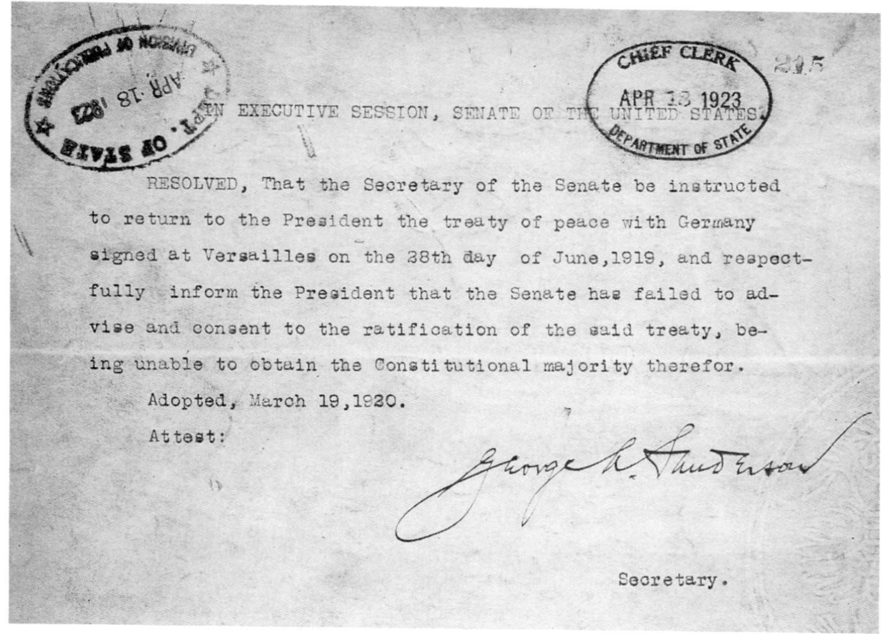

IN EXECUTIVE SESSION, SENATE OF THE UNITED STATES.

RESOLVED, That the Secretary of the Senate be instructed to return to the President the treaty of peace with Germany signed at Versailles on the 28th day of June,1919, and respectfully inform the President that the Senate has failed to advise and consent to the ratification of the said treaty, being unable to obtain the Constitutional majority therefor.

Adopted, March 19,1920.

Attest:

George A. Sanderson

Secretary.

Woodrow Wilson in Paris, 1919. Wilson personally took part in negotiating the Treaty of Versailles.

Opposite: **President Wilson's authenticated, or certified, copy of the Treaty of Versailles, 1919, which ended World War I. The heart of the treaty was the League of Nations Covenant, which was intended to keep the peace and was a forerunner of the United Nations, established in 1945.** *Page 19 of 537 pages, 9 ⅜ by 11 ¾ inches.*

The 1919 Treaty of Versilles, which ended World War I, proposed a new U.S. role in foreign relations. The United States had participated sparingly in world affairs throughout the 19th century. But the Spanish-American War at the close of the century brought the nation to the threshold of a new era and a new role. The acquisition of Puerto Rico and the Philippine Islands as a result of that war thrust the United States directly into the vortex of international politics. Consequently, in 1904 President Theodore Roosevelt had to devise a "corollary" to the venerable Monroe Doctrine, which stated that under certain conditions the United States would act to keep order in the Western Hemisphere. Meanwhile in the Far East, upheaval in China and insurrection in the Philippines had required the use of American troops to restore order. And before the outbreak of World War I in 1914, the Marines were to serve in several places in the Caribbean.

During these tumultuous years, the United States endeavored to play the role of arbiter in international disputes. In 1905 President Roosevelt's good offices helped end the Russo-Japanese War. American diplomats became familiar figures at The Hague peace conferences and elsewhere, but World War I in Europe precluded all efforts to arbitrate a settlement. After 3 years of neutrality, President Woodrow Wilson, who sought to build a lasting peace, led the nation into the war on the side of Great Britain, France, and their allies.

Under the command of General John J. "Black Jack" Pershing, more than 2 million Americans eventually served in Europe. Fighting alongside the tired, dispirited, and sometimes mutinous Allied troops, the Americans became the deciding factor in the war's outcome and supplied Wilson with the opportunity to implement his vision of lasting peace. This vision was embodied in his Fourteen Points and in the creation of an organization of all nations to act as a permanent peacekeeper—the League of Nations.

But Wilson's vision of permanent peace was not to be. Despite his personal presence and his great popularity with the people of Europe, he was unable to prevent France and Great Britain from writing self-defeating punitive measures against Germany into the Treaty of Versailles. Yet Wilson still hoped that the proposed League could establish a peaceful international order.

Here, too, he was thwarted. Significant opposition to the League developed in the Senate. Senator Henry Cabot Lodge, a longtime opponent of Wilson, and a group of "irreconcilable" Senators led by William E. Borah and Robert LaFollette demanded that reservations be added to the Versailles Treaty. Wilson believed these changes would cripple U.S. participation in the League. Unwilling to compromise, exhausted, and ill, Wilson took his case to the American people. He was not successful, and on March 19, 1920, the Senate refused to ratify the treaty.

Wilson's vision had been uniquely his, and the unwillingness of the Senate to accept it marked a personal tragedy. But the refusal also marked the fact that the United States, by now an undoubtedly great power, had not yet clearly defined the role it should and could play in world affairs.

American troops battling insurgents in the Philippine Islands in 1899. The acquisition of overseas territories from Spain in 1898 marked the emergence of the United States as a world power.

War savings "Pledge Week" campaign in Chicago, May 31, 1918.

American soldiers in the trenches at Verdun, 1918. During World War I, American troops fought and died on European soil for the first time.

Chinese map from the Boxer Rebellion, 1900. Chinese nationalists, known as Boxers, tried to evict all foreigners. The United States aided other nations in suppressing the rebellion. *16 ⅞ by 23 ½ inches.*

French postcard commemorating the liberation of Belgium by the United States in 1918. The other Allies also participated in freeing the Belgians from German rule. *3 ¾ by 5 ½ inches.*

RIGHT OFF THE BAT!
(Between Games)
Babe Ruth
Hits 'em for Six $100
U. S. TREASURY
SAVINGS CERTIFICATES
(Presented by Pere Marquette Council K. of C. South Boston)
BABE PICKS WINNERS
Why don't You
Invest in
TREASURY SAVINGS CERTIFICATES
and WAR SAVINGS STAMPS
They Pay Over 4% Interest
Buy Them at Your Post Office or Bank

Flier promoting the sale of war bonds, 1919, *4 ½ by 8 ½ inches.*

Babe Ruth receiving a war bond in Boston, 1919.

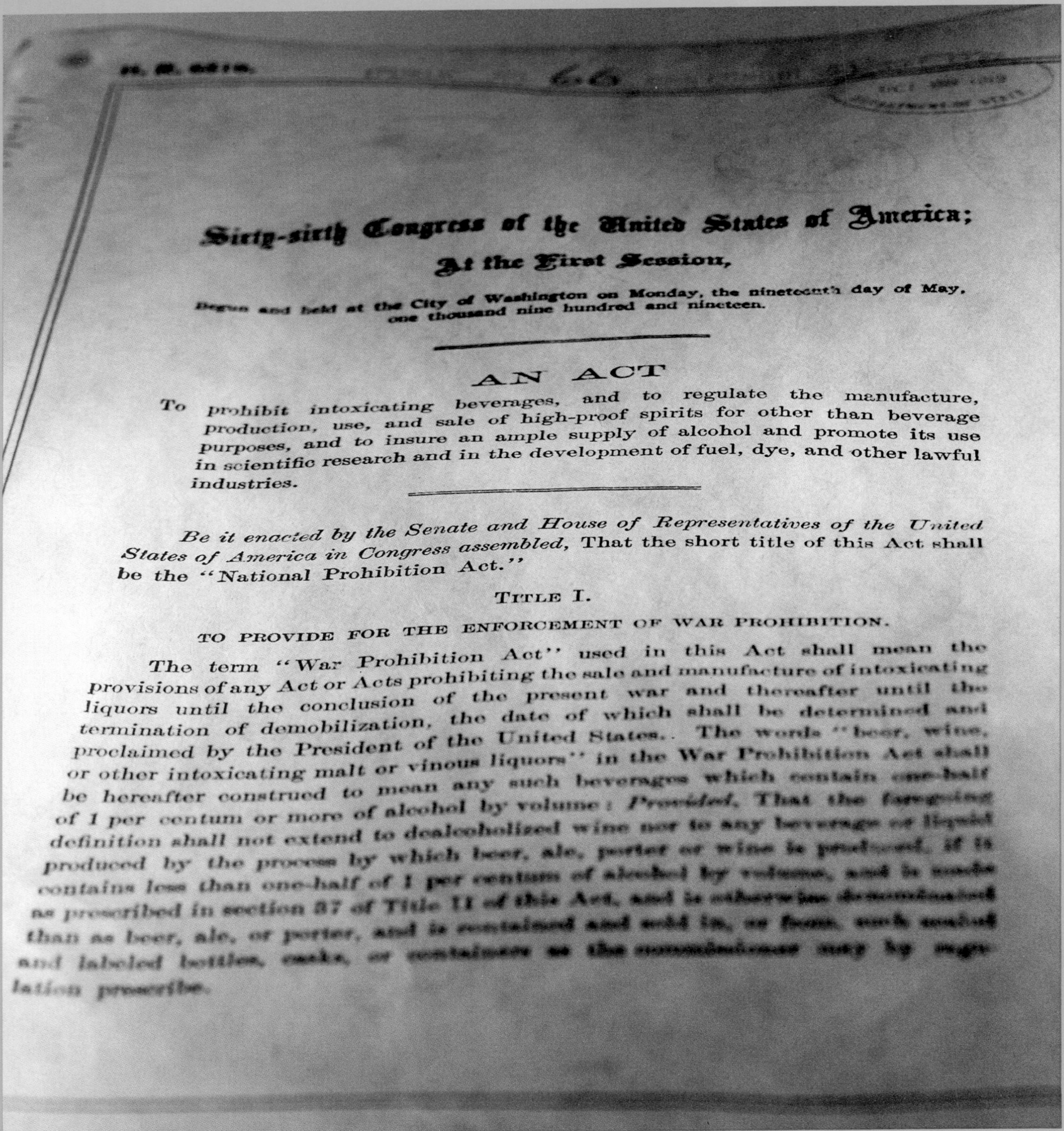

Sixty-sixth Congress of the United States of America;

At the First Session,

Begun and held at the City of Washington on Monday, the nineteenth day of May, one thousand nine hundred and nineteen.

AN ACT

To prohibit intoxicating beverages, and to regulate the manufacture, production, use, and sale of high-proof spirits for other than beverage purposes, and to insure an ample supply of alcohol and promote its use in scientific research and in the development of fuel, dye, and other lawful industries.

Be it enacted by the Senate and House of Representatives of the United States of America in Congress assembled, That the short title of this Act shall be the "National Prohibition Act."

TITLE I.

TO PROVIDE FOR THE ENFORCEMENT OF WAR PROHIBITION.

The term "War Prohibition Act" used in this Act shall mean the provisions of any Act or Acts prohibiting the sale and manufacture of intoxicating liquors until the conclusion of the present war and thereafter until the termination of demobilization, the date of which shall be determined and proclaimed by the President of the United States. The words "beer, wine, or other intoxicating malt or vinous liquors" in the War Prohibition Act shall be hereafter construed to mean any such beverages which contain one-half of 1 per centum or more of alcohol by volume: *Provided,* That the foregoing definition shall not extend to dealcoholized wine nor to any beverage or liquid produced by the process by which beer, ale, porter or wine is produced, if it contains less than one-half of 1 per centum of alcohol by volume, and is made as prescribed in section 37 of Title II of this Act, and is otherwise denominated than as beer, ale, or porter, and is contained and sold in, or from, such sealed and labeled bottles, casks, or containers as the commissioner may by regulation prescribe.

The Volstead Act, 1919. The act implemented and provided an enforcement apparatus for the 18th amendment, which forbade the manufacture, transportation, and sale of "intoxicating beverages." Circumvention of the law led to bootlegging, which in turn was a spur to other organized crime. *23 pages, 10 by 14 3/4 inches.*

Various reformers long considered alcoholic beverages a major impediment to America's social and material progress. This conviction generated one of the most vigorous reform movements in our history.

The crusade against liquor originated during the Revolutionary War era in the ideas of men like Benjamin Rush, Surgeon General of the Continental Army. Following the War of 1812, local temperance societies developed a national organization that mounted a campaign against all forms of "toddies," "flips," and "punches." Everyone was enjoined to take the pledge, and by 1851 the movement succeeded in making Maine the first "dry" state in the nation.

After the Civil War, temperance was revived as a major political issue, first by the National Prohibition Party, founded in 1869, and then by the Women's Christian Temperance Union, formed 5 years later. Despite the agitation of these and other antiliquor groups, "demon rum" thrived. Great urban centers, emerging as America industrialized, gave rise to countless saloons that dispensed the beverages more and more people held responsible for the annual increases in industrial accidents and deaths. Yet the combined antiliquor forces failed to staunch the flow of booze.

By the early years of the 20th century, the Anti-Saloon League of America seemed to have developed a successful state-by-state approach for solving "the liquor problem." Yet by 1914 it was clear that the country did not have what one reformer referred to as "prohibition in fact." Moreover, the efforts of the Anti-Saloon League had aroused deep resentment among many of the country's workers and immigrants. Faced with this continuing dilemma, the league and its supporters launched a massive campaign for national prohibition via a constitutional amendment. Backed for the first time by the national business community, the drive became a stunning success in 1919 when the 18th amendment was ratified by the requisite 36 states, less than 2 years after Congress had voted on the proposed amendment. Andrew Volstead, a Congressman from Minnesota, introduced the implementing legislation, and on January 17, 1920, Prohibition became a reality.

Enforcement soon became a major problem.

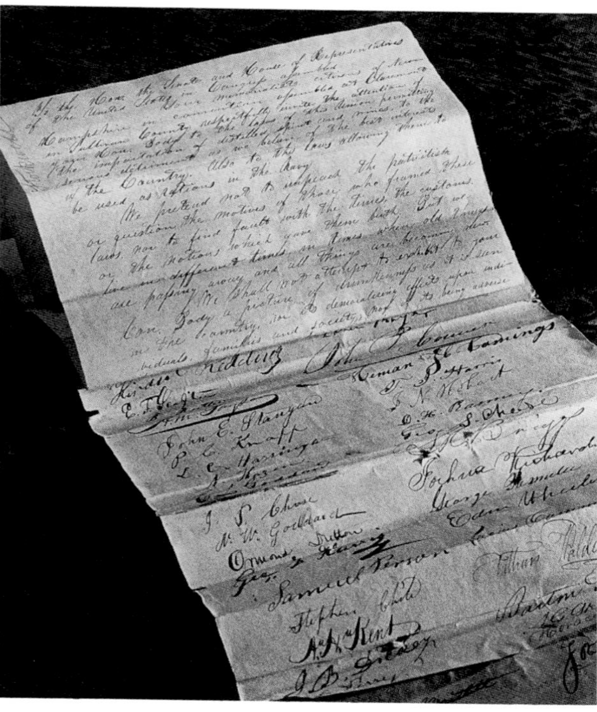

Temperance petition, 1838. In this petition to Congress, New Hampshire citizens stated that intoxicating beverages were "the chief cause of most of the pauperism, crime, wretchedness, and disease which afflicts our country."
Records of the U.S. House of Representatives, National Archives; 7 1/4 by 42 inches.

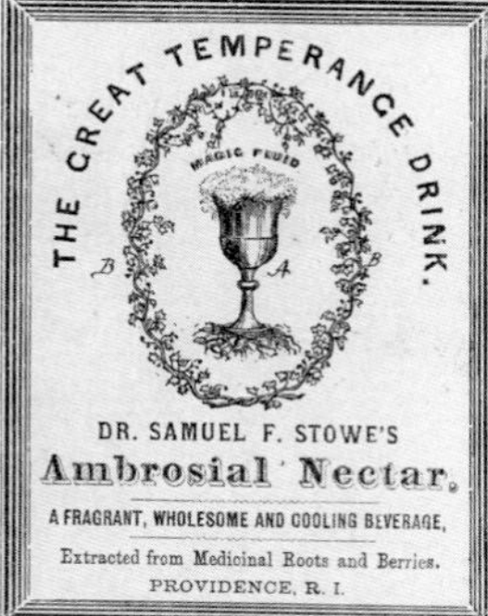

Samuel Stowe's Temperance Drink trademark, 1866. Stowe's practical approach to temperance was to provide an alternative beverage to "demon rum."
13 by 19 3/4 inches.

Los Angeles authorities emptying barrels of rum, 1931. Prohibition was formally ended in 1933 by the 21st amendment, which became the only constitutional amendment to repeal an earlier one.

The Federal Prohibition Bureau of the United States Treasury, charged with enforcing federal prohibition under the Volstead Act, found itself engaged in a lonely battle with determined "wets," who circumvented the law with surprising ease. Under Prohibition, drinking did not stop; it instead shifted from saloons to private homes and speakeasies. To quench the national thirst, moonshiners, bootleggers, and rum runners developed regional networks for the production and distribution of liquor. These networks provided new foundations for criminal empires, and gangsters like Al Capone and "Legs" Diamond amassed personal fortunes that became the basis for organized crime in succeeding years.

Throughout the 1920s the fight to enforce Prohibition proved too difficult for some 1,550 federal agents, including Elliot Ness and his incorruptible unit nicknamed the "Untouchables." Adding to enforcement officers' woes was the

Al Capone. Capone, known as Scarface, was one of the most notorious of the Chicago bootleggers and gang leaders and was said to have grossed as much as $60 million during the 1920s. Unable to build a case against him on major counts, the government was finally able to imprison him on a charge of income tax evasion.

Demonstration in New York in favor of the sale of beer and wine, ca. 1927. One of the arguments used by the "wets" was that the tax revenues that would be obtained from the sale of beer and wine was badly needed.

Federal Prohibition Officer identification cards, 1924 and 1925. Alcoholic beverages continued to be in great demand regardless of the 18th amendment, and some 1,550 agents were unable to halt the illegal liquor traffic. *3 by 4 ¾ inches.*
Newspaper clippings of the 1920s and early 1930s relating to Prohibition and its effects.

Ku Klux Klan. During the 1920s, the sheeted knights of the Ku Klux Klan enjoyed a resurgence as self-appointed enforcement agents for Prohibition and as defenders of white, Protestant, native-born supremacy.

BUFFALO EVENING TIMES

TO BE CHARGED

DAILY COMMERCIAL NEWS

SAN FRANCISCO IS 83 PER CENT AGAINST THE VOLSTEAD ACT

Rum Runner

Indicted in

PHOTOGRAPH

TREASURY DEPARTMENT

THE UNITED STATES INTERNAL REVENUE SERVICE

THIS CERTIFIES THAT

William E. Wright

TREASURY DEPARTMENT

THE UNITED STATES

THIS CERTIFIES THAT

Ralph A. Stearns

vigilante operation of the revived Ku Klux Klan, which added Prohibition enforcement to its anti-Catholic, anti-Semitic, and antiblack activities.

By the mid-1920s whatever enthusiasm for Prohibition had existed was all but gone. By the end of the decade, with the nation caught in the throes of economic collapse, even the most resolute prohibitionists, like John D. Rockefeller, Jr., saw that continuance of the temperance cause was beyond the nation's means. While President Herbert Hoover called Prohibition "an experiment noble in motive and far reaching in purpose," Franklin D. Roosevelt swept to the Presidency in 1932 on a platform that included a strong Prohibition repeal plank.

Following Roosevelt's election, the Congress passed and the states ratified the 21st amendment, December 5, 1933, ending national Prohibition. This is the only constitutional amendment to repeal another.

Simon Crow's whiskey label design patent, 1864. This design was used for barrel labels. *17 ½ inches in diameter.*

Anti-Prohibition forces vigorously opposed a ban on alcoholic beverages in areas such as St. Louis, MO, where this poster originated, ca. 1918. *28 by 40 ¾ inches.*

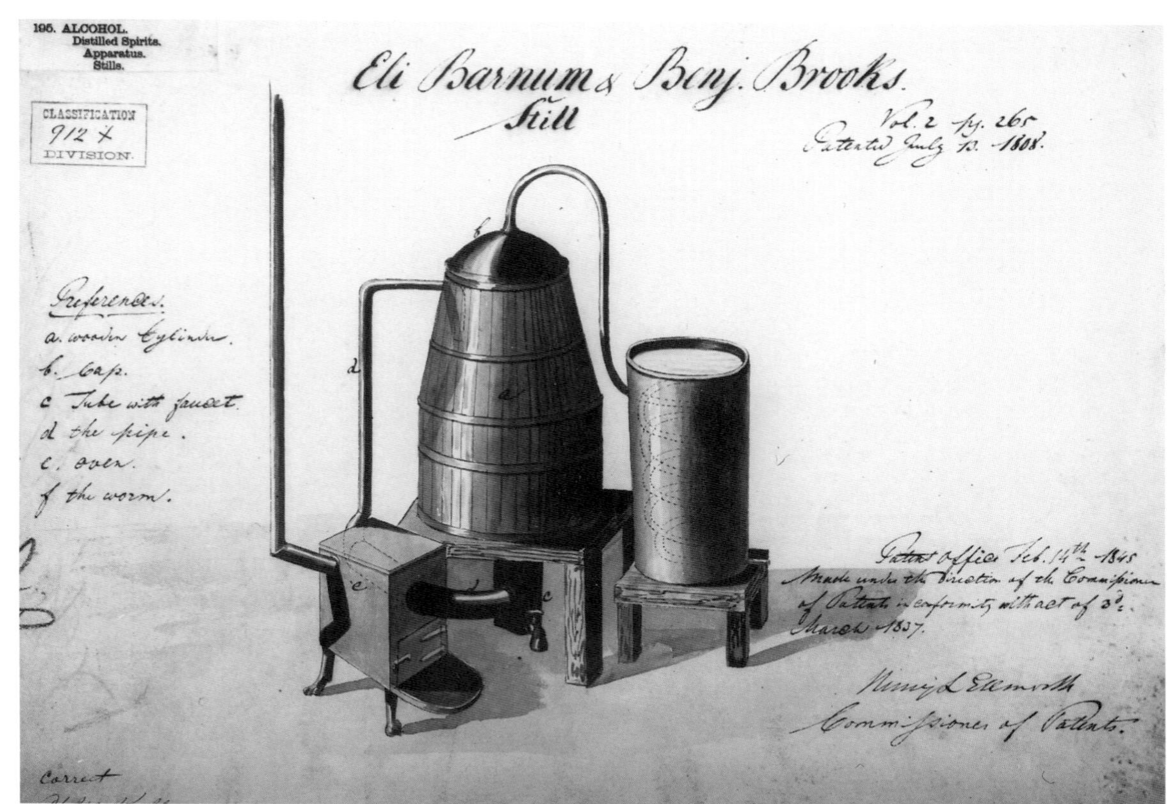

Still patent drawing, 1808. The practice of distilling (moonshining) and selling alcoholic beverages regardless of tax regulations goes back to the very beginning of the nation and continues to this day. *18 ¾ by 13 ¼ inches.*

Sixty-sixth Congress of the United States of America;

At the First Session,

Begun and held at the City of Washington on Monday, the nineteenth day of May, one thousand nine hundred and nineteen.

JOINT RESOLUTION

Proposing an amendment to the Constitution extending the right of suffrage to women.

Resolved by the Senate and House of Representatives of the United States of America in Congress assembled (two-thirds of each House concurring therein), That the following article is proposed as an amendment to the Constitution, which shall be valid to all intents and purposes as part of the Constitution when ratified by the legislatures of three-fourths of the several States.

"ARTICLE ———.

"The right of citizens of the United States to vote shall not be denied or abridged by the United States or by any State on account of sex.

"Congress shall have power to enforce this article by appropriate legislation."

F. H. Gillett

Speaker of the House of Representatives.

Thos. R. Marshall

Vice President of the United States and President of the Senate.

Suffragist with "Kaiser Wilson" banner, 1919. Many feminists opposed what they called President Woodrow Wilson's "too little, too late" support of women's suffrage.

The women's suffrage amendment finally achieved what more than two generations of women had fought for without cessation. Indeed, while her husband John was helping to establish the new American republic, Abigail Adams had perceived the basic injustice of the taxation of women who had no voice in their government.

The intensive campaign to enfranchise women began shortly after the Civil War. Women who had entered public life as advocates of anti-slavery measures resented the inequality that gave the freedman the vote in 1870 while all women, except the few residents of Wyoming Territory, were still excluded. That year, the introduction of a resolution in Congress to permit women to vote marked the beginning of the national legislative history of women's suffrage. Ten years later, Senator A. A. Sargent of California introduced another resolution: "The rights of citizens of the United States to vote shall not be denied or abridged by the United States on account of sex." The resolution passed more than 40 years later with the wording unchanged. The "Susan B. Anthony Amendment," as the measure came to be called, mobilized a broad segment of American womanhood that finally helped win its ratification in 1920.

Women had organized, petitioned, picketed, and even gone to jail as they attempted to correct imbalances and inequality of the American democratic system. They believed that only through the ballot would women establish their legal right to own property, claim their own salaries, have custody of their children, and demand equal pay for equal work. Until 1890 the two most visible national organizations were the American Woman Suffrage Association, which sought state legislation, and the National Woman Suffrage Association, which directed its efforts toward securing an amendment to the Constitution.

In 1890 the two groups merged and became the National American Woman Suffrage Association, with Elizabeth Cady Stanton as its first president. The suffragists underwent numerous hardships in their efforts to obtain signatures on petitions to present to state legislatures and to Congress. Some of the indignities were meted out by other women who "had husbands to look after their interests" and saw no need for a suffrage amendment. The antisuffragists—male and

Woman Suffrage
is a
Curse to Woman
and a
Danger to the State

"Woman Suffrage is a Curse" sticker issued by the National Association Opposed to Woman Suffrage, 1918. *2 ½ by 1 ¼ inches.*

Opposite: **Joint resolution of Congress proposing a constitutional amendment extending the right of suffrage to women, 1919. Beginning in the 1800s, women organized, petitioned, and picketed to win the right to vote, but it took them decades to accomplish their purpose.** *9 ¾ by 14 ½ inches.*

female—organized into the National Association Opposed to Woman Suffrage, which published a newspaper and circulated other literature. Suffragists were successful in some of the Western states. Women received the right to vote in Wyoming as early as 1868, when that territory was organized; Colorado followed in 1893.

When Woodrow Wilson was elected President, Alice Paul organized a massive suffrage demonstration for his inauguration. She later launched the National Women's Party in 1916 and adopted the British practice of picketing. Women picketing the White House were physically abused by opponents, arrested, and sentenced to jail terms.

Congress passed the 19th amendment enfranchising women in 1919. Wisconsin and Michigan were the first states to ratify it; Tennessee's vote on August 18, 1920, delivered the crucial 36th ratification necessary for final adoption. The ratification process had taken 14 months. After the women's suffrage victory, Carrie Chapman Catt attempted to compute human cost:

> *To get the word "male" in effect out of the Constitution cost the women of the country fifty-two years of pauseless campaign. . . . During that time they were forced to conduct fifty-six referenda to male voters, 480 campaigns to get legislatures to submit suffrage amendments to voters, 47 campaigns to get state constitutional conventions to write woman suffrage in state constitutions, 277 campaigns to get state party conventions to include woman suffrage planks, 30 campaigns to adopt woman suffrage planks in party platforms, and 19 campaigns with 19 successive congresses.*

The work of a century did not end with the ratification. In 1919 the National American Woman Suffrage Association had reorganized into the League of Women Voters before women's suffrage was an accomplished fact. The league succeeded in generating considerable enthusiasm among women during the 1924 Presidential election with its "Get-Out-the-Vote" campaign.

Having accomplished one reform by constitutional amendment, leaders of the movement immediately began seeking another by the same device. In 1923 the first Equal Rights Amendment (ERA) was introduced in Congress and in every session thereafter. Finally it passed both houses of Congress in 1972, largely due to the tireless efforts of Congresswoman Martha Griffiths of Michigan, and was sent to state legislatures for their consideration until 1979. In 1978 ERA supporters persuaded Congress to extend the 1979 deadline until 1982. But by the end of 1982, 14 states had still not ratified the amendment, and it died.

The League of Women Voters was part of the coalition that fought for passage of the ERA, but it has also been active on many other fronts. For example, in the late 1920s the league sponsored citizenship schools, and its Radio Committee spearheaded an effort to develop radio as a medium of public education. Throughout the postwar era, the League of Women Voters worked for women's rights by distributing information on candidates and issues, conducting voter registration drives, sponsoring Presidential debates, and lobbying for legislation it deemed to be in the interest of women.

Since the passage of the 19th amendment, more and more women have exercised the right to vote. Sixty-eight percent of women were registered to vote by 1988, making up 54 percent of all registered voters.

Women have also run for, and won, elected offices in increasing numbers. Congress included 15 women, 2 in the Senate and 13 in the House of Representatives, in 1971. By 1991 this total had risen to 31 women, 2 in the Senate and 29 in the House (including 1 nonvoting Delegate). In the 1992 elections, 52 women won congressional office, 5 in the Senate and 47 in the House (including 1 nonvoting Delegate). Three women were serving as state Governors in 1991, and 33 women held top statewide offices. Each of the 99 state legislatures included at least 1 woman member by 1991. The number of women

Voting rights petition to the Senate and House of Representatives, signed by Susan B. Anthony, Elizabeth Cady Stanton, and other suffragists, 1871.
8 1/4 by 17 1/4 inches.

To the Honorable the Senate and House of Representatives of the United States in Congress assembled.

The undersigned Citizens of the United States, believing that under the present Federal Constitution all women who are citizens of the United States have the right to vote, pray your Honorable Body to enact a law during the present Session that shall assist and protect them in the exercise of that right.

And they pray further that they may be permitted in person, and in behalf of the thousands of other women who are petitioning Congress to the same effect, to be heard upon this Memorial before the Senate and House at an early day in the present Session.

We ask your Honorable Body to bear in mind that while men are represented on the floor of Congress and so may be said to be heard there, women who are allowed no vote and therefore no representation cannot truly be heard except as Congress shall open its doors to us in person.

Elizabeth Cady Stanton
Isabella Beecher Hooker
Elizabeth L. Bladen
Olympia Brown.
Susan B. Anthony
Josephine S. Griffing

Hartford Conn.
Dec. 1871.

mayors of cities with populations over 30,000 increased from 7 in 1971 to 151 in 1991.

U.S. Presidents and state Governors have appointed women to many positions. The federal judiciary included 175 women in 1991, and Sandra Day O'Connor, appointed in 1981, was the first female to be appointed a U.S. Supreme Court Justice. By 1991, President Bush had appointed 8 women to the federal bench and 133 women to other Senate-confirmed positions. Female members of state cabinets increased from 64 in 1980 to 113 in 1991. In 1993 President Clinton appointed Ruth Bader Ginsburg to the Supreme Court.

The passage of the 19th amendment gave women a voice in the nation's political arena. Since 1920, whether by serving in elected or appointed office or by casting their votes, increasing numbers of women have made that voice heard.

Officers of the National American Woman Suffrage Association, ca. 1919. Upon enactment of the joint resolution proposing women's suffrage, Carrie Chapman Catt reorganized the National American Woman Suffrage Association into the League of Women Voters and served as its honorary president.

Ninety-second Congress of the United States of America

AT THE SECOND SESSION

Begun and held at the City of Washington on Tuesday, the eighteenth day of January, one thousand nine hundred and seventy-two

Joint Resolution

Proposing an amendment to the Constitution of the United States relative to equal rights for men and women.

Resolved by the Senate and House of Representatives of the United States of America in Congress assembled (two-thirds of each House concurring therein), That the following article is proposed as an amendment to the Constitution of the United States, which shall be valid to all intents and purposes as part of the Constitution when ratified by the legislatures of three-fourths of the several States within seven years from the date of its submission by the Congress:

"ARTICLE —

"SECTION 1. Equality of rights under the law shall not be denied or abridged by the United States or by any State on account of sex.

"SEC. 2. The Congress shall have the power to enforce, by appropriate legislation, the provisions of this article.

"SEC. 3. This amendment shall take effect two years after the date of ratification."

Carl Albert

Speaker of the House of Representatives.

~~*Vice President of the United States and*~~

President of the Senate pro Tempore

First Lady Betty Ford was a stong advocate of women's rights and the Equal Rights Amendment. *From the Gerald R. Ford Library.*

Joint resolution proposing the Equal Rights Amendment, 1972. In 1923 the first Equal Rights Amendment was introduced in Congress and in every session thereafter.

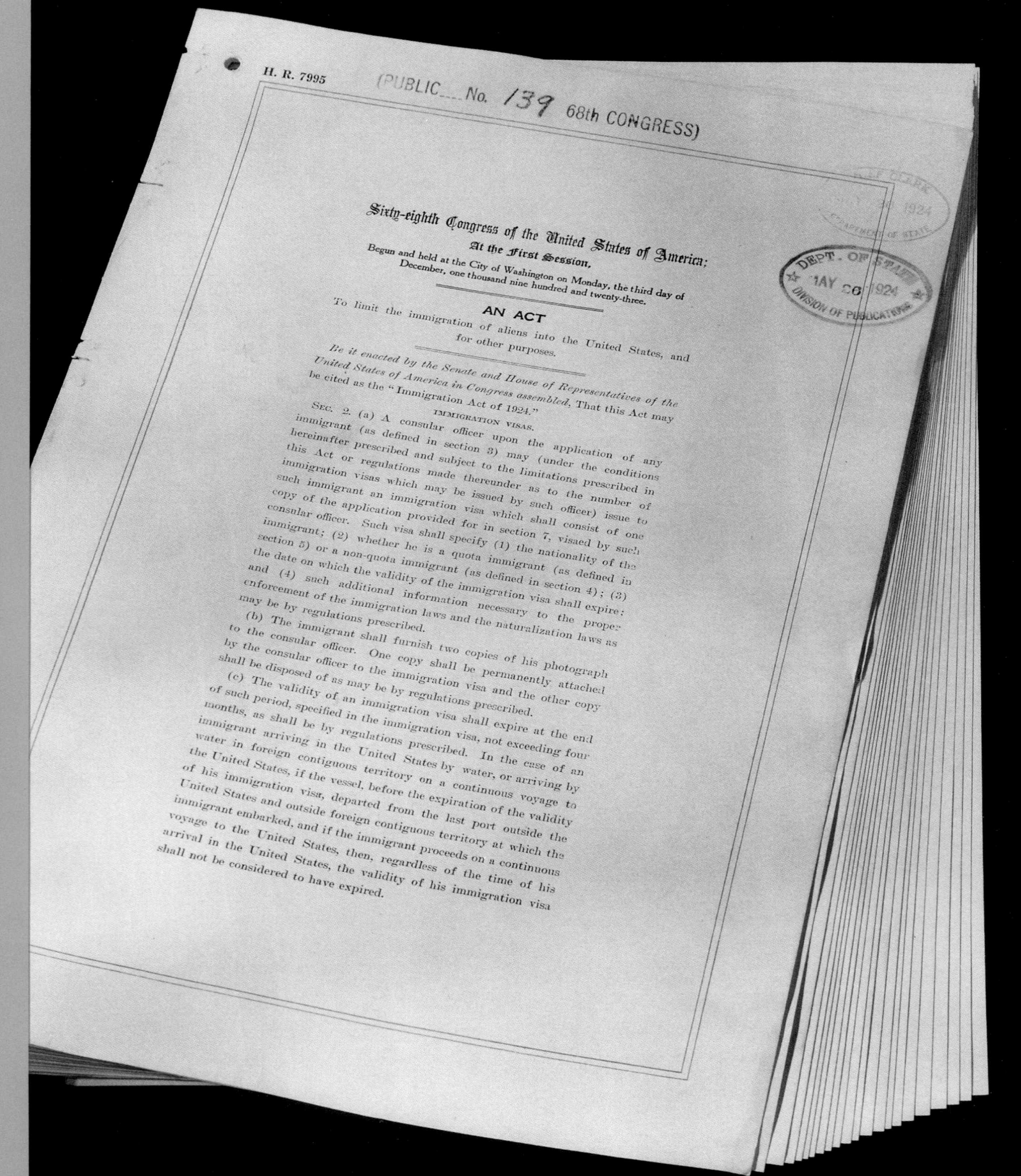
H. R. 7995 (PUBLIC No. 139 68th CONGRESS)

Sixty-eighth Congress of the United States of America;
At the First Session,
Begun and held at the City of Washington on Monday, the third day of December, one thousand nine hundred and twenty-three.

AN ACT

To limit the immigration of aliens into the United States, and for other purposes.

Be it enacted by the Senate and House of Representatives of the United States of America in Congress assembled, That this Act may be cited as the "Immigration Act of 1924."

IMMIGRATION VISAS.

SEC. 2. (a) A consular officer upon the application of any immigrant (as defined in section 3) may (under the conditions hereinafter prescribed and subject to the limitations prescribed in this Act or regulations made thereunder as to the number of immigration visas which may be issued by such officer) issue to such immigrant an immigration visa which shall consist of one copy of the application provided for in section 7, visaed by such consular officer. Such visa shall specify (1) the nationality of the immigrant; (2) whether he is a quota immigrant (as defined in section 5) or a non-quota immigrant (as defined in section 4); (3) the date on which the validity of the immigration visa shall expire; and (4) such additional information necessary to the proper enforcement of the immigration laws and the naturalization laws as may be by regulations prescribed.

(b) The immigrant shall furnish two copies of his photograph to the consular officer. One copy shall be permanently attached by the consular officer to the immigration visa and the other copy shall be disposed of as may be by regulations prescribed.

(c) The validity of an immigration visa shall expire at the end of such period, specified in the immigration visa, not exceeding four months, as shall be by regulations prescribed. In the case of an immigrant arriving in the United States by water, or arriving by water in foreign contiguous territory on a continuous voyage to the United States, if the vessel, before the expiration of the validity of his immigration visa, departed from the last port outside the United States and outside foreign contiguous territory at which the immigrant embarked, and if the immigrant proceeds on a continuous voyage to the United States, then, regardless of the time of his arrival in the United States, the validity of his immigration visa shall not be considered to have expired.

The Immigration Act of 1924 reduced to a trickle the flood of newcomers that had been a prominent feature of American life for more than three centuries. The act established annual quotas limiting immigration to 2 percent of the number of each nationality already part of the population of the United States at the time of the 1890 census. This system weighted immigration quotas heavily against southern and eastern Europe, the source of the "new Immigrants" to the United States. Because these were the peoples most anxious to come to this country at that time, immigration as a whole dwindled when the law took effect. The open invitation, the welcoming hand—symbolized by the Statue of Liberty, France's Centennial gift to the American people—had been withdrawn.

The people of the United States are truly a "nation of immigrants." Immigration was encouraged as far back as the "headright" system of colonial Virginia, which granted land to those financing the passage of new settlers. Frontier communities eager for population as well as ship companies seeking passengers encouraged emigration from Europe with persuasive advertising that extolled opportunities in the New World.

During the Civil War, Secretary of State William H. Seward instructed diplomatic and consular officers of the United States in foreign countries:

> *It may . . . be confidently asserted that, even now, nowhere else can the industrious laboring man and artisan expect so liberal a recompense for his services as in the United States. You are to make these truths known in any quarter and in any way which may lead to the migration of such persons to this country.*

Opposite: **The Immigration Quota Act of 1924. For the first time in American history, broad restrictions were imposed on the number of newcomers permitted from abroad. The act not only greatly reduced the number of persons who could enter the United States but also clearly discriminated against people of color and immigrants from areas outside of northern Europe.** *22 pages, 9 7/8 by 14 3/8 inches.*

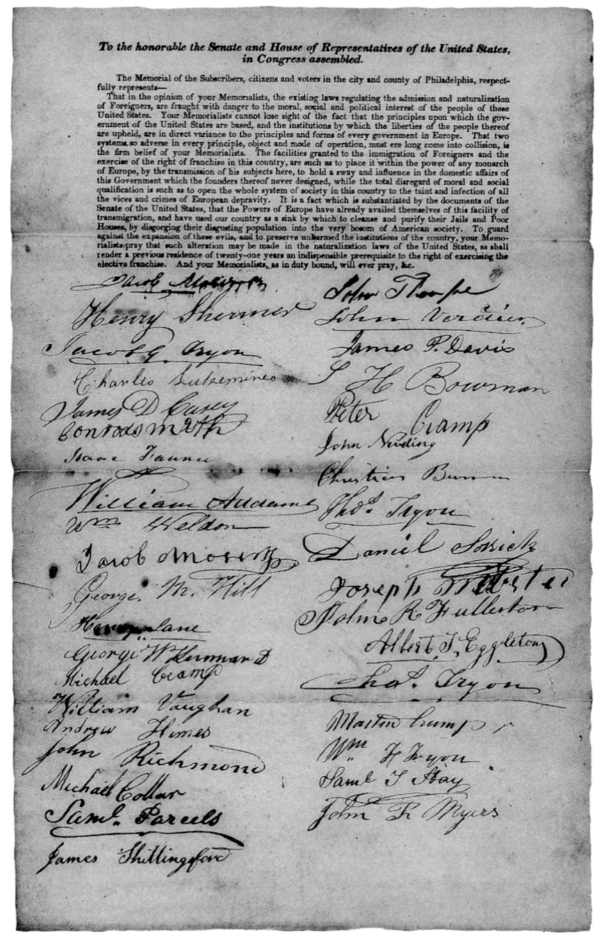

To the honorable the Senate and House of Representatives of the United States, in Congress assembled.

The Memorial of the Subscribers, citizens and voters in the city and county of Philadelphia, respectfully represents—

That in the opinion of your Memorialists, the existing laws regulating the admission and naturalization of Foreigners, are fraught with danger to the moral, social and political interest of the people of these United States. Your Memorialists cannot lose sight of the fact that the principles upon which the government of the United States are based, and the institutions by which the liberties of the people thereof are upheld, are in direct variance to the principles and forms of every government in Europe. That two systems so adverse in every principle, object and mode of operation, must ere long come into collision, is the firm belief of your Memorialists. The facilities granted to the immigration of Foreigners and the exercise of the right of franchise in this country, are such as to place it within the power of any monarch of Europe, by the transmission of his subjects here, to hold a sway and influence in the domestic affairs of this Government which the founders thereof never designed, while the total disregard of moral and social qualification is such as to open the whole system of society in this country to the taint and infection of all the vices and crimes of European depravity. It is a fact which is substantiated by the documents of the Senate of the United States, that the Powers of Europe have already availed themselves of this facility of transmigration, and have used our country as a sink by which to cleanse and purify their Jails and Poor Houses, by disgorging their disgusting population into the very bosom of American society. To guard against the expansion of these evils, and to preserve unharmed the institutions of the country, your Memorialists pray that such alteration may be made in the naturalization laws of the United States, as shall render a previous residence of twenty-one years an indispensible prerequisite to the right of exercising the elective franchise. And your Memorialists, as in duty bound, will ever pray, &c.

Anti-immigration petition from citizens of Philadelphia, 1846. The petition declares "that the Powers of Europe . . . have used our country as a sink by which to cleanse and purify their Jails and Poor Houses, by disgorging their disgusting population into the very bosom of American society." *Records of the U.S. Senate, National Archives; 8 by 13 3/8 inches.*

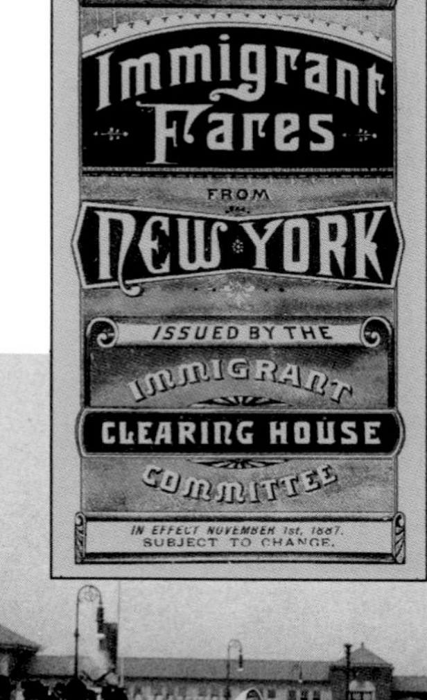

Fare booklet listing ticket prices to many parts of the United States, 1887. *93 pages, 3 7/8 by 6 5/8 inches.*

Immigrants arriving at Ellis Island in New York Harbor, ca. 1895. In the 1890s Ellis Island became the major processing center for immigrants entering the United States.

Industrialists were interested in securing cheap labor: The transcontinental railroads, preceding settlement and financed by federal land grants, sought immigrants to provide business along their routes and to purchase their land. The response was a human tide pouring in through New York City's Castle Garden in the Battery from 1855 to 1892 and then through Ellis Island until immigration restriction became national policy.

On the other hand, patterns of exclusion and outright prejudice against foreigners developed early. Those who arrived first became the aristocrats of the new land. Upward mobility, however, was an immigrant expectation grounded upon the experience of others. "No man continues long a laborer for others," wrote Benjamin Franklin in 1751, "but . . . sets up for himself." Each immigrant generation produced a new generation of native-born Americans who soon joined the older stock in looking askance at the "foreigners" inundating *their* country. Nativist sentiment reached a high point in the 1850s when, coupled with anti-Catholicism, it became the main platform of the American, or Know-Nothing, Party. This movement was partly an attempt to evade the slavery question and partly a reaction to the very real problems created by the sudden arrival of 400,000 Irish, who came in desperate flight from a homeland suffering from famine.

In the 1880s prejudice against Asians precipitated a series of restrictions on Chinese and Japanese immigration that were relaxed only in the 1960s. Immigration restriction became a goal of newly organized American labor, which feared wage-cutting competition for jobs. During the 1880s the national origin of the newcomers began to change from northern Europeans, whose customs, language, and religion made assimilation relatively easy, to southern and eastern Europeans, whose differences seemed greater, particularly in economically hard times. Latent "America for Americans" sentiment emerged and culminated in the 1924 Immigration Act, which intentionally excluded the new immigrants.

Since 1924, compassion for persons displaced by war and revolution around the world has led to some relaxation of the anti-immigration laws. In 1965 a new law abolishing nationality quotas was passed, but as President Lyndon B. Johnson signed it at the Statue of Liberty, he declared, "The days of unlimited immigration are past."

Im Nahmen gottes,
Henrich Muskenug
in Maxedany
Ist nach Christlichen Unterricht unser evangelischen Lutherischen glaubens Lehre, zum erstenmahl zum Heiligen abendmahl gangen in dem Jahr des Herrn 1769 in
Bäth Sontag Rogate; Bey mir sein Pfarrer Daniel Schumacher in Pensylvanien

Sey getreu in deinem glauben
Las dir Satan den nicht rauben

Pennsylvania German *fraktur*, 1769, used to document a Revolutionary War pension claim. The Pennsylvania Germans adorned their private papers—birth, marriage, and baptismal certificates—in highly ornamental styles.
7 3/8 by 13 inches.

Passenger list of the *London*, 1863. One of the passengers was Samuel Gompers, a founder and first president of the American Federation of Labor. His father's occupation is listed as "Segar maker."
13 3/4 by 16 7/8 inches.

A L'AMITIE SECULAIRE DE LA FRANCE ET DES ETATS-UNIS

L'an mil huit cent quatre vingt-quatre, le quatre Juillet, jour anniversaire de la fête de l'Indépendance des Etats Unis.

En présence de Monsieur Jules Ferry, Président du Conseil des Ministres, Ministre des Affaires Etrangères, Monsieur le Comte Ferdinand de Lesseps, au nom du Comité de l'Union Franco-Américaine et de la Manifestation nationale dont le Comité a été l'organe, a présenté la statue colossale de "La Liberté éclairant le Monde" œuvre du statuaire A. Bartholdi, à son Excellence Monsieur Morton Ministre plénipotentiaire des Etats Unis à Paris, en le priant d'être l'interprète des sentiments dont cette œuvre est l'expression.

Monsieur Morton, au nom de ses compatriotes, remercie l'Union Franco-Américaine pour ce témoignage de sympathie du peuple Français; il déclare qu'en vertu des pouvoirs qui lui sont conférés tant par le Président des Etats Unis que par le Comité de l'œuvre en Amérique représenté par son honorable président Mr. William M. Evarts, il accepte la statue et qu'elle sera érigée par le peuple Américain, conformément au vote du Congrès du 22 Février 1877, dans la rade de New-York en souvenir de l'amitié séculaire qui unit les deux nations.

En foi de quoi ont signé:

Au nom de la France. Au nom des Etats Unis.

Au nom du Comité
de l'Union Franco Américaine.

UNION FRANCO AMERICAINE

1776 1876

WASHINGTON

Deed of gift of the Statue of Liberty, 1876. The statue was a Centennial gift from France to the American people. It symbolized this nation's openness to the "huddled masses" of the world and served as a welcoming beacon to generations of immigrants entering New York Harbor. *21 1/8 by 26 5/8 inches.*

Hester Street in New York City's lower East Side, ca. 1898–1903. Hester Street was part of a typical immigrant neighborhood in an urban center. Those who thought immigration should be curbed pointed to the overcrowded, dilapidated conditions in such neighborhoods.

Irish clam diggers and matronly companion, Boston, 1882. Irish immigration to America assumed large proportions in the mid-1800s.

Man working on the Empire State Building, New York City, 1930. Skyscrapers became the city's most visible symbol. *Lewis Hine photograph.*

Crowd of bathers on Lake Michigan beach, Chicago, ca. 1925. In the 1920s, the city became dominant in American political, social, and economic life.

Immigrant couple reading Czech newspaper in an Illinois farm kitchen, ca. 1943.

President Lyndon B. Johnson signing the 1965 Immigration Act at the base of the Statue of Liberty. Although the law abolished national quotas, the total annual immigration remained restricted.
From the Lyndon Baines Johnson Library.

INAUGURAL ADDRESS OF

PRESIDENT FRANKLIN D. ROOSEVELT

MARCH 4, 1933.

I am certain that my fellow Americans expect that on my induction into the Presidency I will address them with a candor and a decision which the present situation of our nation impels. This is preeminently the time to speak the truth, the whole truth, frankly and boldly. Nor need we shrink from honestly facing conditions in our country today. This great nation will endure as it has endured, will revive and will prosper. So first of all let me assert my firm belief that the only thing we have to fear is fear itself, - nameless, unreasoning, unjustified terror which paralyzes needed efforts to convert retreat into advance. In every dark hour of our national life a leadership of frankness and vigor has met with that understanding and support of the people themselves which is essential to victory. I am convinced that you will again give that support to leadership in these critical days.

In such a spirit on my part and on yours we face our common difficulties. They concern, thank God, only material things. Values have shrunken to fantastic levels; taxes have risen; our ability to pay has fallen; government of all kinds is faced by serious curtailment of income; the

...alike. We aim at the assurance
...e.

...sential democracy. The people
...n their need they have registered
...ction. They have asked
...ip. They have made me the
...spirit of the gift I take it.

...ask the blessing of God.
...ay He guide me in the days

Franklin D Roosevelt

This is the original reading copy I used March 4th

Franklin D. Roosevelt's copy of his first inaugural address, March 4, 1933. As Roosevelt took office, the country was gripped by depression and despair. The new President lifted the nation's spirits with his confident style and his statement "the only thing we have to fear is fear itself." *From the Franklin D. Roosevelt Library; pages 1 and 9 of 9 pages, 7 1/4 by 9 1/4 inches.*

"The only thing we have to fear is fear itself," President Franklin D. Roosevelt proclaimed in his first inaugural address. With these words on a gray March 4, 1933, he lifted the spirits of a discouraged people ready for change.

The Great Depression had the nation in its grip in 1933. Traditional methods of response to hard times—voluntarism, private philanthropy, and restricted government aid—had not worked. Following the collapse of the stock market in October 1929, the American economy had plunged downward; the national income fell from $83 billion in 1929 to less than $40 billion 4 years later. By 1933, with the unemployment rate at 24.9 percent and nearly 12 million people out of work, men sold apples on the streets, lined up at soup kitchens, or took to the rails in boxcars. Unrest and a growing inclination to violence spread throughout the United States. Armed farmers resisted foreclosure, destroyed crops, and dumped milk in attempts to drive up prices. Idle men roamed the countryside in search of jobs. Business firms failed daily, and more than 5,000 banks closed between 1930 and 1932. The nation seemed to be on the verge of chaos.

In his Presidential campaign, Franklin Roosevelt had promised a "New Deal." And within a short time, there emerged from Washington a torrent of Executive orders and legislative acts designed to halt the Depression and bring the nation back to an even keel. The first efforts went to saving the banking system and recovering the life savings of hundreds of thousands of Americans.

At the same time, during the first "Hundred Days," the administration created the National Recovery Administration (NRA) to stimulate American industry. Under its provisions, companies were required to draw up codes of fair practice and could ignore antitrust laws, while workers were given the right to bargain collectively and were guaranteed maximum work hours and minimum wages. For a time, the NRA, symbolized by its Blue Eagle, worked reasonably well, but its effectiveness was already on the wane when the Supreme Court declared the act unconstitutional in 1935.

The famous Blue Eagle, symbol of compliance with the National Recovery Administration (NRA) codes intended to revitalize American industry. In 1935 the Supreme Court declared the NRA legislation unconstitutional. *Flag, 4 3/4 by 5 1/2 feet.*

An elderly couple receiving their first Social Security check, ca. 1937.

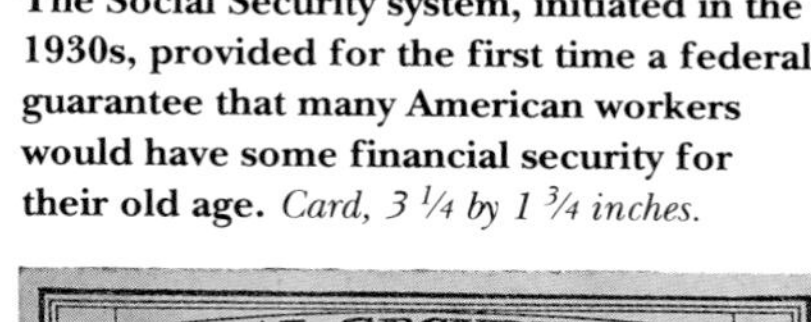

The Social Security system, initiated in the 1930s, provided for the first time a federal guarantee that many American workers would have some financial security for their old age. *Card, 3 1/4 by 1 3/4 inches.*

SOCIAL SECURITY ACT
ACCOUNT NUMBER
109-03-6663
HAS BEEN ESTABLISHED FOR
Meyer Harry Eichbein
12-16-36 Meyer H. Eichbein
DATE OF ISSUE EMPLOYEE'S SIGNATURE

A soup kitchen for the hungry poor in Washington, DC, ca. 1933.

"Alphabet" programs designed to deal with a wide variety of problems proliferated during the New Deal. The PWA (Public Works Administration) expanded construction programs begun under President Herbert Hoover, and the FERA (Federal Emergency Relief Administration) distributed aid to the needy. The WPA (Works Progress Administration) employed writers, artists, and actors; built highways, streets, and airfields; operated recreation centers; and surveyed archives. The CCC (Civilian Conservation Corps) put nearly 3 million young men from urban areas to work in reforestation, fire prevention, and construction of recreational facilities; and the AAA (Agricultural Adjustment Administration) helped to restore the purchasing power of the farmers.

With the passage of the Social Security Act of 1935, the federal government for the first time provided an unemployment, old age, and survivors insurance system. The National Labor Relations Act of 1935, better known as the Wagner Act, protected the right of employees to join labor unions that were organized by craft or by industry and to engage in collective bargaining.

Not to be ignored in any litany of New Deal measures is the Rural Electrification Administration, created by Executive order in 1935. The increased availability of electric power was a boon to America's farm families not only because it brought the electric light and the refrigerator but also because it put these families within the reach of radio. Radio brought in news of the outside world; it brought President Roosevelt's soothing "fireside chats" and the laughter created by Jack Benny and Eddie Cantor. In a troubled time, radio somehow lightened the burden of the Depression.

Many New Deal measures left a permanent imprint on the nation, while others were short-lived. The Depression ended with the onset of the 1940s (and some argue that only the huge wartime expenditures brought back full prosperity). There is no doubt, however, that the New Deal's approach to problems—the use of a strong federal government to remedy economic and social ills and some of its programs, such as social security—fundamentally transformed the way that the American political system would operate in the future.

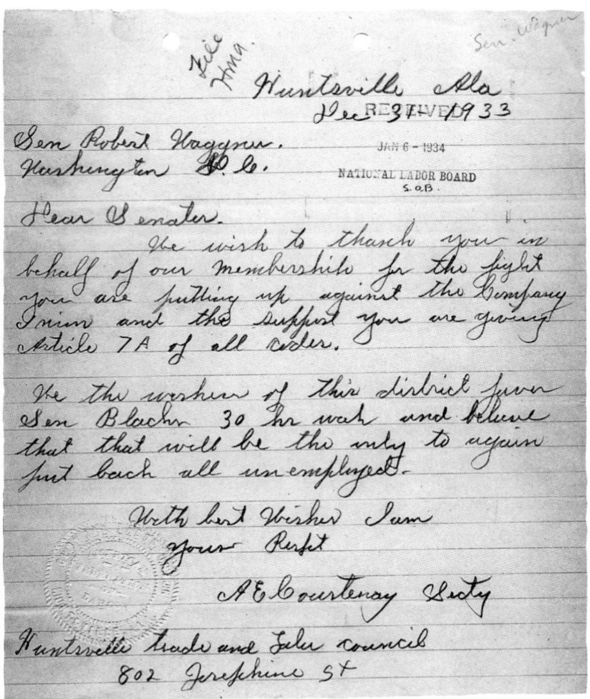

File
Hma.
Sen. Wagner

Huntsville Ala
Dec 31 1933
RECEIVED
JAN 6 - 1934
NATIONAL LABOR BOARD
S.O.B.

Sen Robert Waggner.
Washington D. C.

Dear Senater.
We wish to thank you in behalf of our membership for the fight you are putting up against the Company Union and the support you are giving Article 7A of all order.

We the worker of this district favor Sen Black 30 hr week and believe that that will be the only to again put back all unemployed.

With best Wishes I am
your Respt
A E Courtenay Secty
Huntsville trade and Labor council
802 Josephine St

Letter from A. E. Courtenay, Secretary of the Huntsville, AL, Trade and Labor Council, to Senator Robert Wagner, December 31, 1933. Wagner's efforts to make permanent the right of employees to join unions and to engage in collective bargaining culminated in the National Labor Relations Act of 1935, known as the Wagner Act. *8 3/8 by 10 3/8 inches.*

Mrs. Daniel Flinn of Ashland, IL, celebrating the installation of electricity on her farm, 1943. Rural electrification, a major program of the New Deal, effected a revolution on American farms.

Wisconsin Dells. Wis.
May 12, 1939.
MAY 17 1939

Dear President Roosevelt:
I understand that you have desired to help the farmers obtain cheaper electricity rates. Has anything been accomplished? We live five miles from Wisconsin Dells where the dam and power houses are located. Lines conducting power to other towns are within 50 ft. of our house — yet we would have to pay 4.00 minimum rate per month.
When we get 15 cts. per. dozen for eggs — 25 cts for butter and other produce rates the same
71

fair price, How can we pay 4.00 per. month for a light in our house?
Have you any suggestions to offer.?
I am. Yours Very Truly.
Mina Vickers
Wisconsin Dells
Wisconsin

Letter from Mina Vickers of Wisconsin to President Roosevelt, May 12, 1939. She expressed the fear that even cheap electricity might prove too expensive for farm people such as herself. *8 5/8 by 5 1/8 inches.*

Farmers employed on a bridge-spillway project by the Works Progress Administration near Pierre, SD, 1936. To relieve unemployment, the WPA put hundreds of thousands of Americans to work on various public works projects.

Eighty-eighth Congress of the United States of America

AT THE SECOND SESSION

Begun and held at the City of Washington on Tuesday, the seventh day of January, one thousand nine hundred and sixty-four

An Act

To mobilize the human and financial resources of the Nation to combat poverty in the United States.

Be it enacted by the Senate and House of Representatives of the United States of America in Congress assembled, That this Act may be cited as the "Economic Opportunity Act of 1964".

FINDINGS AND DECLARATION OF PURPOSE

SEC. 2. Although the economic well-being and prosperity of the United States have progressed to a level surpassing any achieved in world history, and although these benefits are widely shared throughout the Nation, poverty continues to be the lot of a substantial number of our people. The United States can achieve its full economic and social potential as a nation only if every individual has the opportunity to contribute to the full extent of his capabilities and to participate in the workings of our society. It is, therefore, the policy of the United States to eliminate the paradox of poverty in the midst of plenty in this Nation by opening to everyone the opportunity for education and training, the opportunity to work, and the opportunity to live in decency and dignity. It is the purpose of this Act to strengthen, supplement, and coordinate efforts in furtherance of that policy.

TITLE I—YOUTH PROGRAMS

PART A—JOB CORPS

STATEMENT OF PURPOSE

SEC. 101. The purpose of this part is to prepare for the responsibilities of citizenship and to increase the employability of young men and young women aged sixteen through twenty-one by providing them in rural and urban residential centers with education, vocational training, useful work experience, including work directed toward the conservation of natural resources, and other appropriate activities.

The Economic Opportunity Act, signed by President Lyndon B. Johnson on August 20, 1964. Part of Johnson's "war on poverty," this program was a lineal descendant of Roosevelt's New Deal. *27 pages, 10 by 15 inches.*

Abandoned farm in South Dakota, 1935. The drought and resultant duststorms in the Great Plains drove thousands from bankrupt farms in the Dust Bowl. These migrants were known as Okies regardless of their place of origin.

Farmer and his son on the way to town, Eufaula, OK, 1940. The struggle with the land left a living record in the faces of those who survived the Dust Bowl.

The instrument of surrender of the Japanese forces, signed in Tokyo Bay on September 2, 1945, on board the U.S.S. *Missouri*. The signing marked the end of World War II.
2 pages, 23 by 32 ¾ inches.

INSTRUMENT OF SURRENDER

We, acting by command of and in behalf of the Emperor of Japan, the Japanese Government and the Japanese Imperial General Headquarters, hereby accept the provisions set forth in the declaration issued by the heads of the Governments of the United States, China and Great Britain on 26 July 1945, at Potsdam, and subsequently adhered to by the Union of Soviet Socialist Republics, which four powers are hereafter referred to as the Allied Powers.

We hereby proclaim the unconditional surrender to the Allied Powers of the Japanese Imperial General Headquarters and of all Japanese armed forces and all armed forces under Japanese control wherever situated.

We hereby command all Japanese forces wherever situated and the Japanese people to cease hostilities forthwith, to preserve and save from damage all ships, aircraft, and military and civil property and to comply with all requirements which may be imposed by the Supreme Commander for the Allied Powers or by agencies of the Japanese Government at his direction.

We hereby command the Japanese Imperial General Headquarters to issue at once orders to the Commanders of all Japanese forces and all forces under Japanese control wherever situated to surrender unconditionally themselves and all forces under their control.

We hereby command all civil, military and naval officials to obey and enforce all proclamations, orders and directives deemed by the Supreme Commander for the Allied Powers to be proper to effectuate this surrender and issued by him or under his authority and we direct all such officials to remain at their posts and to continue to perform their non-combatant duties unless specifically relieved by him or under his authority.

We hereby undertake for the Emperor, the Japanese Government and their successors to carry out the provisions of the Potsdam Declaration in good faith, and to issue whatever orders and take whatever action may be required by the Supreme Commander for the Allied Powers or by any other designated representative of the Allied Powers for the purpose of giving effect to that Declaration.

We hereby command the Japanese Imperial Government and the Japanese Imperial General Headquarters at once to liberate all allied prisoners of war and civilian internees now under Japanese control and to provide for their protection, care, maintenance and immediate transportation to places as directed.

The authority of the Emperor and the Japanese Government to rule the state shall be subject to the Supreme Commander for the Allied Powers who will take such steps as he deems proper to effectuate these terms of surrender.

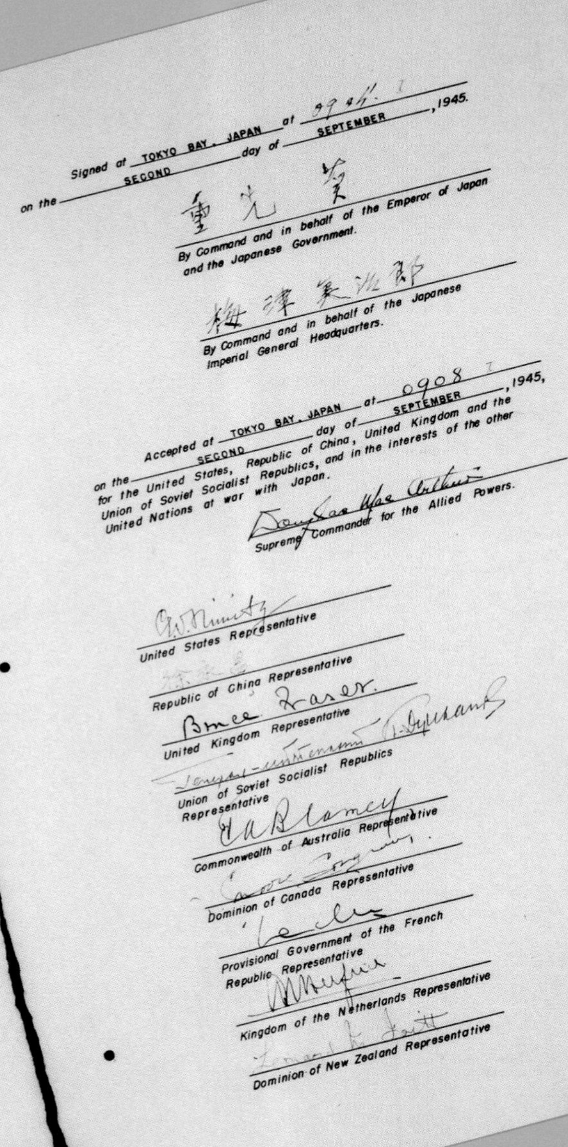

Signed at TOKYO BAY, JAPAN at 0904 I on the SECOND day of SEPTEMBER, 1945.

重光葵

By Command and in behalf of the Emperor of Japan and the Japanese Government.

梅津美治郎

By Command and in behalf of the Japanese Imperial General Headquarters.

Accepted at TOKYO BAY, JAPAN at 0908 I on the SECOND day of SEPTEMBER, 1945, for the United States, Republic of China, United Kingdom and the Union of Soviet Socialist Republics, and in the interests of the other United Nations at war with Japan.

Supreme Commander for the Allied Powers.

United States Representative

Republic of China Representative

United Kingdom Representative

Union of Soviet Socialist Republics Representative

Commonwealth of Australia Representative

Dominion of Canada Representative

Provisional Government of the French Republic Representative

Kingdom of the Netherlands Representative

Dominion of New Zealand Representative

From the sands of North Africa and the hedgerows of France to the steppes of Russia and the jungles of Asia, the world was at war. On December 7, 1941, when the Japanese attacked Pearl Harbor, the United States became a part of World War II, adding its manpower and industrial might to the Allied cause.

By late 1941 Germany dominated the continent of Europe and had penetrated deep into Soviet territory. Quick victories on Wake Island and in Thailand, Malaya, Guam, and the Philippines gave its Axis partner, Japan, dominance over an area stretching from the borders of India to the mid-Pacific by the summer of 1942.

By then, American military induction centers and training camps were rapidly filling. Eventually, nearly 16 million men and women would serve in the Armed Forces. Shipyards and factories had begun to produce unprecedented numbers of liberty ships, tanks, B-17 bombers, and Browning automatic rifles. America was rapidly turning into what President Roosevelt called the "great arsenal of democracy." Civilians were growing accustomed to bond drives and blackouts, gasoline rationing cards and meat shortages. World War II had become everyone's cause.

A wave of national hysteria right after Pearl Harbor led to the shipping of 120,000 persons of Japanese ancestry, both American citizens and noncitizens, from the Pacific states to relocation, or internment, camps in the interior on the premise that if they were left unguarded, they would create a "security" problem. Later, in a great national irony, a regiment of Japanese-American (*nisei*) soldiers in Italy became the most decorated unit in the war.

The gloom created by the early defeat of American forces was lifted slightly by Gen. James H. Doolittle's bomber raid on Tokyo on April 18, 1942. Nevertheless, the tide of the war did not begin to turn until the defeat of the Japanese Navy at the Battle of Midway in June 1942. Later that year, American sea, air, and land forces began the process of recapturing the Pacific islands that would lead them to Japan: Guadalcanal in 1942, Tarawa in 1943, Saipan and the Philippines in 1944, and Iwo Jima and Okinawa in 1945. When Gen. Douglas MacArthur stepped ashore in the Philippines in October 1944, he fulfilled his promise—"I shall return"—made when he was

Hitler, Göbbels, and Göring, ca. 1942. This painting was part of the American campaign to promote hemispheric cooperation against the common Nazi threat. *Watercolor by Arias, 14 by 17 1/4 inches.*

Japanese troops on Bataan, Philippine Islands, ca. 1942. The Japanese attempt to establish "The Greater East Asia Co-Prosperity Sphere" began with an attack on Manchuria in 1931 and continued for the next 14 years. *Captured Japanese photograph.*

forced to evacuate Corregidor 2½ years earlier.

In the European theater, the road to an Allied victory began when the British repelled the German Afrika Korps at El Alamein in November 1942. American forces landed in North Africa that same November and, following the defeat of German armies there, joined the British in the invasion of Sicily and Italy in the summer of 1943. On D-day, June 6, 1944, the Allies carried out the invasion of France and established the long awaited "second front" in western Europe.

On the eastern front, the Russians halted the German advance at Stalingrad in the single bloodiest battle of the war, 1942–43. Soviet forces then counterattacked, pushing the German forces ever backward toward their own borders. Finally, in April 1945, Russian and American troops met at the Elbe River inside Germany. The Nazi war machine, finally outgunned and outmanned, was forced to surrender unconditionally on May 8, 1945.

Victory would soon come in the Pacific, where an awesome new weapon, the atomic bomb, was about to be used. As early as 1939, physicist Albert Einstein had written President Roosevelt that the development of an atomic bomb was feasible. Early in 1942, the secret Manhattan project had been launched, and in closely guarded sites at Hanford in Washington, Los Alamos in New Mexico, and Oak Ridge in Tennessee, scientists raced to create a practical atomic weapon ahead of the Germans.

In August 1945 President Harry S. Truman gave the order to drop the world's first two atomic bombs on the Japanese cities of Hiroshima and Nagasaki, and on September 2, 1945, the Japanese forces surrendered to the Allies aboard the U.S.S. *Missouri* in Tokyo Bay.

Japanese Americans in a control station in Byron, CA, prior to evacuation, May 1942. In the wake of national wartime hysteria, tens of thousands of Japanese Americans were moved from their homes in the Pacific Coast states to internment camps farther inland. *Dorothea Lange photograph.*

Preparing the flight deck of the U.S.S. *Lexington* for an air strike in the Pacific, November 1943. *Edward Steichen photograph.*

Albert Einstein
Old Grove Rd.
Nassau Point
Peconic, Long Island

August 2nd, 1939

F.D. Roosevelt,
President of the United States,
White House
Washington, D.C.

Sir:

Some recent work by E.Fermi and L. Szilard, which has been communicated to me in manuscript, leads me to expect that the element uranium may be turned into a new and important source of energy in the immediate future. Certain aspects of the situation which has arisen seem to call for watchfulness and, if necessary, quick action on the part of the Administration. I believe therefore that it is my duty to bring to your attention the following facts and recommendations:

In the course of the last four months it has been made probable - through the work of Joliot in France as well as Fermi and Szilard in America - that it may become possible to set up a nuclear chain reaction in a large mass of uranium,by which vast amounts of power and large quantities of new radium-like elements would be generated. Now it appears almost certain that this could be achieved in the immediate future.

This new phenomenon would also lead to the construction of bombs, and it is conceivable - though much less certain - that extremely powerful bombs of a new type may thus be constructed. A single bomb of this type, carried by boat and exploded in a port, might very well destroy the whole port together with some of the surrounding territory. However, such bombs might very well prove to be too heavy for transportation by air.

-2-

The United States has only very poor ores of uranium in moderate quantities. There is some good ore in Canada and the former Czechoslovakia, while the most important source of uranium is Belgian Congo.

In view of this situation you may think it desirable to have some permanent contact maintained between the Administration and the group of physicists working on chain reactions in America. One possible way of achieving this might be for you to entrust with this task a person who has your confidence and who could perhaps serve in an inofficial capacity. His task might comprise the following:

a) to approach Government Departments, keep them informed of the further development, and put forward recommendations for Government action, giving particular attention to the problem of securing a supply of uranium ore for the United States;

b) to speed up the experimental work,which is at present being carried on within the limits of the budgets of University laboratories, by providing funds, if such funds be required, through his contacts with private persons who are willing to make contributions for this cause, and perhaps also by obtaining the co-operation of industrial laboratories which have the necessary equipment.

I understand that Germany has actually stopped the sale of uranium from the Czechoslovakian mines which she has taken over. That she should have taken such early action might perhaps be understood on the ground that the son of the German Under-Secretary of State, von Weizsäcker, is attached to the Kaiser-Wilhelm-Institut in Berlin where some of the American work on uranium is now being repeated.

Yours very truly,
A. Einstein
(Albert Einstein)

Letter from Albert Einstein to President Franklin D. Roosevelt, August 2, 1939. This letter precipitated American efforts to build an atomic bomb before the Germans. *From the Franklin D. Roosevelt Library; 2 pages, 8 1/2 by 11 inches.*

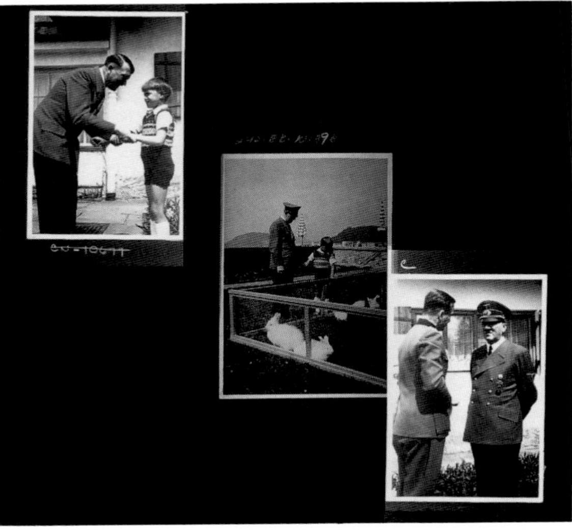

One of the photograph albums of Eva Braun, Hitler's mistress. This album was among the German records seized by American forces and later deposited in the National Archives. *12 by 9 inches.*

Original artwork for World War II poster, 1943. *Watercolor by H. Koerner, 38 7/8 by 17 3/4 inches.*

Civilians load the dead from Gusen (a part of the Mauthausen concentration camp near Linz, Austria) into wagons to remove them for burial, May 15, 1945.

German prisoners of war on the western front, 1944.

Battleship U.S.S. *Missouri* in action. The shells can be seen in the upper left of the photograph.

American troops advance inland on Kwajalein Atoll, February 1, 1944.

SUPREME HEADQUARTERS
ALLIED EXPEDITIONARY FORCE

Soldiers, Sailors and Airmen of the Allied Expeditionary Force!

You are about to embark upon the Great Crusade, toward which we have striven these many months. The eyes of the world are upon you. The hopes and prayers of liberty-loving people everywhere march with you. In company with our brave Allies and brothers-in-arms on other Fronts, you will bring about the destruction of the German war machine, the elimination of Nazi tyranny over the oppressed peoples of Europe, and security for ourselves in a free world.

Your task will not be an easy one. Your enemy is well trained, well equipped and battle-hardened. He will fight savagely.

But this is the year 1944 ! Much has happened since the Nazi triumphs of 1940-41. The United Nations have inflicted upon the Germans great defeats, in open battle, man-to-man. Our air offensive has seriously reduced their strength in the air and their capacity to wage war on the ground. Our Home Fronts have given us an overwhelming superiority in weapons and munitions of war, and placed at our disposal great reserves of trained fighting men. The tide has turned ! The free men of the world are marching together to Victory !

I have full confidence in your courage, devotion to duty and skill in battle. We will accept nothing less than full Victory !

Good Luck ! And let us all beseech the blessing of Almighty God upon this great and noble undertaking.

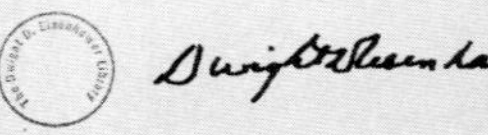

Gen. Dwight D. Eisenhower's D-day proclamation, June 6, 1944. As the Allies landed in Normandy, Eisenhower declared, "Soldiers, Sailors and Airmen. . . . The hopes and prayers of liberty-loving people everywhere march with you." *From the Dwight D. Eisenhower Library; 6 3/8 by 9 5/8 inches.*

On August 14, 1945, San Franciscans celebrate the first news of Japan's surrender, ending the fighting in World War II.

The European Recovery Act, 1948, called the Marshall plan after Secretary of State George C. Marshall, who proposed it the previous year. Assistance under the Marshall plan helped to rebuild and stabilize postwar Europe. *Pages 1 and 32 of 32 pages, 9 3/4 by 14 3/4 inches.*

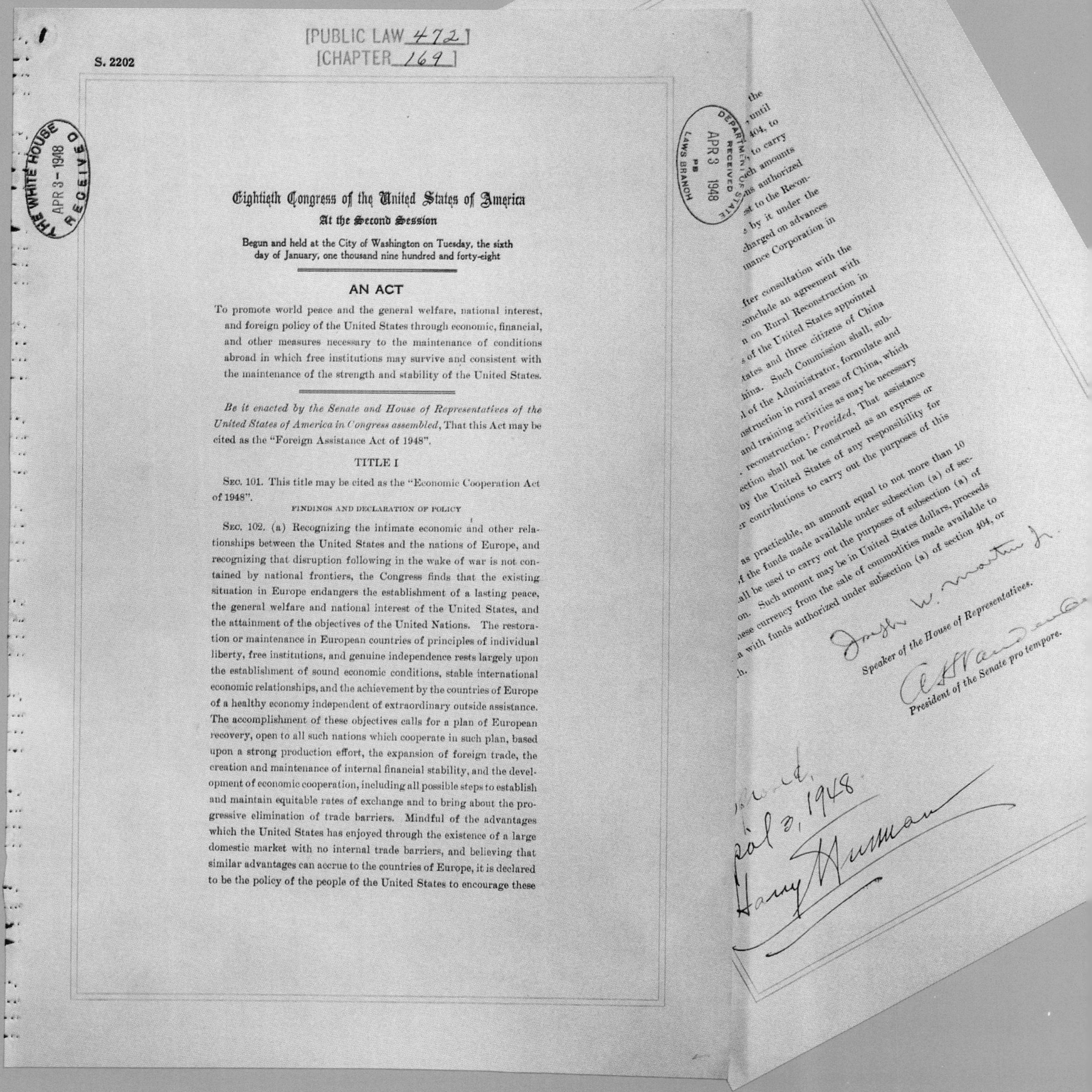

[PUBLIC LAW 472]
[CHAPTER 169]

S. 2202

THE WHITE HOUSE
APR 3 – 1948
RECEIVED

DEPARTMENT OF STATE
RECEIVED
APR 3 1948
LAWS BRANCH

Eightieth Congress of the United States of America

At the Second Session

Begun and held at the City of Washington on Tuesday, the sixth day of January, one thousand nine hundred and forty-eight

AN ACT

To promote world peace and the general welfare, national interest, and foreign policy of the United States through economic, financial, and other measures necessary to the maintenance of conditions abroad in which free institutions may survive and consistent with the maintenance of the strength and stability of the United States.

Be it enacted by the Senate and House of Representatives of the United States of America in Congress assembled, That this Act may be cited as the "Foreign Assistance Act of 1948".

TITLE I

SEC. 101. This title may be cited as the "Economic Cooperation Act of 1948".

FINDINGS AND DECLARATION OF POLICY

SEC. 102. (a) Recognizing the intimate economic and other relationships between the United States and the nations of Europe, and recognizing that disruption following in the wake of war is not contained by national frontiers, the Congress finds that the existing situation in Europe endangers the establishment of a lasting peace, the general welfare and national interest of the United States, and the attainment of the objectives of the United Nations. The restoration or maintenance in European countries of principles of individual liberty, free institutions, and genuine independence rests largely upon the establishment of sound economic conditions, stable international economic relationships, and the achievement by the countries of Europe of a healthy economy independent of extraordinary outside assistance. The accomplishment of these objectives calls for a plan of European recovery, open to all such nations which cooperate in such plan, based upon a strong production effort, the expansion of foreign trade, the creation and maintenance of internal financial stability, and the development of economic cooperation, including all possible steps to establish and maintain equitable rates of exchange and to bring about the progressive elimination of trade barriers. Mindful of the advantages which the United States has enjoyed through the existence of a large domestic market with no internal trade barriers, and believing that similar advantages can accrue to the countries of Europe, it is declared to be the policy of the people of the United States to encourage these

Joseph W. Martin Jr.
Speaker of the House of Representatives.

A H Vandenberg
President of the Senate pro tempore.

Approved, April 3, 1948
Harry Truman

At the end of World War II, Americans came to understand that as a nation, they would have to play a much larger role in international politics than ever before. In 1945 the United States, the single great power to emerge stronger at war's end than at its beginning, faced the urgent task of the relief and reconstruction of a prostrate Europe. As Americans confronted the enormous magnitude of the task, the specter of the Soviet Union, whose vast armies had marched across eastern Europe to the Elbe River, appeared to threaten what remained of Europe's stability.

Winston Churchill gave voice to this concern in his famous speech at Fulton, MO, on March 5, 1946. "From Stettin in the Baltic to Trieste in the Adriatic," warned Britain's wartime leader, "an iron curtain has descended across the continent." Thus was acknowledged the existence of the cold war with the United States and its Western European Allies aligned against the Soviet Union and its satellite nations east of the iron curtain.

The new world order compelled the United States to put aside basic postulates of foreign policy that had influenced its foreign relations since the beginning of the republic. In those earlier days, when Europe was racked by revolutionary upheaval, George Washington had counseled his countrymen not "to implicate ourselves, by artificial ties, in the ordinary vicissitude's of [Europe's] politics, or the ordinary combinations and collisions of her friendships, or enmities." In short, Washington had urged that American policy should avoid the "insidious wiles of foreign influence" and "steer clear of permanent alliances."

The first major turning away from this counsel came in 1945 when the United States and other countries formed the United Nations. But with the development of the cold war, other measures were needed to strengthen and protect Europe. On June 5, 1947, at Harvard University, Secretary of State George C. Marshall proposed a plan for

Secretary of State Dean Acheson signing the North Atlantic Treaty, as President Harry Truman and Vice President Alben Barkley watch, 1949. The nation's greatest peacetime military alliance, NATO was organized as a mutual defense pact among the United States, Canada, and 10 nations of Western Europe.

Cartoon by James Berryman on American foreign policy, courtesy of Berryman and the *Washington Star*, ca. 1947. *From the Harry S. Truman Library; 14 1/4 by 13 3/8 inches.*

major economic aid to bring about "the revival of a working economy in the world so as to permit the emergence of political and social conditions in which free institutions can exist." The Secretary said that his proposal was aimed "not against any country or doctrine but against hunger, poverty, desperation, and chaos." Subsequently, on April 3, 1948, President Harry S. Truman signed into law the European Recovery Act, popularly known as the Marshall plan, which channeled $12 billion in aid to Western Europe over the next 4 years. The Soviet Union and its satellite nations chose not to participate in the Marshall plan.

To establish a strong military presence in Western Europe, the United States joined the North Atlantic Treaty Organization (NATO) on April 4, 1949. This was the United States' greatest peacetime military alliance. NATO marked the first of a series of collective security agreements that gave substance to the 1947 Truman Doctrine pledging to "help free peoples maintain . . . their national integrity against aggressive movements."

These commitments, plus a series of Presidential decisions and orders aimed at containing communism, involved the nation in a prolonged period of diplomatic and military crises throughout the world, including major conflicts in Southeast Asia, particularly in Korea and Vietnam. Europe, the Soviet Union, and nuclear weapons remained the focal point of American concern, though Middle East peace was a continuing problem.

At the same time, some of Washington's precepts have served to guide American policy. In his farewell address, Washington had warned that "The Nation, which indulges toward another habitual hatred or habitual fondness, is in some degree a slave . . . to its animosity or to its affection, either of which is sufficient to lead it astray from its duty and its interest." Negotiations like the Strategic Arms Limitations Talks, which resulted in a Strategic Arms Limitation Treaty (SALT I) with the Soviet Union in 1972, reflected the wisdom of that admonition. SALT I, which placed ceilings on some categories of nuclear arms, was ratified by an overwhelming majority in the Senate.

SALT II called for Soviet and U.S. reductions in existing stockpiles of missiles and bombers, but even though its terms were favorable to the United States, this treaty did not meet with the

Food and fuel being airlifted into Berlin during the 1948–49 Russian blockade. Berlin became a symbol of American commitment to Western Europe during the cold war.

Пролетарии всех стран, соединяйтесь!

Постановление Совета Народных Комиссаров

Scroll presented to the American Relief Administration, 1923, by Russians grateful for food shipments after World War I. The United States helped various war-torn areas after World War I.
From the Herbert Hoover Library; text in Russian, 19 by 30 inches.

same enthusiasm as SALT I. U.S.-Soviet relations were increasingly antagonistic during the late 1970s, and ill feelings between the two nations were exacerbated by the Soviet invasion of Afghanistan in 1979. Despite protracted negotiations that resulted in the signing of SALT II in June 1979, President Jimmy Carter could not persuade the Senate to ratify the treaty. President Carter announced in 1980 that the United States would comply with the provisions of the unratified agreement as long as the Soviets did the same, and Communist Party General Secretary Leonid Brezhnev made a similar announcement regarding Soviet compliance.

In May 1982 President Ronald Reagan declared that he would do nothing to jeopardize either of the SALT agreements, and again, the Soviets made a similar pledge. On May 26, 1986, President Reagan announced that he had reviewed the status of the policy of restraint and that the Soviet Union had not complied with the SALT agreements (including SALT II) or pursued a policy of true restraint. The President said: "Given this situation, . . . in the future, the United States must base decisions regarding its strategic force structure on the nature and magnitude of

President Harry S. Truman meets Gen. Dwight D. Eisenhower on the general's return from Europe, January 31, 1951.

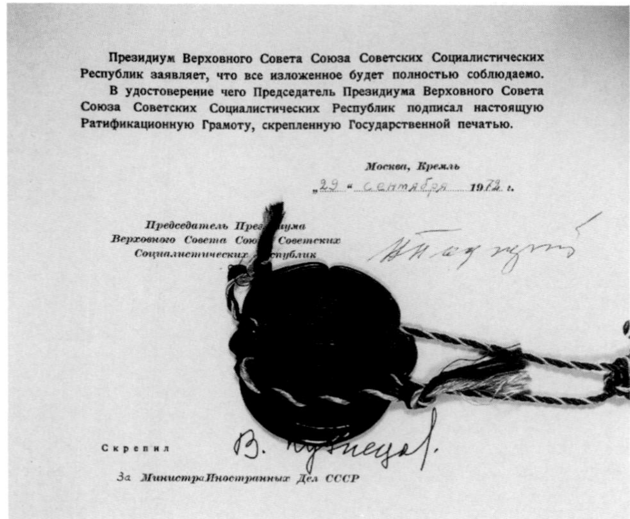

Президиум Верховного Совета Союза Советских Социалистических Республик заявляет, что все изложенное будет полностью соблюдаемо.

В удостоверение чего Председатель Президиума Верховного Совета Союза Советских Социалистических Республик подписал настоящую Ратификационную Грамоту, скрепленную Государственной печатью.

Москва, Кремль

„29" сентября 1972 г.

Председатель Президиума Верховного Совета Союза Советских Социалистических Республик

Скрепил

За Министра Иностранных Дел СССР

SALT (Strategic Arms Limitation Talks) Treaty signed by President Nixon and Soviet Communist Party Chairman Leonid Brezhnev in Moscow on May 6, 1972. The treaty restricted strategic offensive arms. *Soviet exchange copy, 18 pages, 10 ½ by 15 inches.*

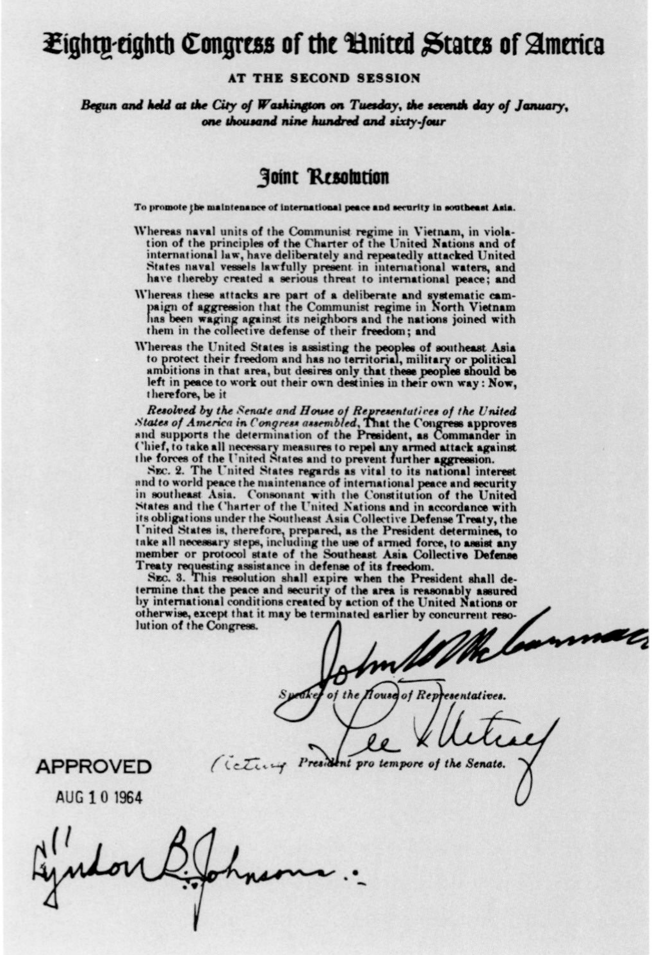

Eighty-eighth Congress of the United States of America

AT THE SECOND SESSION

Begun and held at the City of Washington on Tuesday, the seventh day of January, one thousand nine hundred and sixty-four

Joint Resolution

To promote the maintenance of international peace and security in southeast Asia.

Whereas naval units of the Communist regime in Vietnam, in violation of the principles of the Charter of the United Nations and of international law, have deliberately and repeatedly attacked United States naval vessels lawfully present in international waters, and have thereby created a serious threat to international peace; and

Whereas these attacks are part of a deliberate and systematic campaign of aggression that the Communist regime in North Vietnam has been waging against its neighbors and the nations joined with them in the collective defense of their freedom; and

Whereas the United States is assisting the peoples of southeast Asia to protect their freedom and has no territorial, military or political ambitions in that area, but desires only that these peoples should be left in peace to work out their own destinies in their own way: Now, therefore, be it

Resolved by the Senate and House of Representatives of the United States of America in Congress assembled, That the Congress approves and supports the determination of the President, as Commander in Chief, to take all necessary measures to repel any armed attack against the forces of the United States and to prevent further aggression.

Sec. 2. The United States regards as vital to its national interest and to world peace the maintenance of international peace and security in southeast Asia. Consonant with the Constitution of the United States and the Charter of the United Nations and in accordance with its obligations under the Southeast Asia Collective Defense Treaty, the United States is, therefore, prepared, as the President determines, to take all necessary steps, including the use of armed force, to assist any member or protocol state of the Southeast Asia Collective Defense Treaty requesting assistance in defense of its freedom.

Sec. 3. This resolution shall expire when the President shall determine that the peace and security of the area is reasonably assured by international conditions created by action of the United Nations or otherwise, except that it may be terminated earlier by concurrent resolution of the Congress.

Speaker of the House of Representatives.

President pro tempore of the Senate.

APPROVED

AUG 10 1964

Tonkin Gulf Resolution passed by Congress on August 7, 1964, and signed by President Lyndon B. Johnson. The joint resolution, which approved President Johnson's initiatives to "repel any armed attack against the forces of the United States and to prevent further aggression," opened the way for a large commitment of American troops to Vietnam. *10 by 15 inches.*

the threat posed by Soviet strategic forces and not on standards contained in the SALT structure." President Reagan also promised that the United States would "continue to exercise the utmost restraint" and called on the Soviet Union to help "in establishing an interim framework of truly *mutual* restraint." The "interim framework" that President Carter had presented in SALT II was, for all practical purposes, dead.

President Carter had been more successful with his Middle East peace initiative. By the time that he took office in 1977, the Middle East had become a hotbed of religious, racial, ideological, and economic warfare between Israel and the Arab nations. In 1978, at the Presidential retreat in Maryland, President Carter was able to negotiate the Camp David Accords, a settlement of Israeli-Egyptian hostilities that threatened to explode again into all-out war. He suffered a setback to his efforts to bring peace to the region when revolutionaries overthrew the Shah of Iran and turned their hostilities toward the United States, which had placed the shah on his throne and supported him throughout his reign. After the United States admitted the exiled shah, on November 4, 1979, militant Iranians seized the U.S. embassy in Tehran and took 90 people hostage, 63 of them Americans. These Americans were not released until January 20, 1981, the day of President Ronald Reagan's inauguration.

Terrorism in the Middle East continued to be a problem throughout the 1980s. In 1984 a terrorist attack on U.S. Marine headquarters in Beirut killed 241 Americans, and in the 1985 hijacking of the cruise ship *Achille Lauro,* 1 American was killed. In April 1986, the United States bombed several targets in Libya in retaliation for the Libyan bombing of a West Berlin disco that killed 2 people and injured over 200. On December 21, 1988, a plane en route to New York, carrying 38 Syracuse University students and many U.S. military personnel, exploded over Lockerbie, Scotland, as a result of a Libyan terrorist bomb. The death toll was 270: 259 aboard the plane and 11 on the ground.

Continuing Middle Eastern conflicts escalated into war in August 1990 when Iraqi forces, under the leadership of dictator Saddam Hussein, invaded Kuwait. Attempts by the United States and the United Nations to negotiate with the Iraqis

President Jimmy Carter and Soviet President Leonid Brezhnev signed the SALT II Treaty in June 1979, but the treaty was rejected by the U.S. Senate.
From the Jimmy Carter Library.

President Jimmy Carter with Egyptian President Anwar Sadat and Israeli Prime Minister Menachem Begin at the White House for the signing of the Arab-Israeli peace treaty, March 26, 1979. President Carter had negotiated a settlement of Israeli-Egyptian hostilities in 1978.
From the Jimmy Carter Library.

President George Bush and Gen. H. Norman Schwarzkopf in Saudi Arabia during President Bush's visit to the American troops stationed there during Operation Desert Storm, November 22, 1990. *From the Bush Presidential Materials Project.*

President George Bush receives a piece of the Berlin Wall from West German Foreign Minister Hans-Dietrich Genscher at the White House, November 21, 1989. *From the Bush Presidential Materials Project.*

failed, and on January 12, 1991, Congress gave President George Bush the authority to use force to resolve the situation. On January 16 an international force led by the United States launched air and missile attacks on Iraqi-occupied Kuwait in what became known as Operation Desert Storm. The air attacks continued throughout January, and after a failed Iraqi-Soviet peace initiative, on February 23, the allies began a ground assault. By February 28 Iraq had announced a cease-fire, and on March 2, 1991, the United Nations Security Council approved a resolution to set the terms for a formal end to hostilities. In response to Iraq's violation of the U.N. resolution, the United States bombed several Iraqi military targets in January 1993.

U.S. foreign relations in the late 1980s and early 1990s were also complicated by events in Eastern Europe that drastically changed the delicate balance of power forged during the cold war and remade the international political order. In 1989–90 revolutions in Hungary, Poland, Czechoslovakia, and Romania forced the Communist Party out of power in those countries. Political upheaval, including the resignation in October 1989 of Erich Honecker as leader of the East German Communist Party, and public demands for reform in East Germany led to the opening of the Berlin Wall on November 9, 1989. The movement for a unified Germany gained momentum, and with the cooperation of the United States, England, France, and the Soviet Union, the treaty for the monetary, economic, and social union of the two Germanys was signed in Bonn on May 18, 1990. On July 1 of that year, when the treaty took effect, all border controls around Berlin were dismantled, uniting the city.

Meanwhile in the Soviet Union, growing unrest in the republics undermined the Communist regime. Mikhail Gorbachev, Communist Party General Secretary since 1985, had followed a policy of *perestroika,* a restructuring of Soviet institutions that was praised by Western leaders. He established an unprecedented level of communication with the United States, holding seven summits and two other meetings with U.S. Presidents during his tenure. But by the late 1980s, nationalist ties in the republics and frustration with the economic failure of the Soviet system gave rise to movements in almost all of the republics for autonomy or even complete independence. In August 1991, hard-line Communist Party leaders attempted a coup against Gorbachev. International condemnations and the defiance of pro-democracy Soviets led by Russian President Boris Yeltsin prevented the coup's success. On August 29, 1991, the Soviet national legislature ended Communist Party rule. In December of that year Russia, Ukraine, and Belarus entered an agreement to form a "Commonwealth of Independent States" to replace the Union of Soviet Socialist Republics. By December 21, all the other republics except Georgia had signed commonwealth pacts. Gorbachev resigned on December 25, 1991, and the U.S.S.R. officially disbanded later that day.

Before the upheaval in the Soviet Union had run its course, U.S. President George Bush and Soviet President Mikhail Gorbachev had signed an important Strategic Arms Reduction Treaty (START I) on July 31, 1991. Bush and Russian President Boris Yeltsin signed START II on January 3, 1992. Although these two treaties represent a step forward in post–cold war U.S. foreign relations, their fate is uncertain. START I cannot take effect until Ukraine ratifies it, and the reductions called for in START II cannot begin until those specified by START I are completed. In the face of the new world order created by the end of the cold war, the United States faces many new challenges in its continuing search for a peaceful future.

In June 1990 President George Bush held a summit meeting with Soviet President Mikhail Gorbachev. *From the Bush Presidential Materials Project.*

Russian President Boris Yeltsin with President George Bush in the White House, June 20, 1991. *From the Bush Presidential Materials Project.*

Historical Highlights

Declaration of Independence

July 4, 1776

The Second Continental Congress adopted the Declaration of Independence, breaking the colonial tie to Great Britain and marking America's advent as a sovereign state.

Northwest Ordinance

1787

The Northwest Ordinance outlined how the Northwest Territory would be settled, organized, and prepared for statehood and represents a great political innovation in avoiding a colonial empire in new territory.

Constitution

1789

The Constitution replaced the Articles of Confederation and further unified the independent states of America by establishing a more centralized federal system. The Constitution is the oldest written document of its kind.

Cotton Gin Patent

1794

Eli Whitney invented a device to separate cotton fiber from the seed—an invention that expanded the cotton industry, encouraged the growth of slavery, and ultimately acted as a catalyst for the Civil War.

Louisiana Purchase Treaty

1803

Obtained from Napoleon Bonaparte of France, the Louisiana Territory doubled the size of the United States, advancing its boundary to the Rocky Mountains.

Marbury v. Madison

1803

Chief Justice John Marshall and the Supreme Court established the principle of judicial review and completed the system of checks and balances when the Court declared unconstitutional a law passed by Congress and signed by the President.

Monroe Doctrine

1823

In an annual message to Congress, President James Monroe established the Monroe Doctrine by warning European nations against further involvement and colonization in the Western Hemisphere. Various Presidents have invoked the doctrine in developing U.S. foreign policy.

Oregon Treaty

1846

President James K. Polk forged the Oregon Treaty with Great Britain and peacefully obtained the territory that became Oregon, Washington, Idaho, and parts of Montana and Wyoming.

Treaty of Guadalupe Hidalgo

1848

In a conflict over lands west of Texas, President Polk went to war, and the United States defeated Mexico in 1847. The resulting Treaty of Guadalupe Hidalgo gave the United States California and the Southwest to complete the transcontinental expansion of the nation.

Emancipation Proclamation

1863

Issued in the middle of the Civil War, the Emancipation Proclamation announced the freedom of slaves in the areas still in rebellion in January 1863 and changed the war into a crusade for human liberty.

Homestead Act

1862

The Homestead Act provided any adult citizen with 160 acres of public land provided he or she payed a small registration fee and farmed the land for 5 years. The act did not fully achieve its aim to provide land for small freeholders, and it had an adverse effect on western Native Americans.

Morrill Act

1862

The Morrill Act set aside land in each township for the support of public schools and marked the first federal aid to higher education. Congress passed other legislation in the 20th century to expand higher educational opportunities.

Fifteenth Amendment

1870

The 15th amendment gave black males the right to vote but was only the beginning of the African-American struggle for equality in American public and civic life.

Incandescent Lamp Patent

1879

The patent for Thomas A. Edison's incandescent lamp symbolizes American ingenuity and the creation of a modern industrial society. In the 20th century, such patented inventions led to industrialization, urbanization, and many unintended consequences, such as in the environment and in the quality of life.

Sixteenth Amendment

1913

The 16th amendment provided for the first constitutionally mandated income tax in 1913, but the full potential of such a tax for revenue and the redistribution of wealth was only realized during the era of the New Deal and World War II. The economic circumstances of the 1980s led to new approaches to taxation that are still hotly debated.

Treaty of Versailles

1919

The Treaty of Versailles ended World War I, and its League of Nations Covenant articulated President Woodrow Wilson's vision for lasting peace.

Volstead Act

1919

Andrew Volstead, a Congressman from Minnesota, introduced the legislation that led to Prohibition and the 18th amendment.

Nineteenth Amendment

1920

The "Susan B. Anthony Amendment" mobilized American women to fight for their right to vote, and its ratification opened the door to women's participation in American politics and government.

Immigration Quota Act

1924

The Immigration Quota Act established annual limits on immigration to the United States and reduced the flood of newcomers to America to a trickle. The act clearly discriminated against immigrants from areas outside northern and western Europe.

FDR's Inaugural Address

1933

President Franklin D. Roosevelt lifted the spirits of a nation beaten down by the Great Depression when he told its citizens "the only thing we have to fear is fear itself." His New Deal programs left a permanent imprint on the nation.

Japanese Surrender

1945

The Japanese forces surrendered to the Allies aboard the U.S.S. *Missouri* after President Harry S. Truman gave the order to drop atomic bombs on Hiroshima and Nagasaki. The bombs inaugurated the nuclear age and the haunting possibility of global destruction.

Marshall Plan

1948

After World War II, the Marshall plan, also known as the European Recovery Act, signed into law on April 3, 1948, channeled $12 billion in aid to Western Europe over the next 4 years to strengthen and protect war-torn Europe from communism. The U.S. continued to fight the cold war until the collapse of the Soviet Union in 1991.

Suggestions for Further Reading

General

Boorstin, Daniel. *The Americans.* Vol. 1, *The Americans: The Colonial Experience.* Vol. 2, *The Americans: The National Experience.* Vol. 3, *The Americans: The Democratic Experience.* New York: Random House, 1958–1973.

Miller, William. *A New History of the United States.* 3d ed. New York: Dell Publishing Company, 1969.

Morison, Samuel E. *The Oxford History of the American People.* 3 vols. New York: Oxford University Press, 1965.

Norton, Mary Beth, David M. Katzman, Paul D. Escott, Howard P. Chudacoff, Thomas G. Patterson, and William M. Tuttle, Jr. *A People and a Nation: A History of the United States.* 2 vols. 3d ed. Boston: Houghton Mifflin, 1990.

Tindall, George Brown. *America: A Narrative History.* New York: W. W. Norton, 1984.

Williams, William. *The Contours of American History.* New York: New Viewpoints, 1973.

Milestone Documents in the National Archives

This ongoing series of booklets published by the National Archives focuses on some of the great documents that have shaped the course of U.S. history. Each booklet includes a historical introduction and transcriptions and facsimiles of the featured documents.

The Declaration of Independence. 1992.

A More Perfect Union: The Creation of the U.S. Constitution. 1978, 1986.

The Great Seal of the United States. 1986.

Washington's Inaugural Address of 1789. 1986.

The Judiciary Act of 1789. 1989.

The Bill of Rights. 1986.

The Louisiana Purchase. 1987.

The Emancipation Proclamation. 1986.

Records of Impeachment. 1987.

The Right to Vote. 1988.

Patent Drawings. 1986.

Prohibition: The 18th Amendment, The Volstead Act, The 21st Amendment. 1986.

Franklin D. Roosevelt's Inaugural Address of 1933. 1988.

On War Against Japan: Franklin D. Roosevelt's "Day of Infamy" Address of 1941. 1988.

Germany Surrenders, 1945. 1990.

Japan Surrenders, 1945. 1990.

Atoms for Peace: Dwight D. Eisenhower's Address to the United Nations, 1954. 1990.

Kennedy's Inaugural Address of 1961. 1987.

The Cuban Missile Crisis: Kennedy's Address to the Nation. 1988.

Revolutionary Era

Bailyn, Bernard. *The Ideological Origins of the American Revolution.* Cambridge: Harvard University Press, 1967.

Greene, Jack P. *The American Revolution: Its Character and Limits.* New York: New York University Press, 1978.

Higginbotham, Don, ed. *Reconsiderations on the Revolutionary War: Selected Essays.* Westport, CT: Greenwood, 1978.

Kerber, Linda K. *Women of the Republic: Intellect and Ideology in Revolutionary America.* Chapel Hill: Institute of Early American History and Culture, University of North Carolina Press, 1980.

Maier, Pauline. *The Old Revolutionaries: Political Lives in the Age of Samuel Adams.* New York: Alfred A. Knopf, 1980.

Main, Jackson Turner. *The Social Structure of Revolutionary America.* Princeton, NJ: Princeton University Press, 1965.

Morgan, Edmund S. *The Birth of the Republic, 1763–1789.* Chicago: University of Chicago Press, 1977.

Wood, Gordon S. *The Creation of the American Republic, 1776–1787.* Chapel Hill: Institute of Early American History and Culture, University of North Carolina Press, 1969.

Early National Era

Adams, Henry. *History of the United States of America During the Administrations of Jefferson and Madison.* 9 vols., 1889–1891. Edited by Earl N. Harbert, 2 vols. The Library of America. New York: Literary Classics of the United States, 1986.

Appleby, Joyce. *Capitalism and a New Social Order: The Republican Vision of the 1790s.* New York: New York University Press, 1984.

Banning, Lance. *The Jeffersonian Persuasion: Evolution of a Party Ideology.* Ithaca, NY: Cornell University Press, 1978.

Bloom, Sol. *The Story of the Constitution.* 1937. Reprint. Washington, DC: National Archives, 1986.

Charleton, James H., Robert G. Ferris, and Mary C. Ryan, eds. *Framers of the Constitution.* Rev. ed. Washington, DC: National Archives, 1986.

Finkelman, Paul. *An Imperfect Union: Slavery, Federalism, and Country.* Chapel Hill: University of North Carolina Press, 1981.

Jensen, Merrill. *The New Nation: A History of the United States During the Confederation, 1781–1789.* New York: Alfred A. Knopf, 1950.

Larkin, Jack. *The Reshaping of Everyday Life, 1790–1840.* New York: Harper and Row, 1988.

McDonald, Forrest. *Novus Ordo Seclorum: The Intellectual Origins of the Constitution.* Lawrence: University of Kansas Press, 1985.

Malone, Dumas. *Jefferson and His Time.* Vol. 1, *Jefferson the Virginian.* Vol. 2, *Jefferson and the Rights of Man.* Vol. 3, *Jefferson and the Ordeal of Liberty.* Vol. 4, *Jefferson the President: First Term, 1801–1805.* Vol. 5, *Jefferson the President: Second Term, 1805–1809.* Vol. 6, *The Sage of Monticello.* Boston: Little, Brown and Company, 1948–1981.

Peck, Robert S., and Ralph C. Pollock, eds. *The Blessings of Liberty: Bicentennial Lectures at the National Archives.* Washington, DC: American Bar Association and the Constitution Study Group of the National Archives, 1986.

Remini, Robert. Vol. 1, *Andrew Jackson and the Course of the American Empire, 1767–1821.* Vol. 2, *Andrew Jackson and the Course of American Freedom, 1822–1832.* Vol. 3, *Andrew Jackson and the Course of American Democracy, 1833–1845.* New York: Harper and Row, 1977–1984.

Stagg, J.C.A. *Mr. Madison's War: Politics, Diplomacy, and Warfare in the Early American Republic, 1783–1830.* Princeton, NJ: Princeton University Press, 1983.

Tyler, Alice Felt. *Freedom's Ferment: Phases of American Social History from the Colonial Period to the Outbreak of the Civil War.* New York: Harper and Row, 1962.

Varg, Paul A. *Foreign Policies of the Founding Fathers.* East Lansing: Michigan State University Press, 1963.

Antebellum and Westward Expansion

Berlin, Ira. *Slaves Without Masters: The Free Negro in the Antebellum South.* New York: Pantheon, 1974.

Billington, Ray A., and Martin Ridge. *Westward Expansion: A History of the American Frontier.* 5th ed. New York: Macmillan, 1982.

Blassingame, John W. *The Slave Community: Plantation Life in the Antebellum South.* New York: Oxford University Press, 1972.

Bustard, Bruce. *Western Ways: Images of the American West.* Washington, DC: National Archives, 1992.

Craven, Avery O. *Growth of Southern Nationalism, 1848–1861.* Baton Rouge: Louisiana State University Press and the Littlefield Fund for Southern History of the University of Texas, 1953.

Dangerfield, George. *Awakening of American Nationalism, 1815–1828.* New York: Harper and Row, 1965.

Davis, David B. *The Problem of Slavery in Western Culture.* Ithaca, NY: Cornell University Press, 1966.

DeVoto, Bernard. *The Year of Decision, 1846.* Boston: Little, Brown and Company, 1943.

Fish, Carl Russell. *The Rise of the Common Man, 1830–1850.* New York: Macmillan, 1927.

Fox-Genovese, Elizabeth. *Within the Plantation Household: Black and White Women of the Old South.* Chapel Hill: University of North Carolina Press, 1988.

Gates, Paul W. *The Farmer's Age: Agriculture, 1815–1860.* Vol. 3 of *The Economic History of the United States.* New York: Harper Torchbooks, 1968.

Genovese, Eugene. *Roll, Jordan, Roll: The World the Slaves Made.* New York: Pantheon Books, 1974.

Luchetti, Cathy, and Carol Olwell. *Women of the West.* Berkeley, CA: Antelope Island Press, 1982.

Merk, Frederick. *History of the Westward Movement.* New York: Alfred A. Knopf, 1978.

Merk, Frederick, and Lois Bannister Merk. *The Monroe Doctrine and American Expansionism, 1843–1849.* New York: Alfred A. Knopf, 1966.

Parkman, Francis. *The Oregon Trail: Sketches of Prairie and Rocky-Mountain Life.* New York: Greystone Press, 1847.

Prucha, Francis Paul. *American Indian Policy in Crisis: Christian Reformers and the Indian, 1865–1900.* Norman: University of Oklahoma Press, 1976.

Rose, Willie Lee. *Slavery and Freedom.* Edited by William W. Freehling. New York: Oxford University Press, 1982.

Singletary, Otis A. *The Mexican War.* Chicago: University of Chicago Press, 1960.

Stampp, Kenneth. *The Peculiar Institution: Slavery in the Ante-Bellum South.* New York: Alfred A. Knopf, 1956.

Sydnor, C. S. *Development of Southern Sectionalism, 1819–1848.* Baton Rouge: Louisiana State University Press, 1948.

Turner, Frederick Jackson. *The Frontier in American History.* New York: Henry Holt and Company, 1920.

Viola, Herman J. *Exploring the West.* Washington, DC: Smithsonian Books, 1987.

Wade, Richard C. *The Urban Frontier: Pioneer Life in Early Pittsburgh, Cincinnati, Lexington, Louisville, and St. Louis.* Chicago: University of Chicago Press, 1964.

Webb, Walter Prescott. *The Great Plains.* Boston: Ginn and Company, 1931.

Worster, Donald. *Rivers of Empire: Water, Aridity, and the Growth of the American West.* New York: Pantheon Books, 1985.

Civil War and Reconstruction

Cole, Arthur C. *The Irrepressible Conflict, 1850–1865.* New York: Macmillan, 1934.

Filler, Louis. *The Crusade Against Slavery, 1830–1860.* New York: Harper, 1960.

Foner, Eric. *Reconstruction: America's Unfinished Revolution, 1863–1877.* New York: Harper and Row, 1988.

Foner, Philip S. *Business and Slavery: The New York Merchants and the Irrepressible Conflict.* Chapel Hill: University of North Carolina Press, 1941.

Franklin, John Hope. *The Emancipation Proclamation.* Garden City, NY: Doubleday, 1963.

Franklin, John Hope. *Reconstruction After the Civil War.* The Chicago History of American Civilization. Chicago: University of Chicago Press, 1961.

Gates, Paul W. *Agriculture and the Civil War.* New York: Alfred A. Knopf, 1965.

Gillette, William C. *The Right to Vote: Politics and the Passage of the Fifteenth Amendment.* Studies in History and Political Science, ser. 83, no. 1. Baltimore: Johns Hopkins University Press, 1965.

Kutler, Stanley I., ed. *The Dred Scott Decision: Law or Politics?* Boston: Houghton Mifflin, 1967.

McPherson, James M. *Battle Cry of Freedom: The Civil War Era.* New York: Oxford University Press, 1988.

Nevins, Allan. *Ordeal of the Union.* Vol. 1, *Fruits of Manifest Destiny,. 1847–1852.* Vol. 2, *A House Dividing, 1852–1857.* Vol. 3, *The Emergence of Lincoln: Douglas, Buchanan, and Party Chaos, 1857–1859.* Vol. 4, *The Emergence of Lincoln: Prologue to Civil War, 1859–1861.* Vol. 5, *The War for the Union: The Improvised War, 1861–1862.* Vol. 6, *The War for the Union: War Becomes Revolution, 1862–1863.* Vol. 7, *The War for the Union: The Organized War, 1863–1864.* Vol. 8, *The War for the Union: The Organized War to Victory, 1864–1865.* New York: Charles Scribners Sons, 1947–1971.

Nichols, Roy F. *The Stakes of Power, 1845–1877.* New York: Hill and Wang, 1961.

Perman, Michael. *Reunion Without Compromise: The South and Reconstruction, 1865–1868.* Cambridge: Cambridge University Press, 1973.

Quarles, Benjamin. *Black Abolitionists.* New York: Oxford University Press, 1969.

Stampp, Kenneth. *The Era of Reconstruction, 1865–1877.* New York: Alfred A. Knopf, 1965.

Industrialization and the Progressive Era

Abrams, Richard M. *The Burdens of Progress, 1900–1929.* Scott, Foresman American History Series. Glenview, IL: Scott, Foresman, 1978.

Campbell, Charles S. *The Transformation of American Foreign Relations, 1865–1900.* New York: Harper and Row, 1976.

Cochran, Thomas C., and William Miller. *The Age of Enterprise: A Social History of Industrial America.* New York: Macmillan, 1942.

Coffman, Edward M. *The War To End All Wars: The American Military Experience in World War I.* New York: Oxford University Press, 1968.

Coletta, Paolo E. *The Presidency of William Howard Taft.* Lawrence: University Press of Kansas, 1973.

Commager, Henry Steele. *The American Mind: An Interpretation of American Thought and Character Since the 1880's.* New Haven, CT: Yale University Press, 1950.

Degler, Carl N., ed. *The Age of the Economic Revolution, 1876–1900.* 2d ed. The Scott, Foresman American History Series. Glenview, IL: Scott, Foresman, 1977.

Destler, Charles M. *American Radicalism, 1865–1901: Essays and Documents.* New London: Connecticut College, 1946.

Fine, Sidney. *Laissez Faire and the General-Welfare State: A Study of Conflict in American Thought, 1865–1901.* Ann Arbor: University of Michigan Press, 1956.

Ginger, Ray. *Age of Excess: The United States from 1877 to 1914.* New York: Macmillan, 1965.

Goodwyn, Lawrence. *Democratic Promise: The Populist Movement in America.* New York: Oxford University Press, 1976.

Hofstadter, Richard. *The Age of Reform: From Bryan to F.D.R.* New York: Alfred A. Knopf, 1955.

Josephson, Matthew. *The President Makers: The Culture of Politics and Leadership in an Age of Enlightenment, 1896–1919.* New York: Harcourt Brace and Company, 1940.

Kennedy, David M. *Over Here: The First World War and American Society.* New York: Oxford University Press, 1980.

LaFeber, Walter. *The New Empire: An Interpretation of American Expansion, 1860–1898.* Ithaca, NY: Published for the American Historical Association by Cornell University Press, 1963.

Link, Arthur S. *Woodrow Wilson and the Progressive Era, 1910–1917.* New York: Harper, 1954.

McKelvey, Blake. *The Urbanization of America, 1860–1915.* New Brunswick, NJ: Rutgers University Press, 1963.

Mayer, Arno J. *The Politics and Diplomacy of Peacemaking: Containment and Counterrevolution at Versailles, 1918–1919.* New York: Alfred A. Knopf, 1967.

Morgan, H. Wayne, ed. *The Gilded Age.* Rev. and enl. ed. Syracuse, NY: Syracuse University Press, 1970.

O'Neill, William L. *Everyone Was Brave: The Rise and Fall of Feminism in America.* Chicago: Quadrangle Books, 1969.

Rothman, Sheila M. *Woman's Proper Place: A History of Changing Ideals and Practices, 1870 to the Present.* New York: Basic Books, 1978.

Wiebe, Robert H. *The Search for Order, 1877–1920.* The Making of America. New York: Hill and Wang, 1967.

Woodward, C. Vann. *The Origins of the New South, 1877–1913.* Vol. 9 of *A History of the South.* Baton Rouge: Louisiana State University Press, 1951.

———. *Reunion and Reaction: The Compromise of 1877 and the End of Reconstruction.* Boston: Little, Brown and Company, 1966.

The Modern Era, 1921–1990

Agee, James, and Walker Evans. *Let Us Now Praise Famous Men.* Boston: Houghton Mifflin, 1941.

Allen, Frederick L. *Only Yesterday: An Informal History of the Nineteen-Twenties.* New York: Harper and Brothers, 1931.

Ambrose, Stephen E. *Rise to Globalism: American Foreign Policy Since 1938.* Baltimore: Penguin Books, 1971.

Athearn, Robert G. *The Mythic West in Twentieth Century America.* Lawrence: University of Kansas Press, 1986.

Blum, John Morton. *V Was For Victory: Politics and Culture During World War II.* New York: Harcourt Brace Jovanovich, 1976.

Braeman, John, Robert H. Bremner, and David Brody, eds. *Change and Continuity in Twentieth Century America: The 1920s.* Modern America, no. 2. Columbus: Ohio State University Press, 1968.

Conkin, Paul K. *The New Deal.* Edited by John Hope Franklin and Abraham S. Eisenstadt. The Crowell American History Series. New York: Thomas E. Crowell, 1967.

Davis, Kenneth S. *FDR: Into the Storm, 1937–1940: A History.* New York: Random House, 1993.

Degler, Carl N. *Affluence and Anxiety, 1945 to the Present.* The Scott, Foresman American History Series. Glenview, IL: Scott, Foresman, 1968.

Diggins, John. *The Rise and Fall of the American Left.* New York: W. W. Norton, 1992. Originally published as *The American Left in the Twentieth Century.* 1973.

Gilbert, James. *Another Chance: Postwar America, 1945–1968.* New York: Alfred A. Knopf, 1981.

Goodwin, Doris Kearns. *The Fitzgeralds and the Kennedys: An American Saga.* New York: Simon and Schuster, 1987.

———. *Lyndon Johnson and the American Dream.* New York: Harper and Row, 1976.

Halberstam, David. *The Best and the Brightest.* New York: Random House, 1972.

Heath, Jim F. *Decade of Disillusionment: The Kennedy-Johnson Years.* America Since World War II. Bloomington: Indiana State University Press, 1975.

Heilbroner, Robert L. *The Limits of American Capitalism.* New York: Harper and Row, 1966.

Hicks, John D. *Republican Ascendancy, 1921–1933.* The New American Nation Series. New York: Harper, 1960.

Higham, John. *Strangers in the Land: Patterns of American Nativism, 1860–1925.* Rev. ed. New York: Atheneum, 1963.

Hodgson, Godfrey. *America In Our Time: From World War II to Nixon: What Happened and Why.* Garden City, NY: Doubleday, 1976.

LaFeber, Walter. *America, Russia, and the Cold War.* 4th ed. New York: Wiley, 1980.

Leuchtenburg, William E. *The Perils of Prosperity, 1914–1932.* Chicago: University of Chicago Press, 1958.

———. *A Troubled Feast: American Society Since 1945.* Rev. ed. Boston: Little, Brown and Company, 1979.

———. *Franklin D. Roosevelt and the New Deal, 1932–1940.* The New American Nation Series. New York: Harper and Row, 1963.

———. *In the Shadow of FDR: From Harry Truman to Ronald Reagan.* Ithaca, NY: Cornell University Press, 1983.

McCullough, David. *Truman.* New York: Simon and Schuster, 1992.

Preston, William. *Aliens and Dissenters: Federal Suppression of Radicals, 1903–1933.* Cambridge: Harvard University Press, 1963.

Sale, Kirkpatrick. *Power Shift: The Rise of the Southern Rim and Its Challenge to the Eastern Establishment.* New York: Random House, 1975.

Schell, Jonathan. *The Time of Illusion.* New York: Alfred A. Knopf, 1975.

Schlesinger, Arthur M., Jr. *The Age of Roosevelt.* Vol. 1, *The Crisis of the Old Order, 1919–1933.* Vol. 2, *The Coming of the New Deal.* Vol. 3, *The Politics of Upheaval.* Boston: Houghton Mifflin, 1956–1960.

Sheehan, Neil. *A Bright Shining Lie: John Paul Vann and America in Vietnam.* New York: Random House, 1988.

Smith, Hedrick, Adam Clymer, Leonard Silk, Robert Lindsey, and Richard Burt. *Reagan: The Man, the President.* New York: Macmillan, 1980.

Smith, Nancy Kegan, and Mary C. Ryan, eds. and comps. *Modern First Ladies: Their Documentary Legacy.* Washington, DC: National Archives, 1989.

Waskow, Arthur I. *From Race Riot to Sit-In, 1919 and the 1960s: A Study in the Connections Between Conflict and Violence.* Garden City, NY: Doubleday, 1966.

White, Theodore H. *America in Search of Itself: The Making of the President, 1956–1980.* New York: Harper and Row, 1982.

Wills, Garry. *Reagan's America: Innocents at Home.* Garden City, NY: Doubleday, 1987.

Yergin, Daniel. *Shattered Peace: The Origins of the Cold War and the National Security State.* Boston: Houghton Mifflin, 1977.

Index

Items in **bold** refer to milestone documents; page numbers in **bold** refer to entire chapters (text and captions), and page numbers in *italic* refer to captions.